COGNITIVE THERAPY IN PRACTICE

A case formulation approach

COGNITIVE THERAPY IN PRACTICE

A case formulation approach

Jacqueline B. Persons, Ph.D.

W. W. NORTON & COMPANY · *NEW YORK · LONDON*

The author wishes to gratefully acknowledge permission for the following:

Excerpt on page 87 from J. R. Cautela, Covert sensitization, *Psychological Reports, 20,* pp. 461–2. Used by permission of the author and publisher.

Published simultaneously in Canada by Penguin Books Canada Ltd., 2801 John Street, Markham, Ontario L3R 1B4.

Printed in the United States of America.

Library of Congress Cataloging-in-Publication Data

Persons, Jacqueline B.
  Cognitive therapy in practice : a case formulation approach / by
  Jacqueline B. Persons. — 1st ed.
     p.   cm.
  "A Norton professional book."
  Bibliography: p.
  Includes index.
  1. Cognitive therapy.   I.   Title.
  [DNLM: 1.   Behavior Therapy—methods.   2.   Cognition.   WM 425
P466c]
RC489.C63P47   1989
616.89′142—dc19
DNLM/DLC

ISBN 0-393-70077-1

W. W. Norton & Company, Inc., 500 Fifth Avenue, New York, N. Y. 10110
W. W. Norton & Company Ltd., 37 Great Russell Street, London, WC1B 3NU

                    7 8 9 0

For Jeffrey

Foreword

It has been nearly three decades since the cognitive model was first eluci-
dated by Drs. Albert Ellis and Aaron Beck. In recent years, cognitive
therapy has emerged as one of the most widely practiced forms of psychotherapy in the world. Clinical and basic research on the relationship
between cognition and emotion has achieved a dominant presence in
psychiatric and psychological journals in the United States and abroad.
Numerous studies have demonstrated the efficacy of cognitive therapy in
the treatment of depression, and encouraging preliminary reports suggest
that it may also be effective for many other disorders. These include
suicide and parasuicidal behavior, generalized anxiety, panic attacks,
agoraphobia and other phobias, some personality disorders, eating disorders, hypochondriasis and somatization and pain disorders, drug and
alcohol abuse, sexual dysfunction, some childhood disorders and marital
conflict. In addition, cognitive and behavioral approaches have been
useful in teaching people to cope with serious medical problems and to
comply with treatment regimes. Future studies will be needed to provide
empirical confirmation of the efficacy of cognitive therapy in the treatment of these disorders, and to provide more precise information about
the applications and limits of this modality.

Dr. Jacqueline Persons' *Cognitive Therapy in Practice: A Case Formu-*

lation Approach makes a timely and much needed contribution to this rapidly evolving paradigm. Working at the interface of research and clinical practice, Dr. Persons has produced an outstanding book which should be invaluable to the novice and to the advanced practitioner as well.

One of the strengths of *Cognitive Therapy in Practice* is the balanced focus on the therapeutic relationship as well as on the techniques of cognitive therapy. Drawing on many examples from her own practice, Dr. Persons illustrates cognitive interventions for a wide variety of emotional difficulties in a clear and understandable manner. Practitioners will find the book to be comprehensive and helpful.

Dr. Persons provides a conceptual framework for understanding the patient as a human being, and not simply as a cluster of symptoms to be treated with a bewildering array of highly technologic interventions. Over and over she urges you, the therapist, to formulate your hypothesis about why your patient is suffering. What is the essence of the difficulty? Why is this individual experiencing depression, panic attacks or relationship difficulties at this time? The case formulation approach she describes will help you to conceptualize the patient's many complaints from a cognitive perspective so that you can develop a systematic and coherent treatment plan.

A basic assumption of cognitive therapy (or any therapy) is that the patient and therapist work together as a collaborative team. The goal of this effort is to help the patient to achieve greater self-esteem, improved functioning at work or school, and more satisfying personal relationships. But what can the cognitive therapist do when the spirit of collaboration is lost or cannot readily be achieved? Virtually every therapist has numerous patients who have difficulties making an active commitment to the therapeutic endeavor. These patients may repeatedly "forget" to do self-help assignments between sessions and they may appear oppositional, fighting and arguing with their therapists at every juncture. They complain that their therapists aren't helping, but they seem to dig in their heels when any change is suggested.

These resistant individuals challenge our feelings of competence and can rapidly deplete our creative resources. How can cognitive therapists understand and respond successfully to these patients? How can we encourage trust and motivate individuals who seem ambivalent about the treatment process? How can we deal with the feelings of anxiety and frustration these patients can sometimes stir up in us? I am pleased that Dr. Persons focuses on these transference and countertransference issues in great depth from a theoretical and from a practical perspective.

Dr. Persons brings to this book the clinical perspective of a seasoned therapist and highly esteemed teacher, as well as the discipline of an outstanding researcher. I anticipate that *Cognitive Therapy in Practice* will illuminate your clinical practice and provide you with the latest developments in this promising therapeutic modality.

DAVID D. BURNS, M.D.
Presbyterian-University of
Pennsylvania Medical Center

Contents

Preface

The impetus to write this book came from my daily work. As a practicing cognitive behavior therapist, I found myself grappling with difficulties, obstacles, glitches, setbacks and failures not mentioned in the standard guidebooks. How does the therapist proceed when patients present a long list of serious problems? What can the therapist do if the patient regularly comes late to sessions? If she does not do her homework? If the patient becomes angry at the therapist? If the therapist is angry with the patient?

As I struggled with these difficulties, I found I didn't want simply another list of techniques. Instead, I wanted a general model that would allow me to understand problems and generate solutions to them, based on this understanding, in a coherent, systematic way. This search led to the case formulation model that is the centerpiece of this book.

Behavior therapists have been criticized for being too quick to intervene on the basis of too little understanding. This criticism has some validity, I believe. The emphasis here is on intervention based on understanding. In the approach presented here, interventions depend on the case formulation—that is, the therapist's hypothesis about the psychological mechanisms underlying the patient's problems.

Chapter 1 outlines the case formulation model of psychological problems. Problems are conceptualized as occurring on two levels: the level of overt difficulties and the level of underlying psychological problems.

Overt difficulties are problems that occur in "real life," the kinds of difficulties that bring patients to therapy: depression, procrastination, panic attacks. These problems can be viewed as having three components: mood, cognitions, and behaviors. For example, a young executive who comes to therapy for treatment of "depression" is also inundated with self-critical thoughts and avoiding meetings with his boss. The underlying psychological problems are the deficits that produce the mood, cognitive, and behavioral components of the problem. They can usually be expressed as irrational beliefs. For example, the idea "I must do perfect work; if I do not, I deserve criticism and abuse" can generate the mood, cognitive, and behavioral components of this young man's depression.

Development of a detailed case formulation is the therapist's first task, and Chapters 2 and 3 focus on the two major parts of this task: arriving at a problem list and developing the formulation. Strategies for making a problem list, including measures for assessing problems, are provided in Chapter 2. Methods useful for obtaining and testing a case formulation are detailed in Chapter 3.

The goal of treatment is to solve the behavioral, cognitive, and mood difficulties that bring the patient to treatment, and to modify the underlying irrational beliefs. To accomplish this, the behavior therapist works "top down." That is, interventions are directed primarily at the overt difficulties themselves; changes in cognitions, behavior, and mood are expected to produce changes in underlying beliefs. In fact, cognitive behavior therapists focus on only two of the components (cognitions and behaviors) because direct mood interventions have not yet been developed. The body of the book describes behavioral (Chapters 4 and 5) and cognitive (Chapters 6 and 7) dysfunctions and intervention strategies. The case formulation guides the therapist's understanding of these dysfunctions, decisions about where and how to intervene, and the management of any difficulties that arise.

Chapter 8 addresses homework, a common bugaboo for both patients and therapists. The use of the case formulation to make a good homework assignment and to understand and manage compliance is described and illustrated.

Chapter 9 is devoted to the therapeutic relationship. The use of the case formulation to establish an effective working relationship and to understand and manage difficulties that arise in the relationship is illustrated.

Next comes a chapter on the assessment and treatment of suicidality, one of the most troublesome "difficulties" encountered by clinicians. This presentation focuses on the use of the case formulation and cognitive behavioral strategies.

The last chapter addresses the therapist's discomforts: anxiety about a suicidal patient, anger at a passive or hostile patient, uncertainty about competence. This chapter emphasizes the therapist's understanding of her own vulnerabilities and irrational beliefs, as well as the way they interfere with effective therapeutic work, and suggests some strategies for managing them.

The title of the book uses the term "cognitive therapy" rather than "cognitive behavior therapy" for simplicity; my presentation of cognitive therapy emphasizes its historical origins and current contacts with behavioral traditions and interventions.

The material presented here is intensely personal. Although I place a high value on empirical data, the data often provide little guidance to the clinician struggling with day-to-day difficulties. As a result, much of the material presented here is based largely on my own experience and training. I hope it is helpful to my readers.

Acknowledgments

Thanks go first of all to my husband, Jeffrey Perloff, for his unfailing support of all my professional efforts. I also owe a large debt to my patients, from whom I continue to learn daily. Descriptions of my work with them have been altered to protect their privacy.

I've been fortunate to have many fine teachers who made important contributions to my development, and I hope they will see their influence in this book. My first exposure to cognitive therapy came from Aaron T. Beck, at the Center for Cognitive Therapy in Philadelphia. As I believe this book reflects, Dr. Beck's ideas continue to provide a central and solid foundation for my work. My approach to cognitive therapy has been importantly influenced by David Burns, who served first as a very creative and helpful clinical supervisor and later as a valued research collaborator, as we carried out several studies of cognitive therapy. My identity as a behavior therapist was firmly established during my post-doctoral internship year at the Behavior Therapy Unit, Temple University Department of Psychiatry, where I was influenced most by Joseph Wolpe and Edna Foa. Dr. Wolpe's contribution appears in the approaches to the treatment of fear and anxiety described here and in the emphasis on the case formulation. In addition to her contributions to my understanding and treatment of anxiety, Edna Foa served as an important model of a clinician-researcher. Finally, although I have not worked personally with Ira Turkat, his prolific writings have had a profound impact on my thinking and practice, and the case formulation approach he describes is a centerpiece of this book.

Many colleagues gave useful comments on draft chapters and provided encouragement. The most enduring source of support for the writing of this book came from colleagues at the Depression Clinic of the Department of Psychiatry, University of California at San Francisco, at San Francisco General Hospital. Without Ricardo Muñoz's invitation to participate in his depression seminar at the clinic in 1982, this book probably would not have been written. Jeanne Miranda, first as a student and later as research collaborator, and Charles Garrigues, thoughtful and self-taught cognitive therapist *par excellence*, made helpful comments on early versions of the book. Feedback from students in the clinic was also quite useful. Jill Caire has been a special and valued friend as well as a perceptive and helpful reader of these chapters. I also appreciate incisive, encouraging comments from Rhoda Olkin, and thoughtful suggestions from Susan Krantz.

Cognitive Therapy
in Practice

A case formulation
approach

CHAPTER 1

The case formulation model

This chapter describes the case formulation model of psychological problems that serves as the basis for the assessment and intervention strategies described in the remainder of the book. The first sections of the chapter describe the model itself; later parts of the chapter describe the role of the case formulation in clinical work.

PSYCHOLOGICAL PROBLEMS OCCUR AT TWO LEVELS

The case formulation model conceptualizes psychological problems as occurring at two levels: the *overt difficulties* and the *underlying psychological mechanisms*. *Overt difficulties* are "real life" problems, such as depressed mood, panic attacks, procrastination, difficulty getting along with others, suicidal thoughts, shoplifting, or inability to drive on freeways and bridges. *Underlying psychological mechanisms* are the psychological deficits that underlie and cause the overt difficulties. The underlying mechanisms can often be expressed in terms of one (or a few) irrational beliefs about the self. For example, a young accountant who was socially isolated, anxious about his work, and depressed held the belief, "Unless I'm perfect in everything I do, I'll fail." This belief produced his overt difficulties. It led him to avoid social interactions because he feared any blunder in interacting with others would lead to rejection. Similarly, his fear of making a mistake led to anxiety (and paradoxically, to poor performance as a result) at work. His depression resulted from his social isolation and his feelings of incompetence at work.

The first part of the chapter describes overt difficulties and underlying mechanisms in detail, beginning with overt difficulties.

OVERT DIFFICULTIES

At a "macro" level, overt difficulties include such things as depression, relationship difficulties, poor work performance, obesity, and fear of going out alone. These are problems as they might be described in the patient's own terms.

At a "micro" level, problems can be described in terms of three components: cognitions, behaviors, and moods (Lang, 1979). For instance, a secretary's difficulties working with a supervisor might involve distorted cognitions ("If I make a mistake, he'll fire me"), behavioral problems (poor attendance, palpitations, and sweating), and negative moods (fear and anger). All three components of problems usually reflect the irrational, maladaptive nature of the underlying mechanism. The cognitive, behavioral, and mood components of three typical overt difficulties are illustrated in Table 1.1.

Cognitions

A cognitive component can be found for nearly every problem patients report — even problems that do not appear to involve cognitions. As Beck (1972) pointed out, negative mood states usually involve negative automatic thoughts. For example, a depressed, hopeless patient might report cognitions like, "I can't cope — suicide is the only solution."

Automatic thoughts are also related to problematic behaviors like procrastination, poor work performance, interpersonal squabbles, overeating, and so on. For example, when a piece of laboratory equipment failed, an engineer experienced a barrage of automatic thoughts, including: "I'll never solve this problem, I'm incompetent in the lab, I'm going to be fired, I'll never be a success in my field, Everyone else who works here is more competent than I am." These self-critical thoughts inhibited her from searching for solutions to the problem; instead, she burst into tears and ran out of the lab.

In addition to thoughts, cognitions can also include images, dreams,

Table 1.1 Psychological problems represented as constellations of cognitions, behaviors, and moods

Problem	"Generalized anxiety"	School problems	Confusion about career goals
Cognitions	"I'm trapped." "I don't want to be here."	"I must be perfect." "My Dad insists I get A's."	"If I try working at something I enjoy, I might fail."
Behaviors	Palpitations, sweating, tightening of facial muscles, dizziness, requests for reassurance, avoidance	Stomach cramps, procrastination	Lack of energy, excessive sleeping, overinvolvement with household errands and duties, procrastination
Mood	Fear, anxiety, resentment	Anxiety, depression	Depression, boredom, anhedonia

daydreams, and memories. For instance, a bank clerk experienced feelings of rage and a powerful image of dripping blood whenever she thought about her supervisor.

Behavior

Three types of behaviors are considered here: overt motor behaviors, physiological responses, and verbal behaviors.

Overt motor behaviors that play a role in psychological problems include such things as spending hours lying in bed reading novels, overeating, arguing with others, and avoiding bridges.

Physiological responses relevant to psychological problems often include increased heart rate, sweating, dizziness, and other symptoms associated with panic. Physiological aspects of depressed mood can include insomnia, anorexia, and fatigue. Physiology tends to get short shrift in discussion of problems of depression, but often plays a central role in anxiety.

Problematic verbal responses include continual requests for reassurance, frequent hostile demands, or suicidal threats. Pain complaints can constitute a significant part of the clinical problem (Fordyce & Steger, 1979).

Behavioral components of patient's problems are usually best described as problematic or maladaptive, although the term *irrational*, usually reserved for cognitions, can sometimes be helpful in describing behaviors as well.

Mood[1]

The term "mood" is used here to refer to the patient's subjective report of his emotional experience. Moods that play a role in psychological problems are typically negative and unpleasant: depression, anxiety, panic, boredom, frustration, anger, jealousy, hopelessness, and so on. Depressed patients often seek treatment for their mood problem, unaware that cognitions and behavior are important aspects of their problem.

Relationships among the components

SYNCHRONY. Usually a problem in one component indicates that problems in other components are also present. An underlying deficit is usually manifested in all three components at the overt level, not just one or two. Thus, a person complaining of depressed mood typically shows closely related behavioral and cognitive problems as well.

Occasionally this does not happen; and in that case the components of a problem are said to be desynchronous (Rachman, 1978, Chapter 1). Thus, a person may have a severely depressed mood, but little or no disruption of normal behavioral patterns, or a physiological fear response to cats, but no avoidance.

INTERDEPENDENCE. The synchronous relationships between cognitive, behavioral, and mood components of problems suggests that a change in any one component is likely to produce changes in the other components. These interdependent relationships are indicated by the arrows connect-

[1]Although in the model presented here the term "mood" refers to the patient's subjective report of his emotional experience, this view is an oversimplification of Lang's (1979) model, which suggests that mood is more accurately described in terms of all of the systems described here: cognitions, motor behavior, physiology, and verbal behavior.

ing behavior, cognitions, and mood in Figure 1.1. Thus, if a depressed, inactive person increases his activity level, we would expect an improvement in mood and a reduction in negative thinking as well.

The notion that changes in cognitions can produce changes in mood is the key idea of Beck's cognitive therapy, and the idea that behavioral changes can produce changes in mood is central in Lewinsohn's behavioral treatment and in exposure treatments for fears. The interdependence of the components makes this possible.

The interdependence of the cognitive, behavioral, and mood aspects of problems is particularly important to the clinician treating a mood problem, because therapists have not developed strategies for directly manipulating mood (Rachman, 1981). Thus, although later chapters in this book focus on interventions directed at the behavioral and cognitive aspects of problems, there is no comparable chapter for mood interventions.

The interdependence hypothesis is supported by studies showing that interventions directed at one system appear to produce changes in all systems. Zeiss, Lewinsohn, and Muñoz (1979) treated depressed patients with cognitive therapy, behavior therapy, or social skills interventions. Patients did not show a superior treatment response in the system that was treated; instead, they showed changes in all systems. Rehm, Kaslow, and Rabin (1987) and Simons, Garfield, and Murphy (1984) reported similar results.

Figure 1.1   A two-level model of psychological problems.

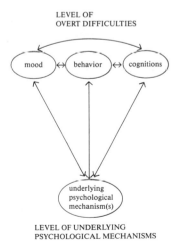

LEVEL OF
OVERT DIFFICULTIES

mood behavior cognitions

underlying
psychological
mechanism(s)

LEVEL OF UNDERLYING
PSYCHOLOGICAL MECHANISMS

UNDERLYING MECHANISMS

The underlying psychological mechanism is a problem or deficit that produces, or is responsible for, the individual's overt difficulties. Direct, objective measures of underlying psychological mechanisms are not yet available. As a result, the therapist's ideas about the underlying cognitions operating in any given case are best viewed as working hypotheses.

Underlying beliefs are often well-expressed in an "if-then" format, such as, "If I get approval and caring from others, I'll be happy," "If I do what others want and expect of me, they'll give me the approval and caring I want," or "If I'm extremely successful, others will accept me." However, sometimes underlying beliefs are simpler, blanket statements, such as, "I'm worthless," "No one cares about me," or "I can't cope." Young (1987) has suggested that patients with personality disorders hold this type of unconditional belief, which he labels an early maladaptive schema (EMS). We might expect these types of underlying beliefs to be more difficult to change than the conditional ones.

Sometimes the patient's central problem is not efficiently described in terms of an underlying belief. For example, the central problem of an impulsive, violent young adolescent may be a lack of problem-solving skills. Empirical work by Linehan and her colleagues (Linehan, Camper, Chiles, Strosahl, & Shearin, 1987) suggests that deficits in problem-solving may underlie suicidal behavior.

Although the therapist attempts to arrive at one clear statement of the proposed underlying mechanism, this can be difficult to do. Various forms and permutations of the mechanism may be operative, depending on the external situation arousing the mechanism and the associated behaviors, cognitions, and moods (cf. Horowitz, Marmar, Krupnick, Wilner, Kaltreider, & Wallerstein, 1984). Or the individual may have more than one problem. When this happens, one problem usually plays a central, dominant role, and the others seem to be somewhat less important.

The question of the malleability of the underlying irrational beliefs is a fascinating topic about which we unfortunately know very little. Many patients, discussing their automatic thoughts, and irrational beliefs, can say, "I *know* I'm not worthless, but I just keep buying into feeling worthless and inadequate." These patients appear to have alternatives to their pathological beliefs already available to them — although they may take some looking for.

Other patients do not seem to have any available alternatives to their central pathological beliefs. In response to the therapist's proposal that the patient is not worthless, this type of patient may say, "What you say makes intellectual sense, but it just doesn't have any emotional impact for me." For these patients, their self-concept and worldview are entirely determined by their irrational ideas. Christine Padesky (personal communication, April, 1986) has suggested that the unavailability of healthy self-perceptions might be a definitive characteristic of people with personality disorders, and others (Young, 1987; Guidano & Liotti, 1983) have made similar suggestions. Obviously, patients who do not have alternative, healthy, cognitive structures will be much more difficult to work with. The therapist's task is not simply to teach the patient to look for or access these structures; instead, they must be created from whole cloth (Padesky, 1988).

An example

The model states that the underlying central problem produces the overt difficulties. For example, the depression, social isolation, and overeating problems experienced by a newspaper writer can be understood as a result of his belief, "If anyone really gets to know me, he/she will see how repulsive I am and reject me." He is socially isolated because his belief causes him to avoid others. He is depressed both because his social isolation causes him to lose out on lots of positive reinforcers and because his isolation reinforces his negative thinking, as he concludes, "The fact that I don't have any friends just proves how unacceptable I am." He overeats because he uses eating as a way of coping with depression and loneliness. The resultant weight gain, of course, exacerbates his fear of rejection.

Common underlying mechanisms

Several writers have described the psychological mechanisms underlying various psychological symptoms and problems. This section reviews some of the most widely known proposals, with the caveat that little empirical evidence is available to support these propositions as yet (exceptions include Hammen, Marks, Mayol, & deMayo, 1985; Persons & Miranda, 1988; Zuroff & Mongrain, 1987). However, they may assist the therapist in generating hypotheses about the mechanisms underlying patients' symptoms.

Cognitive (and psychodynamic) theorists have described two types of irrational beliefs that underlie depressive symptoms: problems of autonomy and problems of social dependency (Arieti & Bemporad, 1980; Beck, 1983; Blatt, 1974).

Persons with problems of autonomy require independence, accomplishment, and achievement in order to feel worthwhile. They have beliefs along the lines, "Unless I am extremely successful and accomplish a lot, I am worthless." Depressive symptoms are precipitated by experiences of failure, and when they become depressed, these individuals are self-blaming and self-critical.

Persons with problems of dependency must be liked, loved, approved of, and cared for by others in order to feel worthwhile. They have beliefs along the lines, "Unless I am loved, I am worthless." Depressive symptoms are precipitated by rejection and other interpersonal difficulties, and when they become depressed, these individuals feel lonely and isolated and are quite concerned about their attractiveness to others, a concern that stems directly from their view that acceptance and love from others are central to their well-being.

In their description of the cognitive view of anxiety, Beck and his colleagues (Beck, Emery, & Greenberg, 1985) proposed that anxious individuals irrationally view themselves as vulnerable to danger and unable to cope.

Jeffrey Young (1987) recently proposed 15 early maladaptive schema (EMS), divided into four groups: autonomy, connectedness, worthiness, and limits and standards. The 15 EMS are summarized in Table 1.2.

RELATIONSHIP BETWEEN OVERT DIFFICULTIES AND UNDERLYING MECHANISMS

A schematic of the relationships between the elements of the model is presented in Figure 1.1. The arrows pointing from the underlying mechanism to the overt difficulties indicate that the underlying difficulties cause, or generate, the overt difficulties. The arrows in the opposite direction indicate that the overt difficulties support, or maintain, the underlying difficulties. The bi-directional arrows suggest that changes at one level can produce changes at the other level.

The overt and underlying levels of problems are closely related. Thus, for example, the patient who has the central pathological underlying belief, "I'll fail at everything I do," has a large set of cognitions, behaviors, and moods consistent with this belief. She repeatedly experiences the automatic thoughts, "I won't be able to do it, it's too much for me, I'm inadequate, I don't measure up, I never could handle responsibility," and so on. She procrastinates on challenging tasks at work, avoids interac-

Table 1.2   Early maladaptive schemas

AUTONOMY

1. DEPENDENCE. The belief that one is unable to function on one's own and needs the constant support of others.

2. SUBJUGATION/LACK OF INDIVIDUATION. The voluntary or involuntary sacrifice of one's own needs to satisfy others' needs, with an accompanying failure to recognize one's own needs.

3. VULNERABILITY TO HARM OR ILLNESS. The fear that disaster is about to strike at any time (natural, criminal, medical, or financial).

4. FEAR OF LOSING SELF-CONTROL. The fear that one will involuntarily lose control of one's own behavior, impulses, emotions, mind, body, etc.

CONNECTEDNESS

5. EMOTIONAL DEPRIVATION. The expectation that one's needs for nurturance, empathy, affection, and caring will never be adequately met by others.

6. ABANDONMENT/LOSS. Fear that one will imminently lose significant others and then be emotionally isolated forever.

7. MISTRUST. The expectation that others will willfully hurt, abuse, cheat, lie, manipulate, or take advantage.

8. SOCIAL ISOLATION/ALIENATION. The feeling that one is isolated from the rest of the world, different from other people, and/or not a part of any group or community.

WORTHINESS

9. DEFECTIVENESS/UNLOVABILITY. The feeling that one is *inwardly* defective and flawed or that one is fundamentally unlovable to significant others if exposed.

10. SOCIAL UNDESIRABILITY. The belief that one is *outwardly* undesirable to others (e.g., ugly, sexually undesirable, low in status, poor in conversational skills, dull and boring).

11. INCOMPETENCE/FAILURE. The belief that one cannot perform competently in areas of achievement (school, career), daily responsibilities to oneself or others, or decision-making.

12. GUILT/PUNISHMENT. The belief that one is morally or ethically bad or irresponsible, and deserving of harsh criticism or punishment.

(continued)

Table 1.2   (Continued)

13. SHAME/EMBARRASSMENT. Recurrent feelings of shame or self-consciousness experienced because one believes that one's inadequacies (as reflected in schemas 9, 10, 11, or 12) are totally unacceptable to others and are exposed.

LIMITS AND STANDARDS

14. UNRELENTING STANDARDS. The relentless striving to meet extremely high expectations of oneself, at the expense of happiness, pleasure, health, sense of accomplishment, or satisfying relationships.
15. ENTITLEMENT/INSUFFICIENT LIMITS. Insistence that one be able to do, say, or have whatever one wants immediately. Disregard for: what others consider reasonable; what is actually feasible; the time or patience usually required; or the costs to others. Or difficulty with self-discipline.

This table is reprinted with permission from Jeffrey Young, Schema-focused cognitive therapy for personality disorders, 1987, unpublished manuscript available from Jeffrey Young, Cognitive Therapy Center of New York, 111 W. 88 Street, New York, New York 10024.

tions with others, and puts off doing her therapy homework. She feels lonely, anxious, and depressed. Thus, the cognitive, behavioral, and mood components of her overt difficulty are tightly linked, mutually supportive, and consistent, because they are all reflecting, and linked by, the central underlying irrational belief. The link between the cognitive component of the overt difficulties and the underlying mechanism often seems particularly direct, perhaps because both are expressed as cognitions. Thus, the anxious woman's recurrent automatic thoughts are often derivatives, or even direct statements, of her central, underlying belief.

ROLE OF ENVIRONMENTAL FACTORS

Dysfunctional cognitions, behaviors, and moods, and irrational underlying beliefs alone do not cause problems. Environmental factors play a powerful role. For example, if a person who holds the belief, "Unless I'm loved, I'm worthless," is receiving daily infusions of love and caring from a close family, he may not experience any emotional distress or problems in living. If, however, his wife leaves him for another man, he may plunge into depression, despair, and suicidal behavior. Similarly, a person who believes, "I can't cope alone," may do well in a structured, supportive working environment, but not at home, where she lives alone and has few friends. Thus, situational and environmental factors play a role in triggering and eliciting underlying beliefs and the overt difficulties that accompany them.

The underlying irrational beliefs, according to Beck's cognitive theory, play a long-term causal role in the development of episodes of anxiety and depression. According to the theory, these beliefs are trait-like attributes, that is, relatively fixed, that persist throughout an individual's life. They are latent until activated by a particular life event or experience. For example, the person who believes, "I'm worthless unless I'm extremely successful" may function relatively smoothly, without depression, until her application for a promotion is turned down, when she suffers a loss of self-esteem and a clinical depression.

COMPARISON WITH OTHER MODELS

The model presented here is not particularly original. It draws heavily on Beck's cognitive theories of depression and anxiety (Beck, 1972; Beck, Emery, & Greenberg, 1985), Lang's (1979) multiple systems view of fear, the model of fear and fear reduction presented by Foa and Kozak (1986), and the case formulation approach described by Turkat and others (e.g., Turkat & Maisto, 1985). Similar ideas have also been described by Safran, Vallis, Segal, and Shaw (1986).

However, the model does differ significantly from two other prominent models: the biological model, and a behavioral model that does not discuss underlying mechanisms. The role of diagnosis in this model also differs from the conventional psychiatric approach.

Biological models

The discussion of underlying mechanisms presented here emphasizes psychological mechanisms, but mechanisms underlying psychological problems may also be biological. Recent data suggest that obesity, alcoholism, depression, anxiety disorders, manic depressive illness, among others, may have biological bases. Thus, many patients receiving cognitive behavioral treatment may also benefit from medication or another type of biological treatment as well (see Burns, 1980, Chapter 17 and Klein, Gittelman, Quitkin, & Rifkin, 1980).

The presence of a possible underlying biological problem indicates that biological treatment may be an option, but does not mean that biological treatment is required. One reason for this is that psychological and biological mechanisms are not mutually exclusive. Both may be operating. In addition, psychological and biological mechanisms appear to be closely linked. We know that biological treatment (antidepressant medication) produces cognitive changes (Simons, Garfield, & Murphy, 1984); it seems likely that psychological treatment can produce biological changes as well. In addition, the distinction between causal factors and maintaining factors reminds us that, although a problem may have genetic or biological origins, other factors may be maintaining the problem.

Models without underlying mechanisms

Although a model that includes underlying mechanisms may appear radical to some behaviorists, it is not a new idea. Similar ideas have been proposed by Beck (1972), Wolpe (1973), Turkat (e.g., Turkat & Maisto, 1985) and others. However, this model does differ from behavioral approaches that do not postulate underlying mechanisms. The question of which approach is more effective is unanswered at this point, because the needed empirical studies have not been done.

Role of diagnosis

In physical medicine, the diagnosis is a statement about the nature of the physiological mechanism underlying the symptom (e.g., fever). Treatment decisions are made on the basis of the diagnosis. Thus, fever due to malaria is treated differently from fever due to pneumonia.

If the same rule applied in psychiatry, diagnosis would be based on the nature of the underlying pathological *psychological* mechanism (Boorse, 1976; Persons, 1986b). Unfortunately, the nature of the underlying pathological psychological mechanisms in psychiatric illnesses is largely unknown at this time. Therefore, psychiatric diagnoses are defined largely in terms of symptom clusters, not underlying mechanisms. For this reason, diagnoses are not very helpful in making treatment decisions. Therefore, the assessment process described here focuses on developing a problem list and a hypothesis about the psychological mechanisms underlying the problems.

Validity of the case formulation model

Which model is most accurate? Which leads to most effective treatment? These are empirical questions, and unfortunately, little evidence is available to answer them. Some indirect evidence supporting the Foa and

Kozak (1986) model was reviewed by those authors, and quite a lot of work has been done to test Beck's cognitive theory (cf. Beck, Brown, Steer, Eidelson, & Riskind, 1987; Eaves & Rush, 1984; Hamilton & Abramson, 1983; Hammen, et al., 1985; Persons & Rao, 1985; Silverman, Silverman, & Eardley, 1984), and Lewinsohn's behavioral theory (Lewinsohn & Graf, 1973; Lewinsohn & Libet, 1972; Youngren & Lewinsohn, 1980), but much more evidence is needed.

Of course, although the approach to treatment described in this book relies heavily on the case formulation model, most of the interventions described here are drawn directly from standard cognitive behavioral treatment approaches, and a great deal of evidence supports the efficacy of those approaches (see Barlow & Waddell, 1985; Marks, 1981; Miller & Berman, 1983; Rachman & Wilson, 1980; Steketee & Foa, 1985). Whether reliance on the case formulation makes an important difference remains to be seen.

Implications of the model for the cognitive therapist

What does the case formulation model mean for the practicing cognitive behavior therapist? The case formulation has several important roles in clinical work.

First, the case formulation guides the therapist's choice of intervention strategies. For example, the evidence shows that depressed patients can be effectively treated with pleasant events, cognitive disputation, or medication. Effective treatments for anxious patients include exposure, relaxation, biofeedback, and assertiveness training. How does the therapist choose?

The case formulation model proposes that the therapist's understanding of the three overt components, along with her hypothesis about the mechanism underlying the depression, guide the choice of intervention strategies. The therapist who hypothesizes that Mrs. Jones' depression is a response to a low level of reinforcement and that Mr. Smith's depression is a response to a constant stream of self-critical statements would work to increase Mrs. Jones' pleasant activities and to decrease Mr. Smith's self-critical statements.

For another example, consider two patients with insomnia. One who has insomnia because of a fear of losing control finds relaxation training anxiety-provoking (Heide & Borkovec, 1984) but responds well to a flooding treatment for the fear of losing control (Persons, 1986a). Another, whose sleeplessness is due to overscheduling and overcommitment because of a fear of being unsuccessful in his work, responds well to treatment of the fear of failure.

Consider two patients who sought treatment for their tendency to procrastinate on participating in a regular exercise program. The therapist addressed this problem in both cases with scheduling (p. 71 below), asking the patients to schedule exercise (aerobics in one case, jogging in the other) and to bring the schedule to the next session for review. The intervention was successful for the jogger but not the aerobic exerciser. Why?

A formulation of the jogger's case would have shown that one of his central problems was his inability to make a plan and follow through on it in a consistent way. His failure to jog was due to a chaotic lifestyle in which activities were not scheduled or planned. He simply bounced from one activity to another, depending on the demands of the moment. Use of a schedule addressed this problem and helped him make and follow through on a planned commitment. However, the aerobic exerciser's failure to go to exercise class was due to a fear of how she would look in her leotard and what other members of the class might think about her; because these fears were not addressed by the schedule, the intervention failed.

Thus, the formulation, particularly the therapist's hypothesis about the underlying mechanism, plays a central role in guiding the therapist's choice of interventions. In addition, a major part of a formulation-based treatment involves alerting the patient to the nature of his central irrational belief and the way it causes his behavioral, mood, and cognitive problems, as well as teaching strategies for solving these problems that at the same time produce some adaptive change in the underlying pathological beliefs.

An alternative to using the formulation to plan the treatment is to barrage the patient with all the interventions the therapist can think of, in the hope that one will work. One difficulty with this approach is that it is time-consuming, and the patient may become discouraged and drop out of treatment if the first interventions attempted are unsuccessful. Another disadvantage is that interventions applied in the absence of a formulation may actually be counterproductive and make the problem worse.

Another advantage of the formulation-based approach to treatment, in contrast to the intervention-list approach, is that it allows the clinician to understand and treat unusual problems he may not have encountered before but that may respond well to cognitive behavior therapy: shoplifting, nailbiting, somatic symptoms (e.g., loss of voice or pain) with no physiological basis, and so on.

The formulation also helps the therapist understand and manage difficulties that arise in the therapy, including resistance to behavioral and cognitive change, failure to do homework, misunderstandings or other difficulties in the therapeutic relationship, and treatment failure. The case formulation model suggests that the moods, cognitions, and behaviors making up these problems can be understood in the same way as the moods, cognitions, and behaviors making up all the other problems on the problem list are understood. Furthermore, a collaborative approach to solving them can be undertaken, even — or especially — when problems in the therapeutic relationship are involved. If the case formulation model is correct, these moods, cognitions, and behaviors are likely to spring from the same irrational beliefs as the patient's other problems. This model for understanding and working with these typical difficulties gives the therapist a structure and a way of thinking about and responding to these difficulties that can be surprisingly powerful and satisfying. An example is provided in the next section; additional examples occur throughout the book.

In addition, as the final chapter of the book describes, the therapist's understanding of his own underlying vulnerabilities can be quite helpful in understanding and managing negative reactions and difficulties he encounters in his work with patients.

AN EXAMPLE: THE MAN WHO THOUGHT HE WAS DEFECTIVE

A young man came to therapy complaining of depression. A review of various areas of his life revealed that he was quite inactive. He neither worked nor went to school, although he frequently made forays into the work or student worlds, only to retreat after a few weeks or months. He had been living with a girlfriend for 10 years, but maintained an ambivalent, distant connection, never feeling quite satisfied with the relationship but never making a move to improve it or break it off. Based on this and other information, the therapist hypothesized that this patient's central irrational belief was, "I'm defective and inadequate." In the area of work, this belief was expressed in the fear, "Whatever I attempt, I will fail at." In the area of interpersonal relationships, he felt weak and vulnerable, fearing, "I'll become overdependent on others, and I'll do what they tell me instead of what's in my own best interest."

This patient's central irrational belief appeared in dozens of ways throughout the therapy. A close examination of a single therapy session illustrates the way his central irrational beliefs appear repeatedly in his cognitions and behaviors.

At about the one-year point in treatment, the patient came to the session reporting that he was feeling good and didn't really have much to talk about. He had been doing well for several weeks and wanted to discuss the possibility of decreasing the frequency of his therapy sessions (he was coming weekly at that point). However, he had difficulty raising this topic because of the thought, "If I reduce my therapy, something bad might happen, and I won't be able to cope." This thought can be seen as a restatement of his central irrational belief.

After the therapist pointed this out, and we worked through this problem (he scheduled a session for one month later), we moved to a discussion of his homework for the college courses he had recently begun. He had decided he wanted to make up a schedule for doing his homework, but didn't follow through and do it. When the therapist asked, "When you think about making up a schedule, what thought do you get?" he responded, "I'll make a schedule, but I won't follow it." This statement is also a restatement of his central irrational belief.

Next, he moved to a discussion of an essay he was working on for his geology class. He reported that he had at first thought of doing an essay on a topic that was of particular interest to him, a topic that he had written a related essay on for another course at another college some years before. However, he had abandoned this idea, thinking, "It would be cheating to do that." This idea was closely related to the core idea, "I'm defective," and was linked to a feeling that he did not get from his family the training in mores and ethics that most other people received. Notice the recurring behavioral pattern: thinking of doing something and then pulling back. This behavioral pattern also appears to be directly related to his central underlying belief.

After we discussed the question of whether using the old essay to get started on a new essay on a similar topic was "cheating" (he decided it was not), we moved on to a discussion of another essay for another class. The patient had begun research on an obscure topic, but after reading one book on the subject that fascinated him, he felt at a loss for obtaining new materials. He had the thought, "I can't get an essay out of this topic," and he abandoned the topic, beginning a search for another. Again, his pattern of thinking and behavior is directly related to his underlying belief about himself.

This patient's central underlying belief appeared in dozens of other ways in the therapy. He readily took on homework assignments, but typically came to therapy sessions reporting he had not completed them (frequently he started, but not completed them), and feeling that what he had done was inadequate. He felt he ought to reread *Feeling Good* (Burns, 1980) on a regular basis, so he could learn to analyze and immediately respond to all his thinking errors. He was reluctant to engage in the therapy, for fear of becoming overdependent on the therapist, and at one point insisted on coming every other week so he could afford to see a hypnotherapist on the alternate weeks.

Thus, this patient's central underlying belief about himself was a guiding theme in the therapy, influencing the automatic thoughts and behavioral patterns seen in the therapy, the patient's way of handling homework, and the therapeutic relationship. An understanding of the case formulation helps the therapist understand and manage all these issues.

WHERE DOES THE THERAPIST INTERVENE?

One question the case formulation model raises is: Where does the therapist intervene? If psychological problems occur at two levels, where does the therapist intervene? Does she work to expose and change the underlying mechanisms? Or does she work to change overt behaviors, cognitions, and moods?

The approach to assessment and treatment described in this book emphasizes a "top-down" approach. Cognitive behavior therapists believe that work on overt difficulties produces more change in both overt difficulties and underlying beliefs than work at the underlying level. For example, a depressed man who has the underlying belief, "I must do everything perfectly to get any pleasure or satisfaction at all" can improve his mood and chip away at the underlying belief in one stroke if he carries out a homework plan to play a mediocre game of tennis with a friend. Although the approach presented here emphasizes top-down work, the question of which direction of work is most effective is ultimately an empirical one.

Of course, therapy inevitably involves both types of work. The bidirectional arrows in Figure 1.1 indicate that changes in overt difficulties can produce changes in the underlying attitudes, and changes in underlying attitudes can produce changes in overt difficulties.

Although the intervention strategies described here focus on overt difficulties, treatment does have the goal of changing underlying mechanisms as well. There is evidence that changes at the overt level that do not involve changes at underlying levels may be short-lived. Researchers have shown that depressed patients who terminated treatment with marked improvement in symptoms but little or no improvement in underlying irrational beliefs were more likely to relapse than those who had experienced changes in their underlying beliefs (Simons, et al., 1984). Foa, Steketee, Turner, and Fischer (1980) showed that obsessive-compulsives who were treated with in vivo exposure to their feared situations were more likely to relapse than patients treated with both in vivo exposure and imaginal exposure to their central underlying fears.

If top-down work does in fact produce changes in underlying beliefs, and if the core underlying beliefs do, as postulated, underlie all the patient's overt difficulties, then good therapeutic progress on one problem ought to be accompanied by improvement even in untreated problems. This idea, of course, is subject to empirical test (e.g., Persons, 1986a).

Because of the emphasis on top-down work, intervention strategies described in this book fall into two classes: interventions directed at behavior (Chapters 4 and 5) and those directed at cognitions (Chapters 6 and 7). Interventions directed at mood are not described because they have not been developed.

The two classes of interventions again raise the question: where does the therapist intervene? To change cognitions or to change behaviors? In general, the answer depends on the nature of the relationships between the components, as described by the case formulation. In addition, pragmatic considerations about which component the patient feels most able to change are quite relevant. Sometimes cognitions seem to cause behaviors. For example, a young woman is unable to refuse an unwanted invitation because she thinks, "If I say no, it will be devastating to him." Cognitive interventions to expose the irrationalities in this thinking may facilitate behavioral change. In other situations, behaviors seem to cause cognitions and to be more malleable. For example, a young woman with very low self-esteem worked to improve her self-image by buying some nice clothes for herself, even though she believed she didn't deserve them.

GETTING STARTED

To make clinical use of the case formulation model, the therapist begins by assessing the two levels of the patient's problems: overt difficulties and underlying mechanisms. That is, the therapist obtains a comprehensive problem list and proposes a hypothesis about the psychological mechanism underlying the problems on the list. These two topics are addressed in the next two chapters.

CHAPTER 2

The problem list

The first step in implementing the case formulation model in clinical practice is specifying the patient's problem list. The problem list is an all-inclusive list of the patient's difficulties. The problem list focuses the treatment; without it, therapy may be aimless and unproductive and it will be difficult or impossible to assess its effectiveness. In addition, as described in the next chapter, an exhaustive and detailed problem list is the first step in developing a case formulation.

The first section of the present chapter focuses on identifying the items that belong on the problem list. The second section outlines procedures for obtaining quantitative measures of mood, cognitive, and behavioral components of each problem on the list. The third section describes the use of the problem list to evaluate the results of treatment.

IDENTIFYING PROBLEMS

What problems belong on the problem list?

It is rare for a person seeking treatment to have only one problem; a typical problem list has eight or ten items. Common problems include depression, panic attacks, phobias, inability to drive on freeways, procrastination at work, overeating, drug or alcohol abuse, marital conflict, social isolation, unemployment, financial difficulties, unsatisfactory living arrangements, headaches, and medical problems.

Although many of these difficulties (e.g., unemployment) may not appear to belong on a list of problems to be worked on in psychotherapy, it is useful, for several reasons, to include all these items on the problem list.

The strategy of beginning with an all-inclusive problem list ensures that important problems are not missed; it can also be helpful in the process of proposing an underlying mechanism, as described in the next chapter. Although unemployment, for example, may not at first seem to be a psychological problem, careful investigation often reveals that the patient's psychological difficulties play a role in causing his joblessness and/or in preventing the patient from seeking and finding employment. The same is true for medical problems. Medical problems often have important psychological causes. A common way psychological difficulties contribute to medical problems is via the patient's failure to comply with treatment recommendations; for example, a patient with high blood pressure has been instructed to stop smoking, but feels unable to do so.

Patients are frequently reluctant to provide a comprehensive problem list. Often they seek treatment for the one or two primary problems that are most distressing, and prefer to ignore other issues. Problems may be avoided because they seem overwhelming and insoluble, because they are embarrassing, because tackling them is expected to be unacceptably painful and difficult, or because the patient does not consider the issue a problem and does not want to make a change in this area. Drug and alcohol abuse frequently fall in this last category. Sometimes patients avoid discussing problems because they are genuinely unaware that a problem exists. For example, a young woman seeking treatment for panic attacks and depression did not own a driver's license and did not drive. She did not consider this a problem, even though it inconvenienced many members of her family and caused her to be completely socially isolated. She was so accustomed to the constricted lifestyle she had adopted that she was not aware of a problem. In addition, of course, her constricted lifestyle allowed her to avoid the anxiety she experienced in social situations—in fact, it allowed her to avoid even the awareness that she *had* social anxiety.

Although patients often resist providing a comprehensive problem list, the therapist's failure to obtain one can jeopardize the treatment. Sometimes issues the patient is most reluctant to discuss are vital to the success of the treatment. A middle-aged boutique owner suffering from severe insomnia repeatedly refused to discuss business and financial problems.

When, after several weeks of unsuccessful treatment, she agreed to examine these issues, a clear relationship between sleeplessness and business reverses was discovered; this made an important and effective difference in her treatment.

Although the strategy recommended here involves drawing up a comprehensive problem list, this does not mean that all of the problems are necessarily actively addressed in treatment. Months of therapeutic work might pass before some of the problems on the list are addressed. However, repeated monitoring of all the problems, even the ones that are not worked on actively, is a good idea. If the underlying mechanism is correct and all the problems are related, as predicted in the case formulation model, work on some problems is expected to produce improvement in untreated problems.

The process of identifying problems

Obtaining an exhaustive problem list is a good focus for the initial therapy session. Often a new patient spontaneously begins with a recitation of his difficulties. If this does not happen, the therapist can provide some structure for this process by saying, "I suggest that we work together to develop a list of problems you want to work on in your therapy."

Often more than one session is required to complete the problem list. As a homework assignment for the first session, the patient can be asked to spend a few minutes thinking about what other problems she might like to work on and what other goals she'd like to accomplish in her therapy, or she can be asked to keep a log to collect baseline data on some particular aspects of a problem described in the first session.

Occasionally patients provide a clear statement of their difficulties in the same terms the therapist uses (e.g., "I'm afraid of contamination and I wash my hands constantly"). However, most don't use the model described in Chapter 1 to conceptualize their problems. Instead, they describe difficulties in vague, general terms, saying, for example, "My life is a mess." The therapist's first task is to transform this kind of complaint into one or more discrete problems of the sort that are treated by cognitive-behavior therapists. In particular, the therapist looks for the mood, behavioral, and cognitive components of problems patients report, as in the following example.

PATIENT   My life is a mess!
THERAPIST   What's going on? (The therapist looks for concrete behavioral, cognitive, and mood difficulties.)

PATIENT   I'm not getting anything done at work. I hardly spend any
    time at my office. My mail just piles up and I don't even open it.
    (behavior)
THERAPIST   What kind of work do you do?
PATIENT   I'm a salesman — I sell medical equipment. But sometimes I
    think I want to change jobs — I'm not enjoying my work very much
    at all right now. (mood)
THERAPIST   I see. Can you say more about what work is like for you?
PATIENT   Well, I'm not returning phone calls. I have a pile of pink slips.
    Some of them are weeks old. (behavior)
THERAPIST   So you're not returning phone calls. What about calling on
    your customers and making sure your orders are filled?
PATIENT   I do OK at the things that *have* to get done, the ones that have
    a deadline. But things that can be put off, like developing more
    customers, don't get done. I put off everything that's not urgent
    until it turns into an emergency. (behavior)
THERAPIST   So the vital stuff gets done, but there's a lot of procrastinat-
    ing on non-emergency stuff.
PATIENT   Right.
THERAPIST   Any other problems?
PATIENT   My social life is a disaster.
THERAPIST   Tell me what you mean when you say that. (Again, looking
    for concrete thoughts, behaviors, and moods.)
PATIENT   Well, I spend a lot of my free time in my apartment by myself,
    watching TV and feeling lousy. I guess I should try to get out of the
    house more. (behavior, mood)
THERAPIST   Yes, that's probably a good idea. Any other problems in
    your social life?
PATIENT   Well, I eat dinner three times a week with my grandmother.
    (behavior)
THERAPIST   Tell me more about that.
PATIENT   Well, she's old, and I'm her only relative here in town. I'd like
    to see her less, but I feel guilty about not spending time with her.
    Her husband is dead, and if I don't visit her, she'll be alone and
    unhappy. (mood, cognitions)
THERAPIST   Anything else?
PATIENT   Well, I'm not dating, and that's probably because I'm holding
    onto a relationship with an old girlfriend of mine who moved out of
    town a year ago. I spend holidays and vacations with her, and I sort
    of realize I need to quit doing that. (behavior, cognitions)
THERAPIST   Why do you think you hold on to that relationship? When
    you think about letting her go, what thought do you get?

PATIENT   I think, "I'll never find anyone else. No one would have me."
    (cognition)

Problems not reported by the patient

Frequently patients have important problems they do not report, either because they are not aware of them or because they are ashamed or afraid to mention them. Patients may be unaware of organic deficits or even of serious interpersonal difficulties. They may be ashamed of having financial difficulties or unable to admit that drugs or alcohol are interfering with work or marriage. They may be frightened to own up to repeated suicide attempts for fear the therapist will refuse to continue treatment.

The therapist can obtain information about these types of problems in several ways. Careful observation of the patient's behavior in the therapy session may reveal interpersonal problems that the patient does not perceive or does not perceive as a problem. A person who is irritable and hostile in his interactions with the therapist is likely to act similarly with others, although he may not volunteer this information.

The family and social history can also reveal unstated problems. A personal history with a series of unsuccessful marriages points to interpersonal problems, even if the patient does not report them. Alcohol and drug addictions in several family members suggests the possibility that the patient may be having similar difficulties.

The patient's family, previous therapists, or others may describe problems the patient is not aware of or wishes to hide. The therapist's hypothesis about the underlying mechanism can suggest the presence of problems the patient does not report. For example, a person whose chief problem is a need to gain the approval of others is likely to be unassertive and overly compliant to the wishes of others, be unclear about his own needs, wishes and goals, and feel angry and resentful toward those he seeks approval from.

The mental status examination can be useful in picking up symptoms of formal thought disorder, delusions, or organic deficits. All of these problems belong on the problem list but are rarely reported by the patient.

When the therapist observes problems the patient does not report, it is a good idea to try to point these out so they can be added to the problem list. However, patients may be reluctant to do this. Depending on the nature of the problems, the therapist may wish to make an agreement with the patient to try treating the problems the patient presents and ignoring the ones the patient wants to ignore. However, if this treatment strategy is ineffective, the unaddressed problems may need to be raised again.

At times the therapist may wish to add problems to the list that the patient is unwilling or unable to discuss at the time the problem list is made up. For example, at the beginning of treatment the therapist may not be able to point out to the patient that he has a tendency to manipulate and take advantage of others. When a problem cannot be placed on the mutual problem list, the therapist can keep in mind that a goal of treatment is to add this problem to the patient's list, so that the problem can be addressed in a collaborative way.

Sometimes a failure to agree on a problem list dooms the treatment. This happened to me recently when, after six months of unsuccessful treatment, a discussion of the lack of success of the treatment clearly revealed that the patient didn't really consider her difficulty leaving the house as a problem that needed work. Her view was that she was fragile and delicate and that she needed to stay home and rest. As soon as this difference in our problem lists (and treatment plans) was laid on the table, the patient came to the conclusion that she didn't want to work with me and left treatment. Although this was not a positive outcome, it was actually preferable to the unproductive and uncollaborative treatment we had been carrying out.

Changes in the problem list

The problem list is likely to change as treatment proceeds. When some difficulties are solved, others may appear. For example, a depressed, isolated, inactive patient who is successfully treated for depression may then reveal social anxiety that had been obscured by the social isolation and depression. Sometimes problems, particularly interpersonal ones, become apparent only as treatment proceeds and the relationship with the therapist develops. Thus, the process of arriving at a problem list is an ongoing one.

QUANTITATIVE MEASUREMENT OF PROBLEMS

When an exhaustive list of the patient's problems has been made, detailed, quantitative information about the mood, cognitive, and behavioral aspects of each problem is needed. Information about the multiple components of problems is necessary to understand the problems and formulate the case. Quantitative information about problems is necessary in order to assess progress. Standardized scales and interview approaches to obtaining this information are described here.

Depression

Often the depressed patient reports a difficulty in only one component of the three components of overt difficulties described in Chapter 1: e.g., depressed mood. However, difficulties in one or both of the other components (cognitions, behavior) are likely to be present, and they need to be assessed as well. The Beck Depression Inventory (BDI) assesses mood, cognitive, and physiological aspects of depression. An activity log may be helpful in assessing gross behavioral problems.

BECK DEPRESSION INVENTORY. The BDI is a 21-item self-report inventory of the severity of symptoms of depression (the score on the weight-loss item is not tallied if the patient is trying to lose weight).[1] The BDI score has frequently been found to show high correlations with clinical ratings of depression severity (Beck, 1972; reviewed by Carson, 1986). Beck has set arbitrary cutoff scores for interpreting BDI scores, as follows: BDI less than 10, not depressed; 10 to 15, mildly depressed; 16 to 20, moderately depressed; 25 or greater, severely depressed.

The BDI can be completed in two or three minutes, and I ask my depressed patients to complete one weekly before the therapy session. Most — but not all — patients accept the BDI as a measure of depression, and as a result it serves as a very useful measure of the progress of the therapy. I plot the patient's score on a graph to monitor progress. A typical good treatment response is presented in Figure 2.1; it shows an initial sharp drop in BDI, followed by slower improvements thereafter (Simons, et al., 1984).

In addition to monitoring progress in therapy, the BDI is also useful in guiding the therapy session. A look at the patient's BDI gives a crude index, before the session starts, of how the patient's week went.

ACTIVITY LOG. An activity log can be used to assess a variety of behavioral aspects of problems. Depressed patients are commonly inactive and withdrawn; to quantify this, the therapist can ask the patient to log social activities or interactions, or time spent in bed. A written log is particularly helpful in obtaining a quantitative assessment of problems. Without a

[1]The BDI is reprinted in Beck, Rush, Shaw, & Emery (1979, pp. 398–399) and in Corcoran & Fischer (1987).

Figure 2.1   Changes in Beck Depression Inventory score over the course of a successful treatment.

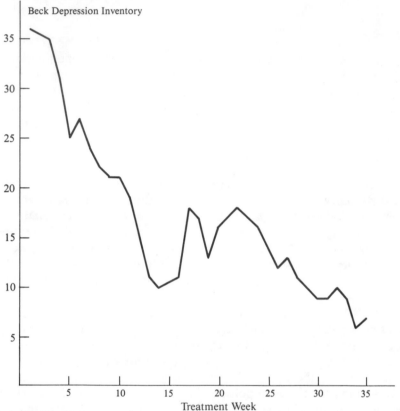

Treatment Week

written log, patients usually cannot give an accurate report, for example, of the number of times they wash their hands daily (for an obsessive-compulsive) or the number of hours they spend at home alone watching TV.

An activity log can be used to record any of a variety of problem behaviors or moods, panic attacks or episodes of suicidal thinking, angry outbursts, overeating, excessive drinking, unwanted sexual activity, shop-lifting, and so on. A simple version of the log can involve simply a count of the frequency of the behavior in question — for example, a count of the number of panic attacks, colitis attacks, angry outbursts, or headaches per week. The log can also include ratings of severity or duration (e.g., for headaches). Ratings of severity can use a simple 0 to 100 scale or whatever type of scale is most appealing to the patient — perhaps she rates her headaches as mild, medium, or severe, for example.

More complex versions of the log can record, for each instance of a problematic behavior, the date, time, situation, mood, thoughts, or consequences. This type of information can provide clues about underlying mechanisms. Through the log, the patient and therapist can learn, for example, that panic attacks regularly occur after the morning cup of coffee or just before therapy sessions.

A log is also useful for keeping an ongoing record of homework exercises. For example, an agoraphobic can record what situations she entered and how anxious she felt. It can be altered to meet the needs of the situation at hand; for example, two anxiety ratings may be helpful, one rating of the *maximum* anxiety in the feared situation, and a second one of the anxiety at the end of the exposure session. In this way, the therapist can determine whether the patient stayed in the feared situation long enough for habituation to occur (see Exposure, Chapter 5).

Although log-keeping is offered here as a way of *assessing* problematic moods and behaviors, there is good evidence that the self-monitoring involved in keeping such a log also produces behavioral *changes*, usually in the desired direction, but these are usually short-lived (Bornstein, Hamilton, & Bornstein, 1986).

Suicidality

Assessment of suicidality is vital, as the failure to assess and treat a serious problem in this area may preclude treatment of any of the patient's other problems! The first interview with depressed patients should include at least one question about suicide. The obvious first question is, "Are you having any thoughts about suicide?"

If the answer to this question is a clear "no," then I often say, "It sounds like suicide is not a problem for you. Let's make an agreement that if it ever becomes a problem, you'll discuss it with me so we can work on it."

If the answer to the question about thoughts of suicide is "yes," additional assessment is needed. Strategies for doing this and for intervening with suicidality are presented in Chapter 10.

Assessment of suicidality is an ongoing process. When patients are completing the BDI weekly, the suicide item (#9) can be used as a quick way of keeping an eye on this issue.

Anxiety and phobic avoidance

The multiple-component view of anxiety (Lang, 1977, 1979) is more prominent than a multiple-component view of depression, and this is reflected in the availability of more measures for assessing anxiety than depression. Several measures of anxiety are presented: the Burns Anxiety Inventory, the Fear Survey Schedule, the fear hierarchy, and the behavioral avoidance test.

BURNS ANXIETY INVENTORY. The Burns Anxiety Inventory, developed by David Burns, is a 32-item self-report scale listing feelings, thoughts and physical symptoms of anxiety. This inventory, reprinted here in Table 2.1, is extremely useful for monitoring the cognitive, mood and physiological (behavioral) symptoms of anxiety. Anxious patients can be asked to complete the BAI weekly.

FEAR SURVEY SCHEDULE. The Fear Survey Schedule (Wolpe & Lang, 1969) lists 108 commonly feared objects or events (e.g., journeys by airplane, looking down from high buildings, fainting). Each item is scored for the amount of "fear or other, related unpleasant feelings" on a scale from 0 (not at all) to 4 (very much). The Fear Survey Schedule is useful for alerting the therapist to fears the patient might not otherwise report. It is widely used in both research and clinical settings.

Internal consistency and test-retest reliabilities for the Fear Survey Schedule are high. However, the scale does not always correlate highly with behavioral and physiological measures of fear. This is not necessarily surprising, given the known desynchrony between the various aspects of fear (Lang, 1977, 1979). In addition, patients' fear ratings may be higher when in the feared situation than when far from it.

FEAR HIERARCHY. A fear hierarchy measures a person's verbal report of fear to a set of related objects and situations. Construction of a fear hierarchy requires the use of a subjective mood scale to obtain a quantitative measure of the patient's subjective experience of negative moods (e.g., anxiety, depression, hopelessness, anger). The ratings may also reflect negative physiological experiences (breathlessness, difficulty swallowing, palpitations, dizziness). Wolpe used such a scale to set up a hierarchy for systematic desensitization (see Wolpe, 1973); he called this the "suds" scale (subjective units of distress). To calibrate the scale he suggested the following instructions, "Think of the worst anxiety you have ever experienced, or can imagine experiencing, and assign to this the number 100. Now think of the state of being absolutely calm and call this zero. Now you have a scale of anxiety. On this scale how do you rate yourself at this moment?" (Wolpe, 1973, p. 120).

A fear hierarchy is extremely useful for guiding exposure homework (the patient can begin exposing herself to the items at the bottom of the

Table 2.1   Burns Anxiety Inventory

Symptom List

Instructions: The following is a list of symptoms that people sometimes have. Put a check (✔) in the space to the right that best describes how much that symptom or problem has bothered you during the past week. If you would like a weekly record of your progress, record your answers on the separate "Answer Sheet" instead of filling in the spaces on the right.

Category I: Anxious Feelings	0 – NOT AT ALL	1 – SOMEWHAT	2 – MODERATELY	3 – A LOT
1. Anxiety, nervousness, worry or fear				
2. Feeling that things around you are strange, unreal or foggy				
3. Feeling detached from all or part of your body				
4. Sudden unexpected panic spells				
5. Apprehension or a sense of impending doom				
6. Feeling tense, stressed, "uptight" or on edge				

Category II: Anxious Thoughts

7. Difficulty concentrating				
8. Racing thoughts or having your mind jump from one thing to the next				
9. Frightening fantasies or daydreams				
10. Feeling that you're on the verge of losing control				

(continued)

	0 – NOT AT ALL	1 – SOMEWHAT	2 – MODERATELY	3 – A LOT

Category II: Anxious Thoughts (continued)

	0 – NOT AT ALL	1 – SOMEWHAT	2 – MODERATELY	3 – A LOT
11. Fears of cracking up or going crazy				
12. Fears of fainting or passing out				
13. Fears of physical illnesses or heart attacks or dying				
14. Concerns about looking foolish or inadequate in front of others				
15. Fears of being alone, isolated or abandoned				
16. Fears of criticism or disapproval				
17. Fears that something terrible is about to happen				

Category III: Physical Symptoms

	0 – NOT AT ALL	1 – SOMEWHAT	2 – MODERATELY	3 – A LOT
18. Skipping or racing or pounding of the heart (sometimes called "palpitations")				
19. Pain, pressure or tightness in the chest				
20. Tingling or numbness in the toes or fingers				
21. Butterflies or discomfort in the stomach				
22. Constipation or diarrhea				
23. Restlessness or jumpiness				
24. Tight, tense muscles				
25. Sweating not brought on by heat				
26. A lump in the throat				

(continued)

Category III: Physical Symptoms *(continued)*	0 – NOT AT ALL	1 – SOMEWHAT	2 – MODERATELY	3 – A LOT
27. Trembling or shaking				
28. Rubbery or "jelly" legs				
29. Feeling dizzy, lightheaded or off balance				
30. Choking or smothering sensations or difficulty breathing				
31. Headaches or pains in the neck or back				
32. Hot flashes or cold chills				
33. Feeling tired, weak or easily exhausted				

Add up your total score for each of the 33 symptoms and
record it here: _____

                                             Date: _____

Grateful acknowledgment is made to David Burns for permission to reprint this table.

list and then work up) and for assessing the effects of treatment. A
hierarchy of feared situations for an agoraphobic young lady is presented
in Figure 2.2. Pre-treatment ratings for all the items and post-treatment
ratings (eight weeks later!) for a few of the items are supplied in the
figure.

BEHAVIORAL AVOIDANCE TEST. The BAT provides a direct, objective,
quantitative measure of the degree of avoidance of phobic objects and
situations (Taylor & Agras, 1981). This is a direct measure of a key
behavioral component of many anxiety problems. The BAT provides
objective, quantitative, and clinically relevant data, and it is ideal for
assessing changes due to treatment.

Figure 2.2   Pre- and post-treatment ratings of fear on a hierarchy for an agoraphobic young woman. Post-treatment scores are in parentheses.

---

100 (50) — holding down a job — being expected to be in one place all day without being able to leave.*

100 — crowded movie, alone

90 — crowded restaurant, alone

80 (0) — riding a crowded bus

80 — crowded movie, accompanied

80 (50) — crowded restaurant, accompanied

70 — elevator, alone

60–65 (50) — crowded, large department store

60 (30) — empty movie, alone

50 (30) — walking the crowded streets in the financial district

50 — shopping mall

40 (20) — elevator, with others

30–40 (15) — small elevator in the building where I live

30 (15) — empty restaurant, alone or accompanied

30 — empty movie, accompanied

30 (10) — spending the afternoon doing volunteer work

20 (10) — grocery store

10 — freeway driving

---

*At post-treatment the patient accepted a part-time job.

A test can be devised for almost any phobia. Acrophobics can be asked to report the maximum number of floors up a tall building they are able to climb. Cat phobics can be asked to approach a cat as closely as possible and report the number of feet between themselves and the cat when this has been done. Bridge phobics can be asked which bridges in the area they cannot drive over. Agoraphobics can be asked how many blocks from home they can go, or what places and situations they avoid — travel by public transportation, movie theaters, auditoriums, and so on. A related measure is duration of exposure to the feared object or situation. Claustrophobia, for example, can be assessed by measuring the length of time the patient can spend in a tiny room with the door closed.

Other measures

In addition to the scales described and reprinted here, many others are reprinted and described in Corcoran and Fischer (1987) and Hersen and Bellack (1988).

Interview strategies

The most commonly used method of collecting information is undoubtedly the clinical interview. Interview strategies for obtaining a quantitative description of the behavioral, mood, and cognitive aspects of several common psychological problems are illustrated here.

"A PROBLEM AT WORK."

THERAPIST   Tell me more about the problem at work.
PATIENT   Well, I got demoted last year, and these days I am always afraid I'll be demoted again. I worry about it all the time, and it makes it hard to get any work done. (mood, cognitions, behavior)
THERAPIST   So things aren't getting done?
PATIENT   No, I tend to procrastinate on important projects.
THERAPIST   I see. Like, for example, what projects are you procrastinating on right now?
PATIENT   Well, I have a project for a big firm in Houston that I'm avoiding dealing with, and the end-of-the-quarter report is getting put off, too.
THERAPIST   Is the end-of-the-quarter report usually a problem for you?
PATIENT   Yes, I always put it off until the last minute, and then I have to have my secretary put in a lot of overtime to finish it on time.
THERAPIST   Does it ever get done late?
PATIENT   Yes, last time it was late.
THERAPIST   And do some of the other big projects run late too?
PATIENT   Yes, I missed the deadline on the Cleveland project by a week!
THERAPIST   What percent of the time would you say that your projects run late?
PATIENT   Oh, maybe 30% to 40%.
THERAPIST   So you'd like to work on that? You'd like to get these projects done on time?
PATIENT   Yes, I would.
THERAPIST   OK, that sounds good, let's make that a goal for you. Now, let's go back to the anxiety you're having. Let me ask you this: On

an average day at work, how strong, from 0 to 100, is your fear that
you'll get demoted?

PATIENT   Oh, it's hard to say. Maybe about 50.

THERAPIST   Well, I'll tell you what I'd suggest. How about keeping a log.
At the end of every workday, how about rating your fear of being
demoted, on average during the day, and just writing the number on
your appointment calendar — can you do that?

PATIENT   Sure.

THERAPIST   Good. Let's review it when you come in next week, and if
you can keep that log on a regular basis, we can use it to evaluate
how effective we're being at working on that problem. Does that
make sense to you?

PATIENT   Sure.

"A PROBLEM AT THE LAB." A depressed (mood) chemist felt incompetent
in his laboratory work (mood) and avoided going to the lab (behavior).
When he was in the lab, he experienced a barrage of self-critical thoughts
(cognitions) assessing his performance as inadequate and inept.

To assess his lack of self-confidence, he rated, on a scale of 0 to 100,
the feelings: "how confident I feel about the quality of my work" and
"how confident I feel about the quality of my work when I talk with my
supervisor." To assess the behavioral aspect of the problem, time spent at
the lab, he kept a log of his hours at the lab. To get more information
about the cognitive aspects of the problem, he recorded automatic
thoughts when he was in the lab or imagined being in the lab, and rated
his degree of belief in the thoughts. As therapy progressed, he spent more
time in the lab, felt more confident about his work, and his automatic
thoughts were less frequent and less believable.

"LONELINESS." A depressed young female computer programmer reported feeling intensely lonely and isolated. She estimated she felt this way
80% of the time. An assessment of her behavior indicated that, except for
time at work, she spent most of her hours alone. Even at work and at
home, where she had a roommate, she avoided social interactions whenever possible. Her typical week included one social event after work or on
the weekend. When she was overwhelmed with loneliness, she had
thoughts like, "I don't belong," "I'll always be alone," and "I'll never be
happy unless I get married and have a family." Social interactions precipitated thoughts along the lines, "I'll get hurt," "I'll lose my autonomy and
my life," and "This is dangerous." She believed these thoughts 100%.
Treatment goals for this patient included reducing the frequency (and
intensity, though that was not measured here) of negative moods of lone-

liness and depression, increasing the frequency of social interactions, and decreasing the frequency and degree of belief of the automatic thoughts.

EVALUATING THE EFFECTS OF TREATMENT

The problem list serves as a basis for evaluating the effects of treatment. Unless detailed, quantitative information about the patient's problems is collected at the beginning of therapy, the patient and therapist cannot know whether progress has occurred. The inability, at the end of many weeks or months of hard work, to clearly determine whether therapy has been helpful, can be extremely demoralizing to both patient and therapist.

Sometimes patient and therapist disagree in their assessment of the effects of the therapy. This type of disagreement may be due to the tendency of depressed patients to have a distorted, negative view of everything, including their progress in therapy. This type of patient may drop out of treatment, believing he has failed in therapy. A plot of weekly Beck Depression Inventory scores that shows steady improvement can remind patients who claim they have not benefitted from treatment that they have in fact improved. The opposite problem can occur as well. Some patients, particularly dependent, passive ones, wish to inflate the view of the progress made in therapy in order to maintain the status quo, particularly the therapeutic relationship. These patients wish to stay in therapy too long. In both these cases, objective, quantifiable data for assessing the effect of treatment are invaluable.

If treatment is unsuccessful, it is important to know this. Without frequent assessments of progress, the patient and therapist may waste valuable time pursuing an unproductive or misguided treatment. Although achievement of the goals of therapy may take years, some evidence of change in the desired direction is usually expected within a matter of weeks. For example, depressed patients who respond to cognitive therapy typically begin to show an improvement in Beck Depression Inventory scores within six weeks (Simons et al., 1984). If this does not happen, reevaluation is indicated.

In my own practice, I try to review progress every three months. I generally raise this issue by saying something like, "We've been working together for three months, so I'd like to review how we're doing. What I'd suggest is that you take some time to think about this during the week, and next time we meet we can spend a few minutes reviewing our progress. We can do this by going over the list of problems we made up when you started, and seeing how we're doing. How does that sound?"

Reviewing progress is often a very stressful event for patients, many of whom are frightened of failure or of being rejected by the therapist. The therapist's awareness of the patient's underlying belief and typical cognitions can be used to anticipate and prepare for negative reactions to the review process. For example, patients who believe, "Unless I please others, they will reject me" may be frightened that the therapist will feel angry at them for failing to improve fast enough; the therapist may wish to predict this fear and offer appropriate reassurance.

Sometimes it is difficult to determine whether progress is occurring. This is particularly true when some progress has taken place but the pace is slow. Is this a treatment failure or a slow treatment success? When faced with this question, I evaluate not only the accomplishment of the treatment goals, but also the process of the therapeutic work. Does change occur within the session? Do the patient and therapist work together in an effective, collaborative, productive way? If the answers to these questions are "yes," and the patient and I are willing to tolerate a slow rate of progress, we can decide to just keep plugging away.

CHAPTER 3

The case formulation

The case formulation is a hypothesis about the nature of the psychological difficulty (or difficulties) underlying the problems on the patient's problem list. This chapter begins with a description of the many roles of the case formulation in treatment. Next, the format of the case formulation is outlined and an example provided. Finally, the process of obtaining a formulation is described in detail, and five strategies for testing a formulation are described.

ROLE OF THE CASE FORMULATION

The case formulation is the therapist's compass; it guides the treatment. In general terms, the most important role of the formulation is to provide the basis for the treatment plan, which follows directly from the hypothesis about the nature of the underlying deficit producing the patient's problems. Clinical examples are used here to illustrate nine important roles of the case formulation. The case formulation helps the therapist:

1. Understand relationships among problems

The case formulation ties together all of a patient's problems. Without the formulation, the therapist may see the problems as a random collection of difficulties. In addition, patients sometimes seek treatment of only some of their problems. The formulation can help the therapist estimate whether this type of treatment plan is likely to be successful, as in the case of a 50-year old bachelor who seeks treatment for fears of contamination and extensive washing rituals dating from early adolescence. The washing rituals currently consume most of his waking hours. Mr. Bachelor is unemployed and has worked only one to two years since graduating from college more than 25 years ago; he has been supported by his family. He is also quite socially isolated. However, he states that he does not want to address the work and social problems in treatment; he wants to focus only on the contamination fears and the washing rituals. At the end of the evaluation session, however, it comes out that he is ambivalent about giving up these symptoms, because then he would face the need to go to work (he is running out of money) and to interact with others. Thus, the patient's contamination fears and washing rituals are reinforced by the fact that they protect him from confronting his fears of work and social interactions. This patient's central irrational fear appears to be, "Going out in the world is too dangerous for me." This formulation suggests that the fears of work and relationships must be included in treatment if it is to be successful. In fact, the formulation suggests that it may be necessary to treat these fears first.

2. Choose a treatment modality

A 35-year-old female assistant professor at a major university sought treatment for anxiety. She reported that she had had two panic attacks about eight months prior to seeking treatment, and high levels of anxiety since. The first panic attack occurred on the day she left the hospital with her new baby. This panic episode was resolved by calling her husband to come to the hospital to get her. The second attack occurred two weeks later, on a Saturday afternoon at home, while she was waiting for her husband to return from a bowling party with his friends. Except in the case of the two panic attacks, she was unable to say what situations or cognitions preceded the anxiety. The problem of assessment was complicated by the fact that as soon as she began treatment, the anxiety largely remitted.

What treatment ought the therapist to suggest? Without a formulation, the therapist might simply treat the symptoms. In this case, because the patient's presenting problem was anxiety, relaxation training might have been prescribed. The therapist did prescribe relaxation training, but it was presented as a helpful strategy, not a complete solution; this would not be possible until a full understanding of the causes of the anxiety was obtained. To search for this information, the patient was asked to keep a log of anxious feelings, the situations in which they occurred, and thoughts occurring at those times. Log-keeping revealed that the patient felt anxious when her husband (a traveling salesman) was out of town.

A discussion of the patient's concerns when her husband was away and an investigation of the marital relationship showed that the patient tended to assume the role of caring for all of her husband's needs and those of the children and household as well. The couple had two children, a large home, and both worked full time at demanding jobs. In addition, the patient was recovering from a recent serious medical problem and major surgery. Her husband was out of town at least three days a week. He was accustomed to spending his weekends socializing with his friends and watching sports events on television.

This information led to the formulation that the young wife's panic was a result of the idea, "I can't get the help I need from my husband." As a result of her belief that she could not get help, she tended to assume excessive burdens and to avoid asking for help from others, assuming she would not get it. As a result, she felt overwhelmed, undersupported, and anxious. This hypothesis is consistent with the fact that the first panic attack was resolved by calling the husband to come to the hospital and that the second attack occurred when he was away from home. The formulation is also consistent with the fact that much of the patient's anxiety remitted when she began treatment (and felt she was receiving some support and help).

This pattern of assuming excessive responsibility had occurred before, in a relationship with a previous boyfriend who was a drug addict and in the patient's relationship with her parents. Her father was a charming but completely unreliable person (he agreed to pay the patient's college tuition; the patient learned he had not done so when when she received a notice cancelling her registration). Her mother depended so heavily on her children for emotional support that they were unable to rely on her.

The husband had a complementary belief, "I expect my wife to take care of my needs," which had its origins in his upbringing as an only child whose mother focused her life around him and his needs. This formulation (or pair of formulations) suggested that marital therapy was indicated. The couple agreed to this, and the outcome was successful.

3. Choose an intervention strategy

A young executive, recently recovered from a depressive episode, came to a therapy session feeling quite distressed, saying, "I've been rejected by a woman." He reported that a young woman he had been dating for several weeks had decided to return to her boyfriend of six years, whom she had left about six months earlier. Although he could see, logically, that her decision to break off the relationship probably had nothing to do with him, he was still caught up in a stream of self-critical thoughts, and he kept repeating, "It must have been something I did. Women don't like me — they never have and they never will." He proposed, "I think I should do cognitive therapy homework for about an hour every morning to improve my mood before I leave my apartment, because I'm frequently in a bad mood in the morning and that turns women off."

The patient's homework suggestion makes a certain amount of sense. This young man did have a tendency to lapse into negative and hostile moods, and there is good empirical evidence that depressed, negative moods push others away (Coyne, 1976). Despite these considerations, the therapist's response was, "No, I don't think that's a good idea. In fact, what would be a better idea would be to go out every day in as negative a mood as possible and have as many interactions with as many people as possible. Keep a careful log of the results."

The patient was astonished by this recommendation. Why did the therapist propose this intervention rather than the one the patient suggested? The answer, of course, comes from the case formulation. This was an intensely self-critical young man who responded to every setback and negative event in life by saying to himself, "It must have been due to a mistake on my part. If I had done things correctly, this wouldn't have happened. My behavior must be perfect at all times or I'll be rejected by others. I must correct all the defects in my personality or I won't receive love from others." This belief had its origin in his relationship with his father, who was extremely critical about every aspect of his young son's behavior and appearance. The young child must have learned, "In order to gain approval and caring, I must be perfect."

He had a similar idea about his work ("My performance must be perfect in order for me to feel happy about my work and accomplish my goals."). The result was that he couldn't make good progress on various technical projects he was working on because he insisted on perfecting the work at every stage. As a result, he never got beyond the initial stages of the project.

If this formulation is correct, what this patient needs to do is not to abolish his negative moods but to learn that he can have caring and successful relationships with others even if he is sometimes in a bad mood. Paradoxically, of course, learning this lesson will improve his mood. The therapist operating with this formulation would recommend against the patient's proposed homework plan, because this plan simply reinforces the patient's perfectionism.

The general point here is that the cognitive-behavioral view that mood changes can be accomplished by changing cognitions and behaviors does not tell the therapist what intervention to choose for any particular problem. More precisely, it does not tell the therapist what the problem is, exactly. Is this patient's negative mood in the morning a problem that needs correction? The goal of eliminating all the patient's negative moods is unrealistic, and in the case presented here, counter-therapeutic. In particular, treatment interventions that are not guided by the case formulation may fall into the trap of accepting the beliefs of patients who state, "I must learn to overcome all my negative moods," "If I experience a negative mood, that means there's something wrong with me," "I shouldn't feel angry," and similar perfectionistic ideas.

4. Choose an intervention point

It is unrealistic for the therapist to attempt to eliminate all the patient's distorted and maladaptive thinking. After all, overgeneralization and all-or-nothing thinking occur all the time in everyone (a distorted thought!). How does the therapist choose which distorted, maladaptive thoughts to take up in therapy? How does the therapist choose which problematic behaviors to work on? The case formulation helps the therapist to answer this question and to focus on problems and aspects of problems that are closely related to the patient's central difficulties.

Sometimes the patient comes to the session with two or three topics he wishes to discuss. Which one is it most useful to work on? The formulation can help the therapist focus on the problem most closely related to the patient's central difficulties. For example, a patient with the belief, "If I attempt something, I'll fail," and a pattern of beginning projects but then dropping them when she gets anywhere near the possibility of failure, comes to her therapy session wishing to discuss recent visits by relatives, but doesn't raise the topic of the status of a new approach to finding a job that she initiated last week. The therapist attending to the formulation knows she needs to ask about that project.

Similarly, a young woman with the beliefs, "I'm unimportant, my needs don't count, no one is interested in me," began her therapy session with the statement, "During the week I made a list of things I wanted to talk about here, but when I was sitting in the waiting room, I decided none of them was important." Without the case formulation, the therapist might respond to this statement by saying, "Well, let's follow up on what we did last time. How did your homework assignment go?" hoping this would lead somewhere productive, which it probably would. However, an awareness of this patient's formulation suggests that a better intervention might be:

THERAPIST   Oh . . . Do you see what's going on here?
PATIENT   No.
THERAPIST   Well, let's go over again what you just said: "During the week I had a list of things to discuss, but now they seem unimportant." Does this statement sound familiar to you?
PATIENT   (silent)
THERAPIST   This idea reminds me of the common idea you have, "No one is interested in me; my needs don't count." Does that ring a bell?
PATIENT   Yes.
THERAPIST   OK, now what does that tell us about what we should do about the thought, "Now the things I wanted to discuss seem unimportant"?
PATIENT   (silent)
THERAPIST   Well, I'd suggest we don't buy into it. What do you think?
PATIENT   (smiles brightly and pulls out the list of topics she had drawn up earlier in the week)

5. Predict behavior

The ability to predict patients' behavior can be extremely useful to the therapist, and the formulation can predict some aspects of patients' behavior. For example: imagine that the therapist gives a new patient, who believes, "Unless I do things perfectly, I'll be unacceptable to others," the homework assignment to keep a log of angry outbursts and bring it to the session. The formulation can be used to predict that the patient is likely to feel quite anxious about presenting his log to the therapist; he is likely to have an automatic thought like, "It's no good — she'll think I'm a bad patient and tell me she can't work with me."

Thus, the formulation predicts the patient will feel anxious about the homework assignment. If the patient also holds the belief, "I can't cope with stress," avoidance responses may be predicted as well: the patient may forget the assignment, precipitate an emergency that takes priority over the assignment, cancel his appointment, or even drop out of therapy. Another more productive avoidance (of anxiety) response might be to spend hours perfecting the homework assignment.

6. Understand and manage noncompliance

Consider the case of a young woman graduate student who habitually reschedules therapy sessions at the last minute and runs in the door five minutes late for nearly every session. Several questions about this behavior arise. First, is this behavior a problem that needs attention, or does it make sense for the therapist to simply accept five minutes' tardiness as within the realm of normal behavior? If it is a problem, what causes it and what is the best way to handle it? The case formulation helps the therapist answer all these questions.

To determine whether the lateness and rescheduling merit discussion in the therapy, the therapist can examine the case formulation and ask: Is the lateness and constant rescheduling that happens with me also happening outside the session? Is this problem one of the problems on the patient's problem list? Might the proposed mechanism underlying all the patient's problems on the problem list underlie this problem as well?

In this particular case, the answer to all these questions was "yes." Similar problems occurred frequently outside the session. In fact, the chaotic, disorganized life that resulted was the patient's chief presenting problem. The therapist had hypothesized that this patient's central underlying irrational belief was, "I can't make a good decision for myself. Any decision I make will be wrong and will lead to a disaster." A closely related idea was, "I must make the optimal use of my time, every moment of the day, or I'll fail." It made sense that the lateness and rescheduling were a result of these ideas.

To verify the supposition that the patient's rescheduling and lateness in the therapy sessions were due to these fears, and to flesh out the way in which the fears led to these problematic behaviors, each time the patient arrived late the therapist reviewed with her the circumstances responsible for the lateness. It became clear that the rescheduling stemmed from the patient's fear of having scheduled the session at a bad time and her inability to tolerate the possibility that she might have made a mistake — she feared a catastrophe would result. Driven by her need to make optimal use of her time, she constantly reorganized her schedule, continually tried to squeeze activities in time slots too small for them; as a result, she arrived late to nearly every destination.

Once the lateness and rescheduling were understood in this way, we proceeded with several therapeutic steps. First, the process of working to understand the lateness was an intervention in itself, because the therapist's initiation of a discussion of the causes of the lateness whenever it happened had the result of making it happen less often, because the patient found these discussions a little punishing; she had other, more important, matters she wanted to work on in therapy. In addition, active work on the types of irrational thoughts that pushed the patient to over-schedule herself decreased this type of behavior. The therapist also announced that she was no longer willing to reschedule the patient's appointments (response prevention), and explained carefully why this plan was necessary (therapeutic for the patient, necessary for the therapist's sanity and for continued good doctor-patient relations). This set of strategies was quite effective; the young woman stopped telephoning to reschedule her appointments and began coming on time regularly. Concomitantly, the therapeutic relationship improved markedly. Similar improvements occurred outside the session.

7. Understand and work on relationship difficulties

A graduate student came to therapy because he was anxious and depressed, was "blocked" in writing his dissertation, and had problems in his relationship with his girlfriend. His therapy sessions were problematic as well. He had difficulty scheduling regular, weekly sessions, saying, "I don't want to become so dependent that I'll have to come to you for the rest of my life." This fear was partly related to his concern about the expense of the therapy.

His interactions with the therapist were also troubled. He had a great deal of difficulty setting an agenda and tended to wander from topic to topic, taking up a subject in an offhand way, as though it weren't really important, and then quickly dropping it for another that he handled in the same way. He spoke in a nearly inaudible tone and mumbled out of the side of his mouth. The therapist began working on the problem by addressing the patient's difficulty setting an agenda.

THERAPIST   When you think about making an agenda, what thought do you get?
PATIENT   I think, "If I choose the wrong topic, I'll waste the session, and I'll waste money, and I won't make progress in the therapy."
THERAPIST   Do you see that this fear you have about choosing the wrong agenda item in the session is similar to your fear of choosing the wrong direction of work on your thesis?
PATIENT   I guess so.
THERAPIST   It also strikes me as similar to the kind of problem you have in your relationship: you're afraid of getting involved before you're sure it will work out. Here, you're afraid of getting involved in

working on a particular topic until you're sure it will be profitable.

PATIENT   I guess it's all the same thing.

THERAPIST   Sounds like it. Let's work on this by working on the problem of setting the agenda in the therapy session. What can you say to yourself, when you get the thought, "This might not be the best thing to work on?"

PATIENT   (blank)

THERAPIST   Let's think about your usual strategy. Seems like what you usually do is to kind of make a tentative start on something, but all the time worry that it's the right thing. How well does that strategy work?

PATIENT   Not too well. I don't get very far.

THERAPIST   OK, now imagine you were to do it differently. How would it go?

PATIENT   I guess I'd just go ahead with something.

THERAPIST   That sounds right to me. Now, what can you say to yourself to help you just go ahead with something?

PATIENT   (pause) I'll try this.

THERAPIST   That's not bad, but it sounds a little like your usual strategy. Any other ideas?

PATIENT   I'll try it and stick with it for a while.

THERAPIST   That sounds better. Now let's try it. What topic should we take up right now?

PATIENT   (blank)

THERAPIST   I know it's hard for you, but at this point you just need to take the plunge.

PATIENT   OK. Let's talk about the writing.

THERAPIST   Fine. Let's go ahead. If you feel the need to change the topic, let me know, and we'll work on it so you can stay with this topic and get something done.

8. Make decisions about "extra-therapy" issues

If the patient asks to delay payment during a financial crisis, should the therapist grant this request? The behavior therapist armed with a list of techniques for particular problems has no way of thinking about this question. In contrast, the case formulation helps him understand what's going on and make a plan for how to handle it. The therapist might decide to refuse the request for the patient whose central problem is the idea, "I can't solve problems on my own; I must get help from others," but to grant it for the patient whose central problem is the idea, "I must never ask anyone for help — this means I'm weak."

9. Redirect an unsuccessful treatment

The formulation provided the therapist with a way of understanding and managing treatment failure in the case of a 30-year old depressed graphic artist who sought cognitive therapy to work on the following problems:

1. Depression. The depression had two prominent aspects: feelings of anger toward others and himself, and feelings of worthlessness, failure, and incompetence.
2. Feeling incompetent as an artist, and working at a level below his potential. He procrastinated on everything and avoided completing important projects.
3. Poor relationships with others: frequent fights with his girlfriend, estrangement from a close friend, estrangement from his parents. Relationship difficulties appeared to arise when the patient became angry at others as a result of his perception of being criticized, put down, taken advantage of, or treated unfairly. He became angry with his father, for example, when his father asked him about his art because he perceived these questions as a put-down.
4. Excessive concern about health and physical problems. The patient ruminated about minor problems, fearing they posed a serious danger to his health.

The depression had begun three years previously, when he had moved to California to accept a new job, leaving behind his network of friends and family. At about the same time, his sister committed suicide. The patient was extremely angry at his parents and stated, "My parents didn't handle the situation adequately; if they had, my sister wouldn't have committed suicide."

The therapist postulated that this patient's central problem was the idea, "Others should do what I want them to do or I'll be miserable."

The proposed mechanism accounted for some — but not all — of the problems on the problem list. The depression (1) and the anger and relationship difficulties with others (3) could be understood as a natural result of the fact that others usually did not do what he expected and insisted they do. The formulation did not account for the concern about physical problems (4), nor did it account for the work problems (2).

The proposed mechanism had its origins in the patient's family history. He was the oldest of six children, reared by a demanding, highly critical father and a rather passive mother. As all six children were born in the space of eight years, we can speculate that the patient did not receive much attention and support from his mother. As a result, he felt mistreated by his parents and was quite angry at them.

Using this formulation, the therapy focused on the patient's anger toward others and his unreasonable expectations of them, using cognitive techniques to decrease the anger and to increase his sense of self-efficacy and his assertiveness. After about eight sessions, it seemed clear that treatment was not very helpful; sessions seemed unproductive and the depression was unabated.

At this point the therapist reviewed the case in an attempt to revise the hypothesis about the underlying belief generating the patient's symptoms and problems. The therapist asked herself, "*Why* is the patient so angry? Perhaps another, more basic problem produces the anger." This line of thinking led to an alternative proposal about the patient's central underlying belief: "I'm worthless." This formulation appeared superior to the previous formulation because it accounted for the patient's work difficulties, as well as for his concern about his physical health, if the problem of poor self-esteem were extended to the physical arena. This formulation differed from the previous one in viewing the anger as secondary—a result of poor self-esteem, rather than the other way around.

Using this formulation, the treatment was refocused on increasing the patient's self-esteem, beginning with asking the patient to keep a log of self-critical thoughts, and then to work to add some positive thoughts and to decrease the number of self-critical thoughts. Patient and therapist reviewed both past and current episodes in which the patient evaluated his conduct as inadequate and unworthy, in order to arrive at a more balanced and less self-punitive view. This treatment approach was rapidly effective, and the patient's depression improved markedly in two months.

This example illustrates the role of the formulation when treatment is unsuccessful. The failure of an intervention based on a case formulation suggests that the formulation may be incorrect. After arriving at a new formulation, the therapist can test this hypothesis and intervene to solve the problem by making an intervention based on the new formulation. Without the case formulation to guide this process, the therapist may make unsystematic, blind changes in the treatment plan, or give up completely.

Summary: The central role of the formulation

Thus, the formulation, particularly the part that describes the patient's central underlying irrational belief, plays several key roles in treatment. If the formulation is so helpful to the therapist, we might also expect it to be helpful to the patient in understanding and managing his behavior. Thus, many of the interventions outlined in the remainder of the book are directed toward teaching the patient the nature of his central problem.

FORMAT OF THE CASE FORMULATION

The case formulation has six parts: (1) the problem list, (2) the proposed underlying mechanism, (3) an account of the way in which the proposed mechanism produces the problems on the problem list, (4) precipitants of current problems, (5) origins of the mechanism in the patient's early life, and (6) predicted obstacles to treatment based on the formulation. The problem list was described in the previous chapter; the remaining parts of the formulation are described here.

Hypothesized mechanism

The hypothesized underlying mechanism is the heart of the formulation, and the term "case formulation" in this book generally refers to the underlying mechanism rather than to the six-part formulation described in this section.

After fleshing out the problem list, the therapist attempts to propose a single psychological problem or underlying mechanism that can account for all of the problems on the list. Often this can be stated in terms of a central irrational belief, such as, "If I get close to someone, I'll get hurt."

An example is provided by the case of a 39-year-old physician who sought treatment for the following problems:

1. Work problems, including procrastination, overpreparation, and performance anxiety. The patient's automatic thoughts had the theme, "Others will see I'm incompetent, and I'll be fired." Assessment of her actual performance suggested that her fears did lead to procrastination and lateness, but that she was quite competent at most of what she did.
2. Ambivalence about her sexuality. The patient had had several sexual relationships with women, but rejected a lesbian lifestyle and wanted a relationship with a man because it was culturally more acceptable and because she felt like a failure for not being able to succeed at relationships with men.
3. Relationship difficulties. Attempts to develop romantic relation-

ships with men never seemed to get anywhere; they either failed altogether or turned into friendships. Relationships with women were pursued in fits and starts.

4. Depression. She felt dissatisfied with her life, disappointed in herself, and hopeless about making any changes.

The central irrational idea underlying these problems appeared to be, "Unless I do things perfectly and conventionally, I will be rejected."

Relation of mechanism to problems

In this part of the formulation, the therapist attempts to specify clearly the way in which the hypothesized central problem leads to all of the problems on the problem list.

In the case of the physician, the work difficulties and the ambivalence about her sexuality (numbers 1 and 2 on the problem list) can be understood as resulting directly from her fear that if she does not do things perfectly she will be rejected; she fears being fired from her job for poor performance and rejected by friends and peers for an unconventional lifestyle. Relationships with men (3) stall both because she does not make a sexual connection with them due to her lesbian sexual orientation and because she distances herself because of her fears that if men she likes get to know her they will think badly of her. Romantic relationships with women (3) stall because her fears of acknowledging her lesbianism and of being condemned and rejected cause her to continually withdraw from relationships. Even non-romantic relationships fail (3) because the patient is so afraid of being judged negatively and rejected that she distances herself from others and leads an essentially solitary lifestyle. The depression (4) can be understood as an indirect result of the lack of gratification and satisfaction she experiences in her life, coupled with the intense self-criticism she levels at herself because of her failures; as the formulation suggests, she perceives her failures as due to her own personal inadequacies and character flaws.

Precipitants of current problems

The attempt to tie the proposed central mechanism to precipitants of the current problems is a test of the hypothesis about the central mechanism. For example, a patient who holds the belief, "Unless I'm loved I'm worthless," might be expected to become depressed following a rejection or a loss of love. If another type of event precipitated the current episode, or if the loss of an important love does not precipitate symptoms, the formulation is called into question. Of course, many events that do not at first appear to involve a loss of love may carry this meaning to the patient, so an investigation not only of the event but also of the meaning of the event to the patient is indicated.

In the case of the physician described here, difficulties were long-standing, but an increased bout of anxiety and depression were precipitated by the occasion of her 39th birthday, which elicited the automatic thought, "I'll never have a baby and a conventional family, and without that I'll be rejected by others."

Origins of the central problem

Finally, the therapist attempts an account of the possible origins of the hypothesized mechanism (central problem) in the patient's history. Usually relationships with parents play a central role here.

The phobic physician had been reared by a father who was criticized harshly on a daily basis by his wife for his failings. The patient may have learned that incompetence of any sort leads to harsh negative judgments and rejection by important others.

Predicted obstacles to treatment

The formulation can be used to make predictions about obstacles that might arise in the course of treatment. The ability to predict difficulties makes it more likely that the therapist can prevent or solve them. In this case, the patient's belief, "Unless I do things perfectly I will be rejected," suggests that she will be unduly anxious about the therapist's evaluation of her performance in therapy. Given her behavioral pattern of coping with anxiety by avoiding, we can expect that she might avoid homework assignments through procrastination or forgetfulness.

Of course, patients with other problems will encounter other obstacles in treatment. The patient with the central belief, "I must gain the approval of others at all costs," might be expected to be extremely — and, in fact, excessively — compliant with any and all requests the therapist makes. In some cases, this can be helpful, as the patient may be willing to, for example, carry out tasks that are quite difficult for her or homework assignments she doesn't believe will be helpful, just because the therapist has requested it. However, the patient's inability to assert herself with the therapist may make it impossible for her to refuse to do a certain task, and the patient may even feel the only alternative is to drop out of treatment. Or, she may become angry and resentful at the therapist for "forcing" her to do things she doesn't want to do. For another example, a patient whose central problem appears to be an impulsive decision-making style as a result of a deficit in responding to long-range consequences of his behavior is likely to wish to terminate treatment impulsively when he doesn't feel he is making immediate important gains. The therapist can intervene preventively, including setting explicit, achievable treatment goals and warning the patient that he may have the urge to end therapy prematurely.

The six-part format for the case formulation outlined here appears in Table 3.1, which can serve as a form for the therapist wishing to integrate the formulation into his writeup. The Table also includes a place for the Treatment Plan, which ought to follow logically from, and be based on, the hypothesized underlying mechanism.

THE PROCESS OF HYPOTHESIZING
AN UNDERLYING MECHANISM

The process of developing a hypothesis about the underlying mechanism is one of the most difficult (and creative) parts of treatment, and some ideas about how to do this are offered here.

Examine the problem list

A good first start to obtaining an idea about the underlying mechanism is a very close look at the problem list. A central theme often becomes apparent when the therapist examines the problem list while asking himself the question, "What do all these problems have in common?"

A fine-grained look at the problem list can reveal nuances that provide clues to the underlying mechanism. For example, a problem described grossly as "depression" conceals many details. Individuals who report lots of self-criticism, feelings of failure, self-hate, and guilt may have central problems along the lines, "I must be perfect or I'm worthless." In contrast, those who are concerned that they are becoming old and unattractive may be dependent and fear rejection from others (Beck, 1983; Persons & Miranda, 1988).

A careful look at the patient's pattern of behavior can be helpful. Examine the patient's behavior, asking the question, "What belief would a person who is behaving like this have?" For example, the person is avoiding bridges, freeways, anxiety. This person must think, as Beck

Table 3.1   The Case Formulation

Identifying information:

Chief complaint:

Problem list:

1.
2.
3.
4.
5.
6.
7.
8.

Hypothesized mechanism:

Relation of mechanism to problems:

Precipitants of current problems:

Origins of the central problem:

Treatment plan:

Predicted obstacles to treatment:

---

points out, "I'm a weak and vulnerable and fragile person, and I cannot cope with anxiety or stress of any kind."

Examine the automatic thoughts

Automatic thoughts—that is, the cognitive components of the problems on the problem list—are often derivatives of the central underlying belief. Thus, a graduate student came to therapy to work on his problem writing his dissertation. His automatic thoughts were: "I haven't done enough, I haven't learned enough, I need to understand everything in the lab and everything in my experiment perfectly before I can write my dissertation." These automatic thoughts are a very close cousin of the therapist's hypothesis about the key underlying belief, which was simply a more general statement of these ideas about the dissertation: "I must be perfect in everything I do or I won't be successful in life."

Study the chief complaint

Careful attention to the chief complaint, as well as the words the patient uses to frame it, can also be informative. I once treated a young man who stated, when he telephoned for an appointment, "I think I'd like to start therapy because I think it would be a good business investment in myself." This phraseology suggested that he was frightened of admitting problems or inadequacies, and that his central fear might be something like, "If I fail at anything, I'm a failure." As it happened, the treatment process indicated that he had both a fear of failure and a fear of rejection, as in the case of the phobic physician above.

Look for antecedents and consequences

Carefully specifying the antecedents and consequences of the problems frequently leads to a formulation. Thus, the case formulation approach to assessment is related to the ABC's (antecedents, behaviors, consequences) of traditional behavioral analysis (Goldfried & Pomeranz, 1968).

An example is provided by the case of a 20-year old man of borderline intelligence (IQ probably about 80) who was brought in for treatment of repeated vomiting episodes for which no physical cause could be found. Episodes, occurring about once a week, had led to a tear in the esophagus which led to life-threatening bleeding during severe vomiting episodes. An interview with the patient yielded little information.

Interviews with the patient's family revealed that when the patient had a vomiting episode, the patient's father, who was otherwise distant and unavailable, mobilized himself to clean up the vomit, prop the patient up on the couch in front of the TV and wait on him hand and foot. When necessary, he spent long hours with him in the emergency room. This information suggested that attention from the father was a consequence of the vomiting behavior. Because this attention was highly valued by the patient, it seemed likely that it was serving as a positive reinforcer for the vomiting.

This model of the contingencies controlling the vomiting suggested that the vomiting behavior could be eliminated by eliminating the attention received for the vomiting, while adding attention for "well" behavior. The patient's father reluctantly agreed to the plan of requiring the patient to clean up his own vomit, sending the patient to the emergency room alone, and withholding attention when the patient vomited. The father was unwilling to give attention when the patient was well, however, so this part of the treatment was done with the assistance of the patient's sister-in-law, who arranged for the patient to attend a rehabilitiation and recreation center for mentally handicapped young adults. Within three months, vomiting had completely stopped.

Although this patient's problem was most easily formulated in terms of antecedents and consequences, it can also be described in terms of underlying beliefs. This young man behaved as though he believed "The only way to get attention from my father is by vomiting," and "My father is the only source of affection and attention available to me."

An example of the importance of understanding antecedents can be drawn from cognitive therapy sessions devoted to eliciting automatic thoughts and answering them with rational responses in order to alleviate negative moods. These sessions are often structured around the Thought Record (see Figure 7.2, Chapter 7). The "Situation" column of this record might be viewed as specifying the environmental antecedents of the negative moods, and the "Thoughts" column as specifying the internal antecedents. Understanding these antecedents makes it much easier to modify negative moods.

Use a standardized measure

Cognitive therapists have begun developing standardized paper-and-pencil measures to assess underlying beliefs. The Dysfunctional Attitude Scale (DAS) was developed by Weissman and Beck (Weissman, 1979; Weissman & Beck, 1978) to measure the dysfunctional beliefs characteristic of depressed patients; the DAS is reprinted in Burns (1980).

Failure to obtain a formulation

Occasionally the therapist is unable to propose a formulation. When this happens, symptom-oriented treatment can be initiated. Sometimes this treatment will be successful; sometimes it is not, but it yields additional information that can eventually lead to a formulation (Turkat & Carlson, 1984).

TESTING THE PROPOSED UNDERLYING MECHANISM

The therapist can never be certain her hypothesis about the underlying mechanism is correct and must always be prepared to revise or change it in the face of evidence. This is a continuous process; in fact, assessment and treatment are a continuous process of proposing, testing, reevaluating, revising, rejecting, and creating new formulations.

Five tests of the underlying mechanism

The first test of the mechanism is: How well does it account for the problems on the problem list? To conduct this test, it's helpful to review, systematically, each problem on the list, and attempt to "tell a story" about how the proposed mechanism might lead, directly, or indirectly, to the problem. If the mechanism does not readily account for all the problems on the problem list, it is unlikely to be correct.

Second, as described above, the patient's report of the events precipitating the current episode ought to fit with the formulation in an easily understandable way.

Third, the therapist can test the mechanism by making predictions based on it, then testing the predictions by collecting the relevant data. For example, the hypothesis that the patient is afraid that if she gets close to others she'll be hurt suggests she was reared in an abusive family. The patient's report that her family was close and harmonious calls either the formulation or the report into question.

Fourth, it's useful to ask for the patient's reaction to the proposed mechanism. If the patient feels the formulation is correct, I view this as a piece of supporting evidence; if the patient feels the formulation is wrong, I begin looking for a new one.

Finally, the outcome of treatment can be viewed as an indirect test of the accuracy of the formulation. Treatment failure can indicate that the mechanism on which the treatment was based is incorrect. Therefore, the therapist using the case formulation approach responds to treatment failure by examining the hypothesis about the underlying mechanism, attempting to propose a new one, and using this new formulation to develop a new treatment plan. Of course, the outcome of treatment cannot be viewed as a foolproof measure of the formulation, because treatment failure can have many other causes.

The process of testing the hypothesis about the mechanism

The process of developing a hypothesis about the underlying mechanism and testing it can begin immediately. If, when the patient telephones to schedule the initial appointment, she provides some information about her problems, I immediately begin taking notes. Then I take a few minutes prior to the initial session to use the notes to generate a hypothesis about the underlying mechanism and to prepare some questions that might test it.

For example, a 40-year-old man telephoned for an appointment, saying, "I have severe neck pain, and I've spent 15 years of my life and visited hundreds of doctors to try to get rid of this pain — without success. I can't do anything until I get rid of it."

The fact that the pain has been present for 15 years leads the therapist to hypothesize that the pain complaints are being reinforced (Fordyce & Steger, 1979). The statement that nothing else can be done until pain relief is obtained suggests that one of the reinforcements is the patient's nonparticipation in life. The therapist might then predict that the patient has important problems in the areas of interpersonal relationships and/or work, most likely both, given the chronicity and severity of the pain problem; this hypothesis can be tested in the process of collecting the personal and social history.

An exploration of this man's work history reveals he has worked for 20 years in a field he doesn't like and has always wanted to be an interior designer but never pursued it. Why not? The therapist might propose several hypotheses:

- fear of failure. Perhaps he avoids pursuing a career in interior design for fear he'll fail at it;
- fear of disappointing others. Perhaps the patient's parents (or other significant others) will criticize and reject him for this choice;
- fear of making the wrong choice. "I'm not sure I should pursue this direction — I might not be happy in it."

To test these hypotheses, the therapist might ask, "If you were going to take one step in the direction of being an interior designer, what would it be?"

PATIENT   I'd take a course at night.

THERAPIST   Where would you take it?

PATIENT   At Johnston College. I've already looked into it — they have some good classes. I just can't get to them.

THERAPIST   Imagine you actually get to class and you begin working with the class on a project, say a living room of a house in the country. What thoughts do you get?

PATIENT   I'll have no talent. I won't be able to do it.

This answer supports the fear of failure hypothesis. Of course, the other hypotheses might also be correct, and the therapist might want to explore them by asking about the parents' or other significant others' likely reactions to the patient's career change.

A detailed family and social history, including information about parents (what were they like, how did they treat the patient), sibs, locale and environment of early upbringing, religious training, school (private or public, did the patient do well or poorly), friends, relationships with the opposite sex, marriage, job history, and children also helps to flesh out and test the formulation.

FROM ASSESSMENT TO TREATMENT

Obtaining the problem list (Chapter 2) and the case formulation (this chapter) are the main goals of the initial assessment process. Once this has been done, active interventions can begin. The next chapters focus on interventions directed at problematic behaviors and cognitions. However, it is important to remember that assessment and treatment occur in tandem, with changes (or failures to change) as a result of treatment leading to revisions in both the problem list and the case formulation.

CHAPTER 4

Behavioral interventions

This chapter and the next discuss interventions intended to accomplish direct behavioral change. The chapter begins with a discussion of the use of the case formulation to plan interventions. Several intervention strategies are presented, beginning with teaching the patient the case formulation model in general and his own formulation in particular. In addition, a strategy labeled "pointing to the underlying problem" is described. Next, the old plan/new plan strategy, scheduling, modeling and role-playing, and relaxation are described. The next chapter describes rewards and punishments, breaking tasks into small parts, exposure, stimulus control, and exercise.

Behavioral interventions are described before cognitive ones because they often come first in treatment. Even when they are extremely distressed, patients often understand and can carry out behavioral changes, whereas subtle cognitive distinctions and changes may be difficult to comprehend at first. Beck et al. (1979) also recommend emphasizing increasing the activity level of a severely depressed patient at the beginning of treatment before tackling cognitive change.

USING THE CASE FORMULATION TO PLAN
BEHAVIORAL INTERVENTIONS

The case formulation model (Chapter 1) proposes that an understanding of the behavioral, cognitive, and mood components of the patient's problem at the overt level and of the patient's central underlying irrational belief guides the therapist's choice of interventions. Several examples are provided here.

Sometimes the chief complaint is not a behavioral problem at all — the patient may be depressed or frightened of contracting AIDS, for example. However, these problems usually have a behavioral component, and awareness of this can aid the therapist in planning an intervention strategy. For example, the depressed person who believes, "I'm no good at anything," has stopped going to work. The person who is frightened of contracting AIDS may be housebound. The close relationships between behavioral, cognitive and mood components of problems indicates that changes in one are likely to lead to changes in the other. Thus, going back to work would help to improve the depressed person's mood and self-evaluation. Similarly, the phobic who is afraid of AIDS would benefit from scheduling daily trips, however small, outside the home.

Behavioral interventions can be useful in dozens of problems that do not immediately appear to be behavioral problems — for example, low self-esteem. People with low self-esteem generally reflect this attitude in their behavior; they tend to treat themselves as if they were worthless. A depressed housewife who held the belief, "I'm inadequate and morally bad," had stopped wearing makeup because of thoughts like, "I don't deserve to look attractive." Once the connection between these thoughts, self-esteem, and makeup-wearing became clear to her, she decided she would work to improve her self-esteem by wearing makeup whether she felt she deserved it or not. The patient reported that this strategy was quite successful and that it appeared to contribute to improved mood, greater assertiveness, and enhanced self-esteem.

Two graduate students sought treatment for difficulty writing their dissertations. One was avoiding writing altogether because of the automatic thoughts, "I haven't done enough lab work to write a good thesis," "I haven't learned enough yet." These ideas are directly related to his central underlying belief, "I must correct all my defects before I can be successful in life." As a result, despite years of laboratory work, he felt he was not ready to write up his results. Another dissertation writer did sit down to write, but became overwhelmed with anxiety and unable to function as a result of the thoughts, "It's not good enough — I should have chosen some other project." This young man held the underlying belief, "I'll make the wrong choice and a disaster will result."

The different cognitive and mood components of the two problems and their underlying mechanisms indicate that different interventions are indicated even though the behavioral problem is crudely similar: inability to write the dissertation. In the case of the young man who avoids writing, cognitive interventions (Chapters 6 and 7) that will expose his irrational thinking and role-playing (Modeling and Role-playing, p. 76 below) might help him discuss his thesis plans with his advisor. In the case of the anxious writer, helpful interventions might include relaxation (p. 78 below) and cognitive interventions to attack his expectations of catastrophe. In both cases, teaching the patient about his own case formulation – the cognitive, behavioral and mood components of his problem, and the central underlying belief is indicated. This is the first intervention described below.

Imagine the depressed executive who works like a madman from 7 a.m. to 7 p.m., but feels he accomplishes too little during his working hours. Is it a good idea to use scheduling (see pp. 71–73 below) to help him make more efficient use of his time? The answer to this question depends on the therapist's hypothesis about the underlying mechanism driving this behavior. If this man's central fear is, "Unless I work three times as hard as others I will fail," the answer to this question is probably "no." In this case, a better strategy would involve helping him test his belief by scheduling *shorter* workdays and taking careful note of the consequences.

These examples illustrate the central role of the case formulation model, and particularly the hypothesis about the underlying mechanism, in guiding interventions. Because of its importance, the case formulation model in general and the patient's own formulation in particular, are taught to patients.

TEACHING THE CASE FORMULATION APPROACH TO BEHAVIORAL PROBLEMS

Teaching the relationship between behavioral, mood, and cognitive components of problems

Sometimes patients are unaware they have a behavioral problem, and simply explaining this is surprisingly helpful. For example, the patient may seek treatment for a mood difficulty – depression or anxiety. When the therapist points out that depressed mood is linked to inactivity and that an increased activity level will probably lead to an improvement in mood, many depressed patients are quite willing to become more active. Some choose to increase their activity level by returning to an abandoned exercise regime (see Exercise, Chapter 5, p. 98 below). Anxious patients, when they understand that avoidance feeds their fear, are often willing to decrease their avoidance activities. When patients do not understand the relationship between behavior and other aspects of their problems, the therapist can demonstrate this connection with skillful questioning, as in the following example.

THERAPIST   What time of the day yesterday did you feel the worst?
PATIENT   In the morning, I guess.
THERAPIST   What were you doing in the morning?
PATIENT   Nothing. I stayed in bed late even though I wasn't asleep. I just couldn't get up.
THERAPIST   And what time of day did you feel the best?
PATIENT   (quickly) Dinnertime.
THERAPIST   What was going on then?
PATIENT   Well, I really enjoyed myself. I went out to dinner with a friend of mine, and I haven't done that for a long time. I was surprised how much I enjoyed it.
THERAPIST   Right. Now are you following the point I'm trying to make here?
PATIENT   You're trying to tell me that when I stay home doing nothing I feel worse, and when I get out and do things, I feel better.
THERAPIST   Exactly. And what do you think?
PATIENT   But I don't *feel like* doing anything! That's why I'm here!
THERAPIST   I see. You don't feel like doing anything. OK, let's see how we can work with that. Let me ask you this; how did it happen that you made a plan to go to dinner with your friend?
PATIENT   Well, he called me up and invited me.
THERAPIST   I see, and how did you feel when he made the invitation?
PATIENT   Well, I didn't really think I wanted to do it, but I couldn't turn him down.
THERAPIST   And when it came time to get dressed and go out, did you feel like doing it?
PATIENT   No, I didn't.
THERAPIST   How did you get yourself out the door?
PATIENT   I just made myself do it — I didn't really have a choice.
THERAPIST   And what do you think about this approach of making

yourself do it even though you didn't feel like doing it? Did it pay
off for you? Did you enjoy the dinner?

PATIENT   Yes, I did.

THERAPIST   Now what can we learn from this?

PATIENT   Well, maybe I should make myself do things even when I don't
feel like doing them.

THERAPIST   Yes, I think this is a good idea for you. I think the usual rule
most people use, of waiting until we feel like doing something
before we do it, is a rule that works if we're not depressed. But when
you're depressed, that rule doesn't work, because you never feel like
doing anything. When you're depressed, you need a new rule: Do
things even though you don't feel like doing them. Then later you'll
feel like doing them. Does this make sense to you?[1]

PATIENT   Yes, I read about that in Dr. Burns' book[2] (see Burns, 1980),
but it seems hard.

THERAPIST   It is hard, but I think it will pay off for you. Are you willing
to try it?

PATIENT   Yes, I'll try it.

THERAPIST   Great. OK, let's think, what's next for you? What would
you like do next week that you don't feel like doing?

The therapist can also teach phobic patients the relationship between
their anxious mood and the avoidance behaviors most of them engage in.
Patients who are anxious about rejection avoid interpersonal contacts,
those afraid of having a panic attack avoid going out alone, those afraid
of failing avoid working, and so on. The avoidance is the patient's behavioral solution to the fear. However, this solution actually worsens the fear.

Imagine a housewife who suffers from high anxiety and believes, "If I
go out alone, I'll have a panic attack, and something terrible will happen." Avoidance feeds her fear in (at least) three ways. First, if the woman
goes home whenever she begins to feel uncomfortable in a shopping mall,
the cues associated with being in the mall are repeatedly paired with
feelings of anxiety, discomfort, and impending doom. Second, the avoidance behavior is consistent with, and thus strengthens, her automatic

---

[1]This intervention is based on the idea that inactive patients will experience an improvement
in mood if they increase their activity level (Beck et al., 1979). This idea is similar to
Lewinsohn's (1985) theory that patients will experience an elevation in mood if they engage
in *pleasant* activities. Of course, the therapist is unlikely to urge the patient to engage in
aversive activities. Nevertheless, these two hypotheses about the relationship between activity and mood do differ, and a study examining this question would be both theoretically and
clinically interesting.

[2]The patient had read *Feeling Good* as homework.

thoughts that she is too frightened to go out alone, and her underlying belief that she is fragile and vulnerable and cannot cope with stress of any kind. Third, the avoidance behavior prevents the patient from collecting information that would contradict the irrational belief ("If I go out alone, I'll have a panic attack and something terrible will happen") that produces the fear.

The same line of thinking can be used to understand the behavioral rituals carried out by obsessive-compulsives. These can be seen as active avoidance strategies; e.g., washing is a way of removing anxiety-provoking dirt and contamination. Patients who make constant requests for reassurance from family or therapists are also engaging in avoidance behavior: they are avoiding taking responsibility for making their own decisions, tolerating uncertainty, or accepting the consequences of their choices. All these behaviors reinforce fear. When patients come to understand the correct relationship between anxiety and avoidance behavior, many are willing to make valiant efforts to change their behavior.

Teaching the relationship between behavioral problems and irrational beliefs

Patients' underlying beliefs cause, and are reflected in, behavioral problems. Thus, the housebound housewife who believes, "If I go out, something terrible will happen," has a central belief along the lines, "I'm a fragile and vulnerable person, and I can't cope." If the therapist can point this out to the patient, she may be able to see that staying home reinforces her beliefs. Sometimes this awareness alone convinces the patient to make a behavioral change. To teach this lesson, the therapist might proceed as follows.

THERAPIST   It sounds like you're afraid to go out of the house.
PATIENT   I know it's irrational, but I'm just afraid.
THERAPIST   Let me show you what's going on here. You know, we've talked about your central problem being a feeling that you're fragile and vulnerable, and easily overwhelmed. Does that make sense to you?
PATIENT   Yes, it does.
THERAPIST   Now, how does that problem relate to your unwillingness to go out of the house? Do you see?
PATIENT   Sort of.
THERAPIST   Imagine you did go out of the house. What would it do for your belief about yourself?

PATIENT   I'd probably start to feel more confident.
THERAPIST   Exactly. You'd start to learn that your idea that you're
    helpless just isn't right. Now, can we make a plan that will get you
    out of the house?

When carrying out this intervention, it can be helpful to draw a diagram of the behaviors, automatic thoughts, moods, and irrational underlying beliefs that make up the problem. An example, for the case of this
phobic patient, is provided in Figure 4.1.

Another example is provided by a depressed student who, when he is
challenged with the task of going to class in the morning, responds, "I
can't do it." In this situation, the therapist might use an idea suggested by
Burns (1980) in order to point out to the patient the irrationality of his
automatic thought; then he can point out the origins of the automatic
thought in the irrational underlying belief.

THERAPIST   Well, let me ask you this: suppose I agreed to give you
    $1,000 if you went to class tomorrow. Do you think you could do
    it?
PATIENT   What?
THERAPIST   I know it sounds crazy, but just imagine it for a moment. If

Figure 4.1

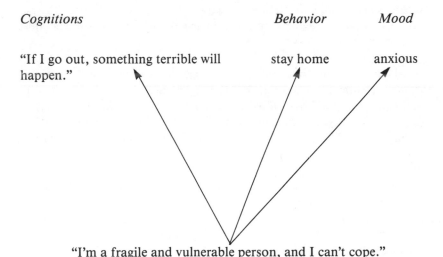

Cognitions   _Behavior_   _Mood_

"If I go out, something terrible will   stay home   anxious
happen."

"I'm a fragile and vulnerable person, and I can't cope."

you go to class tomorrow, I'll give you $1,000 in cash. What do you think? Could you go to class?

PATIENT   Yes, I guess so.

THERAPIST   Are you sure? (smiling)

PATIENT   Yes, pretty sure! (smiling)

THERAPIST   OK, now what does that tell us? When you say to yourself, "I can't do it," is that a correct statement?

PATIENT   I guess not. I *can* do it.

THERAPIST   Yes, you can. Now, where does this idea come from, the idea that you can't do it? Does it sound familiar to you?

PATIENT   (blank)

THERAPIST   Do you remember that we've talked about this idea before? This idea seems to be a central belief you have about yourself: "I'm incompetent; I can't cope."

PATIENT   Yes, I guess so.

THERAPIST   It looks like this idea keeps you from going to class in the morning.

PATIENT   I guess so.

THERAPIST   Do you see that not going to class strengthens this idea? It reinforces your sense of yourself as being incompetent and not able to do things.

PATIENT   Yes, I guess so.

THERAPIST   If this behavior strengthens your irrational belief about yourself, what does that tell you?

PATIENT   I guess I need to go to class.

THERAPIST   It would be a good way to work on your problems.

POINTING TO THE UNDERLYING PROBLEM

When the patient understands the general idea that behaviors reflect and support underlying irrational beliefs, the therapist can use it over and over again to point out maladaptive behavior and thinking of which the patient may not be aware.

The intervention of pointing to the underlying problem is particularly helpful when patients have difficulty accepting the possibility that their behavior is problematic or maladaptive in any way. For example, a young woman whose central belief about herself was that she was incompetent at everything, and whose usual behavior showed a pattern of attempting countless activities, jobs, classes, and so on, but dropping out after a few weeks came to her therapy session saying: "I've decided I'm going to quit my sewing class. The teacher isn't very good."

THERAPIST   I see. Any other reasons for quitting the class?
PATIENT   It's not a convenient time.
THERAPIST   Any other reasons?
PATIENT   No . . . My main reason is that the teacher isn't very good.
THERAPIST   I see. For some reason, I'm hesitating to accept this completely. Do you see why? How am I thinking about this?
PATIENT   You're thinking that I'm quitting something again.
THERAPIST   Yes, I am. What do you think about it?
PATIENT   I guess I am quitting something, but the teacher is really terrible.
THERAPIST   Well, we can talk about how terrible the teacher is, but you and I know that no matter how compelling the reason, there may be some irrational thinking here, because we have talked before about how your tendency to quit things seems to be due to your fear of failing at them. What do you think? Is there any chance this might be going on here?
PATIENT   It doesn't seem that way to me, but I guess it might be happening.
THERAPIST   How can we find out?
PATIENT   (pause) I don't know.
THERAPIST   What would you think about sticking it out a little longer so we can test out this idea?
PATIENT   (pause) Yes, I guess that makes sense. I'll try it out.
THERAPIST   That sounds great. If you stick it out, you might start to get anxious about how you're doing in class, and that would be a clue. Are you willing to try it?
PATIENT   Yes, I'll try it.

This strategy can also be used in reverse. That is, the therapist (or patient) can begin with the underlying belief and ask, "What behaviors would we expect from someone who believed, 'I'm incompetent at everything'?" Brainstorming in response to this question can be quite revealing. Answers might include: seeking out boring, unchallenging friends and relationships who will not challenge my competence; seeking dependent friends who need me and subjugating my needs to theirs; purposely sticking with jobs and classes that are outside my interests and talents, so I don't have to feel threatened about not doing well; procrastinating and forgetting when expected to do something challenging; finding my time consumed with daily chores and errands, so there is no time left for creative work or learning.

This type of exercise can also be used to generate some predictions about future behavioral problems. Thus, the therapist might be able to predict to the patient that she would want to drop out of her sewing class soon after she started it. In some cases, the therapist might also want to point out to the patient that she may wish to terminate treatment prematurely.

OLD PLAN/NEW PLAN

In the examples presented so far, the nature of the behavioral change required in order to attack the underlying belief is fairly obvious. Sometimes the nature of the behavioral change required is not clear. In this case, the old plan/new plan intervention is helpful.

The old plan/new plan strategy can be used to help patients undertake new behaviors that will alleviate current problems and attack the central underlying beliefs. For example, a young woman seeks treatment because she is overwhelmed by anxiety and unable to move ahead in her life because she can't decide whether to go to school or take a job. She frantically expends a lot of energy generating job offers and applying to graduate school, but is unable to make a decision about which route to pursue. She appears to have the beliefs, "I must pursue the best choice, or I won't be successful," and "I can't afford to give up any options, because the loss might ruin my career." These ideas seem to be related to a central fear of being inadequate, weak, vulnerable and unable to cope (cf. Beck et al., 1985).

The patient's frantic attempts to acquire as many options as possible actually reinforce her psychological problem. To point this out, and to help the patient make some behavioral changes that will attack her beliefs, the therapist can use the old plan/new plan intervention. The term "old plan" refers to the pattern of behavior the patient is currently engaged in, with its associated moods, automatic thoughts, and underlying irrational beliefs. The "new plan" refers to alternative mood, automatic thoughts, and beliefs that would generate, be consistent with, and support a more adaptive pattern of behavior. Another useful terminology is "pro-belief" or "counter-belief" behaviors, where belief refers to the underlying irrational belief. Patients can be encouraged to propose and carry out "counter-belief" behaviors. An example follows.

THERAPIST   It sounds like your plan is to generate as many job offers and graduate school acceptances as possible right now.

PATIENT   Yes, I guess it is.

THERAPIST   Let's call that the "old plan." You're actually doing pretty well at that plan. You have several options right now, including some you seem clear about not wanting but hold onto nonetheless. But you still seem quite anxious. Do you see why that is?

PATIENT   I'm anxious about losing out on something important.

THERAPIST   It must seem to you that if you lose out on one of your options, that you might lose something extremely valuable that might make a fantastic difference in your career later.

PATIENT   Yes, it does.

THERAPIST   So, this type of idea, "I must have as many options as possible or I won't be successful" is part of what's producing your anxiety. Does that make sense to you?

PATIENT   Yes, I guess so.

THERAPIST   Let me write this down (see Figure 4.2) Now, do you see how all this is related to your main fear of not measuring up, not being good enough?

PATIENT   Yes, it's all related.

THERAPIST   Well, let me ask you this: if you want to start working on your anxiety, and chipping away at this irrational belief, what behavior change could you make?

PATIENT   (stumped)

THERAPIST   Let me ask you this. Imagine you had the idea, "I am competent and capable, and if I choose from a reasonable number of options, I can probably get what I want and be successful." If you believed that, how would your behavior change? What would you do?

PATIENT   I guess I'd give up a couple of the choices I have that I don't really want. I'd probably also stop looking for new job offers. But I don't think I can do that.

THERAPIST   Well, you may not be able to do everything, but this is a good start. Let's call this the "new plan." Does this "new plan" make sense to you? What part of the "new plan" can you do, do you think?

PATIENT   Well, I can call the telephone company and turn down their job offer. I almost did it this morning.

THERAPIST   Great. Now let me ask you this. After you make that call, how are you going to feel?

PATIENT   I'll feel anxious.

THERAPIST   Yes, you probably will. Do you see why?

PATIENT   Because I'll have given up one of my options.

Figure 4.2   The "old plan/new plan" intervention.

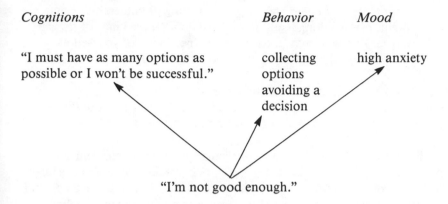

OLD PLAN

Cognitions   *Behavior*   *Mood*

"I must have as many options as   collecting   high anxiety
possible or I won't be successful."   options
                                                avoiding a
                                                decision

                        "I'm not good enough."

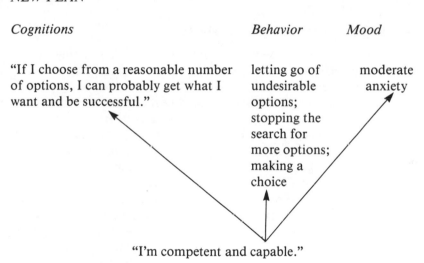

NEW PLAN

Cognitions   *Behavior*   *Mood*

"If I choose from a reasonable number   letting go of   moderate
of options, I can probably get what I   undesirable   anxiety
want and be successful."   options;
                                                stopping the
                                                search for
                                                more options;
                                                making a
                                                choice

                        "I'm competent and capable."

THERAPIST   Right, you'll have given up one of your options, and
     because you're probably still hooked into that old pattern of
     thinking, the one that gives you the idea you won't survive without
     an unlimited number of options, you'll probably feel anxious. Well,
     then, why am I suggesting you do something that will make you
     anxious?

PATIENT   (blank)

THERAPIST   The reason I'm suggesting this move is that this model (refer
    to old plan/new plan sheet (Figure 4.2) tells us that turning down
    the job offer will help break up your feeling of vulnerability, and
    ought, over the long haul, if you keep doing these kinds of things
    and see that you survive, to give you a new sense of yourself as
    competent and a new sense of self-confidence. Does that make
    sense?

PATIENT   Yes, it does, but it's still scary.

THERAPIST   Yes, it is, and I wish I could make it not scary. But this is the
    best way I know to accomplish the result we want.

Even when understanding a particular behavioral problem and the
underlying deficit convinces the patient to make a behavioral change,
similar problems tend to recur over and over again. The patient's central
irrational belief exerts a powerful effect over a wide range of behaviors,
and the therapist will need to point this out repeatedly.

POINTING TO BEHAVIORAL PROBLEMS

If the therapist has a good formulation-based understanding of the
patient's problems, she can often point out behavioral manifestations of
them that the patient may not be aware of.

For example, a young accountant finally overcame her driving phobia
and began driving to work. She avoided telling any of friends about her
success. This reluctance to ask for congratulations from her friends might
be viewed as simple modesty. However, an investigation by patient and
therapist of the thoughts accompanying this behavior and examination of
the case formulation suggested otherwise. The patient's automatic
thought was, "If I tell people, and then have a setback and can't drive
anymore, everyone will think I'm ridiculous." Her central fear was, "I'm
incompetent, I can't cope, and people will reject me for it." The close
relationship among her behavior, the distorted automatic thought, and
the underlying central fear suggests that her reluctance to tell her friends
about her driving success is a behavior that actually reinforces her central
irrational belief and subtly undermines her progress. Of course, this view
of the problem suggests an obvious behavioral attack: the patient might
commit to a homework plan of telling one or two friends about her
driving success.

As in the case of cognitive interventions described later in the book,
often the therapist's main role is simply to point out the patient's falling

into the same old trap again, carrying out a behavior or pattern of thinking that reinforces and is consistent with the pathological world view. Sometimes when this is pointed out, patients can make a clear decision to change and carry it out. Often, of course, they need help changing their behavior, and many of the interventions described in the remainder of this chapter, and in the next, can be helpful here.

SCHEDULING

Scheduling is helpful for a patient who understands the importance of making a behavioral change and says he is willing to do it, but has difficulty actually carrying out the "new plan." Often these patients tend to avoid difficulties, so time passes and the intended behavior changes simply do not take place. Or the patient may have difficulty translating the general rule, "I want to socialize more," into concrete behaviors that occupy a place in the flow of events in his life. "Old plans" fit easily into the flow of life, but "new plans" do not and will fall by the wayside unless explicit plans to carry them out are made. The therapist can help the patient schedule the "new plans" and prevent obstacles from interfering with them, as in the following example.

THERAPIST   We've talked about the general idea of increasing your
    activity level. Let's get concrete. Do you want to make some plans?
PATIENT   OK.
THERAPIST   Why don't you grab that pad of paper and write down what
    we come up with. Now, today is Wednesday. What do you want to
    do between now and the next time I see you?
PATIENT   I don't know.
THERAPIST   Well, let's think about it. What's on the books for
    tomorrow?
PATIENT   Nothing, it's my day off.
THERAPIST   OK, well what's the first thing you'll do tomorrow?
PATIENT   I'll get up.
THERAPIST   Right, and what time is that?
PATIENT   Oh, around 10 o'clock.
THERAPIST   Fine. Let's put that on the schedule. Then what happens?
PATIENT   I don't know.
THERAPIST   What do you usually do on your day off?
PATIENT   I kind of lay around the house all day.
THERAPIST   And how do you feel when you do that?
PATIENT   Lousy.

THERAPIST   Right. Now, what can you do instead?

PATIENT   I could go to the movies.

THERAPIST   Great. When could you do that?

PATIENT   In the afternoon.

THERAPIST   OK, let's put it on the schedule. What movie can you go to?

PATIENT   I don't know, but I can check the entertainment section of the paper to find out. I know there are two or three things I've been wanting to see.

THERAPIST   Terrific. OK, what else can you do?

PATIENT   Well, Friday I'm busy all day because I'm working that day.

THERAPIST   Fine, let's put "work" on the schedule for that day. Now let's think about the weekend.

PATIENT   Well, the weekend is always tough for me.

THERAPIST   Then it's important to make some plans for it. (Therapist waits a bit to see if the patient comes up with something.)

PATIENT   (gloomily) Well, I could call my grandmother and ask her if she wants me to take her to the cemetery. . . .

THERAPIST   That doesn't sound like something you really want to do.

PATIENT   No, it isn't.

THERAPIST   Let's see if we can come up with something you'd enjoy more.

PATIENT   Well, I always enjoy it when I work in my garden, but I haven't done it for a long time.

THERAPIST   Would you like to do it on Saturday?

PATIENT   Yes, if the weather is good.

THERAPIST   OK, fine, let's put it down, and let's also see if we can come up with another plan in case the weather is bad. How long do you want to work in the garden? When do you want to start? (pinning down the details)

PATIENT   I'd like to work two hours, starting at 9.

THERAPIST   (knowing this patient usually doesn't get up until 10) Is this realistic for you? How will this plan feel on Saturday?

PATIENT   Well, I'm not going to want to start at 9. I'll want to sleep late, and then sit around and have breakfast and read the paper.

THERAPIST   OK, let's put that down. What time will you want to start?

PATIENT   At 11.

THERAPIST   Fine, let's put that down. Of course, if you start earlier or later, that's fine, but if you start with a plan that we know is unrealistic, it can be discouraging. OK then, what do you want to do after gardening?

PATIENT   I don't know.

THERAPIST   Well, what's the first thing you'll do when you come in the house?

PATIENT   I'll take a shower.

THERAPIST   OK, let's put that down. Then what?

PATIENT   That's where I get stuck.

THERAPIST   OK, let's see if we can generate some ideas. What could you do on Saturday afternoon? What did you do last Saturday afternoon?

PATIENT   Well, I moped around the house by myself.

THERAPIST   Do you want to do that again?

PATIENT   No, it felt terrible.

THERAPIST   What could you do that would feel less terrible? (The therapist is slow to offer suggestions, working patiently to elicit ideas from the patient.)

PATIENT   I could call up a friend and go out.

THERAPIST   That sounds good. Who could you call up?

PATIENT   I could call Terry, or Jane . . . or Barbara.

THERAPIST   OK, now let's think about it. When could you call them?

PATIENT   I guess I'd better call soon so we can make plans.

THERAPIST   Sounds good. When can you call?

PATIENT   I can call tonight.

THERAPIST   Great. Let's put that down on the schedule.

Difficulties

Although scheduling may seem trivial, it is not trivial in either sense of the word. It's not trivial in the sense of being unimportant. A small task, carried out on a daily basis, whether writing, swimming, self-administering insulin, or backing up computer disks, can have a momentous impact on a person's life. It's also not trivial in the sense of being easy. Scheduling is more difficult than it seems at first. Several types of difficulties can arise.

Patients may have difficulty keeping to their schedule if they have contracted to carry out activities that are onerous, overwhelming, or particularly anxiety-producing for them. These types of plans are easily overturned. Small, manageable plans are more likely to be carried out.

When an activity has been chosen, it's important to spend some time in the session working out some of the details of the plan (what, when, where, with whom). The more specific the plan, the more likely that it will be carried out. The process of working through the plan in detail often uncovers obstacles; the therapist can work with the patient in the session to remove these (e.g., the patient plans to go jogging, but doesn't have any jogging shoes). Compliance is also more likely for activities that do not depend on the weather, the availability of tickets, whether or not others are free, and so on. For example, the patient may come to the next session saying, "I couldn't go to see 'The Music Man', because I couldn't get tickets." To avoid this, the therapist can work to schedule activities that depend only on the patient; if "The Music Man" is something the patient wants to do, the plan can be, "Call two friends to see if they want to go to the show, and call to see if tickets are available. If they're not, just go out to dinner."

Providing the patient with a structured, written schedule also enhances compliance by clarifying what is expected and providing a reminder. In addition, the patient's writing down the proposed plan during the session constitutes a more active commitment to it than would occur in an unstructured discussion. The therapist can suggest that the patient check off each activity as it is done and bring the schedule to the next session for review.

Pleasure-predicting

A common difficulty arises when the depressed patient responds to the suggestion that he schedule more social or other types of activities with the automatic thought, "I won't enjoy it, so what's the point of doing anything?" David Burns (1980) devised a clever intervention, called pleasure-predicting, to address this problem. Pleasure-predicting induces patients to undertake activities to test the hypothesis that they will not enjoy anything. It works because depressed patients' predictions of the amount of enjoyment they will get is generally distorted: usually they enjoy things more than they expect to. In addition, one activity often leads to another, beginning a positive cycle of increased activities and improved mood.

As Burns (1980) has pointed out, the same general idea can be used to work on procrastination that has its origins in the perception that the avoided task is unpleasant, boring, aversive, painful, and that little advantage or satisfaction will result from completing the task. Usually the actual unpleasantness is less than predicted and the actual satisfaction is greater.

To do pleasure-predicting, the therapist works with the patient to list an activity or two that the patient used to do but resists doing now because she wouldn't enjoy it. Next, the therapist asks the patient to predict, for each activity, the amount of enjoyment she expects. The patient's task is to carry out the activities, as homework, and then to rate the amount of enjoyment actually experienced. Here's an example.

PATIENT There's no point in being more active — I don't enjoy anything anymore.

THERAPIST What did you enjoy doing before you became depressed?

PATIENT I haven't done anything for so long that I don't remember.

THERAPIST Well, let's think about it. What did you do when you had time to spend on yourself? (Here the therapist refuses to take "no" for an answer, and essentially repeats the question.)

PATIENT I used to spend time with friends, but now I don't want to see anybody.

THERAPIST Who did you used to spend time with?

PATIENT Well, I had two or three girlfriends. But they're all busy, and they don't have time for me.

THERAPIST What are their names?

PATIENT Well, Lisa, and Jane, and sometimes Angela.

THERAPIST What did you do with them?

PATIENT I'd meet them for lunch, and sometimes we'd spend the day together on Saturday.

THERAPIST OK, now let me ask you this: If you did have lunch with Lisa, how much, on a scale of 0 to 100, would you expect to enjoy it?

PATIENT (slowly) Oh, it's hard to give a number.

THERAPIST Yes, it is hard, but I want to show you something with this sheet, and we need a number to do it. What's the first number that comes to mind?

PATIENT Oh, not much. Maybe 20.

THERAPIST Fine, let's put that down here. Now let me tell you how this sheet works. When people are very depressed, like you are, they often don't do much because they don't feel they will enjoy things. But, if they actually *do* get involved in an activity, they usually enjoy it more than they expected. For example, you think you'll only enjoy lunch 20, but from my experience, my guess is that you'll actually enjoy it much more, maybe 50 or even 70 or 80. What do you think?

PATIENT Well, you might be right.

THERAPIST We can use this sheet to find out. I'd like to suggest that you call Lisa for lunch, and after lunch, rate how much you enjoyed the lunch (draw a column for recording this information). Then let me know next week, and we'll be able to see if this works for you, too. What do you think?

PATIENT   OK, I'll try it.

THERAPIST   Great. Now we need to think about how we can use this idea even if Lisa or Jane or another friend can't meet you for lunch. Can we think of another activity you can try? . . .

MODELING AND ROLE-PLAYING

Modeling and role-playing strategies are useful in helping patients carry out new plans and behaviors. A patient may feel convinced that it's a good idea to learn to say "no" to her mother-in-law, but have no idea how to go about it. The therapist can demonstrate and help the patient practice.

Role-playing can also be useful in identifying behavioral problems. A businessman may complain, for example, that his wife is unresponsive to his requests for sexual variety. A role-play of his interaction with his wife reveals that he begins the discussion by criticizing his wife's weight problem and her lack of imagination.

Next, the patient and therapist can switch roles, and the therapist can demonstrate another approach. Finally, the patient and therapist can switch roles again so the patient can practice the new strategies. Several repetitions of this process may be needed.

Role-playing and modeling are helpful when the patient is clear (or fairly clear—the role-playing can add clarity) about what he wants to do, but doesn't know how to go about it. The therapist can model appropriate, productive behavior in situations that are troublesome for the patient: a productive fight with a spouse, an effective way of handling criticism from the boss, returning an item to a department store, breaking up with a girlfriend. Then the patient can practice, and the therapist can give feedback.

Sometimes patients know what they want to say (e.g., "I'd like to break off the relationship"), but fear they are being cruel and hurtful. The therapist can model the feared behavior in a role-play and then ask, "Was that a cruel thing to say?" Usually the patient views the therapist's statement as assertive and reasonable. Even if the patient is not ready to actually carry out the modeled interaction, the role-play brings her closer to the feared situation and may defuse some irrational fears she has about what will happen.

Breaking up is hard to do

PATIENT (playing the role of himself) Jane, I'm very sorry to say this, and I certainly don't want to hurt you, but I think we should stop going out.
THERAPIST (playing the role of Jane) Why?
PATIENT Well, I'm interested in someone else.
THERAPIST: (out of role) Now, what will happen?
PATIENT She'll probably burst into tears.
THERAPIST So she'll be pretty hurt.
PATIENT I guess so. I'll feel terrible.
THERAPIST Would you like to break off the relationship without hurting her so much?
PATIENT Yes, I would!
THERAPIST OK, let's think about how you could do it. Let's try another approach. You be Jane, and I'll be you.
THERAPIST (playing the role of the patient) Jane, I'm very sorry to say this, because I think you're terrific in a lot of ways, but I feel I need to break off our relationship. It's just not working out.
PATIENT What do you mean, break up? Why?
THERAPIST I just don't think the relationship is working out for me.
PATIENT What do you mean? What's the problem?
THERAPIST I just feel the relationship isn't working out, and I want to break it off. (Here the therapist can point out the strategy of simply repeating his statement, deflecting questions asking for explanations, which can often be quite hurtful or unproductive.)
PATIENT How can you do this to me? We've been together almost a year.
THERAPIST Yes, it has been a long time. But it's not working out for me, and I need to break it off.
PATIENT I think you owe me an explanation.
THERAPIST There isn't really an explanation to give. I just feel it's not working out and I want to break it off.
PATIENT What do you mean, "break it off"? Can't we still be friends?
THERAPIST Well, I don't think I can manage that right now. I just think it's time to end the relationship.

This model for breaking up the relationship may be very different from the way the patient would do it — usually the patient feels he must defend and justify his decision at length. If so, a discussion of the pros and cons of the two approaches may be helpful. The patient may have an automatic thought like, "I *owe* her a full explanation." If so, it may be useful to elicit and respond to the distortions in this thought.

The therapist as model

In addition to the explicit use of modeling described above, the therapist frequently serves as a model for her patients without being explicitly aware of doing so. The therapist frequently has opportunities to model assertive statements ("I suggest you spend 15 minutes working on this during the week"), refusing requests ("No, I won't be available on Tuesday at 4 — I could meet at 2 or at 3"), giving compliments ("You look nice in that color"), accepting compliments, responding to criticism, handling errors, and so on.

RELAXATION

Relaxation is helpful for patients who complain of bodily and psychological tension and anxiety. It is also helpful for patients who feel unable to cope and would benefit from learning some active coping strategies. It can be useful as a procedure in and of itself or as part of a larger plan. In systematic desensitization, described in the Exposure section of Chapter 5, patients are asked to relax while imagining fearful scenes. In anxiety management training (Suinn and Richardson, 1971), patients are asked to imagine fearful scenes and then practice using relaxation to cope with the anxiety they experience in the difficult situations.

Many approaches to relaxation have been developed. Well-known procedures include those developed by Wolpe (1973) and Bernstein and Borkovec (1973), both of which use instructions for tensing and relaxing muscles based on Jacobson (1938). Many patients have relaxation procedures they know and like, including meditation and self-hypnotic procedures. There is no clear evidence that these procedures differ in efficacy. Cassette tapes of relaxation procedures can be obtained from many sources (see the *Psychology Today* tapes listings). I often give my patients one or two tapes and ask them to listen to both, choose the one they like best, and begin practicing.

Relaxation improves with practice, ideally daily. Patients can be asked to keep a log of their relaxation sessions for review in the therapy session.

Difficulties

A common difficulty is the failure to practice. Practice is important to achieving substantial benefit and in having the ability to marshall the procedure when it might be helpful in anxiety-provoking situations. To solve this difficulty, the therapist can explore why the patient does not practice. Often this problem is directly related to the patient's central problem, and this can be pointed out, as in the following example.

PATIENT   I think the relaxation helps me. I just don't get it done.

THERAPIST   Let's think about what keeps you from getting it done.

PATIENT   I just don't have time.

THERAPIST   "I just don't have time." This sounds familiar to me. Do you see how this is related to some of the other problems we've talked about — how it's hard for you to say no to other people and hard to take time to do things that you enjoy doing, or want to do, just for yourself? This is your idea, "I don't count" again, isn't it?

PATIENT   Yes, I guess it is.

THERAPIST   OK then, what does that tell you? Do you see what I'm driving at?

PATIENT   You're going to say I can work on that idea by doing the relaxation.

THERAPIST   Right. Does that make sense to you?

PATIENT   Yes, it does. But I still feel like I don't have time.

THERAPIST   Of course you feel like you don't have time. That's your idea about yourself: "I don't have time to take care of my needs." But maybe we need to start finding some time. What do you think?

PATIENT   I guess so.

THERAPIST   Good. Now where can we find the time? (see Scheduling earlier in this chapter)

Some patients find relaxation to be anxiety-producing (Heide & Borkovec, 1984). Often these patients have a central fear of losing control, and relaxation exacerbates the fear. For these patients, cognitive coping strategies or exposure are likely to be more helpful than relaxation.

CHAPTER 5

Additional behavioral interventions

This chapter describes five behavioral interventions: rewards and punishments, breaking tasks into small parts, exposure, stimulus control, and exercise. These strategies are useful in helping patients make behavioral changes they want to make but have difficulty accomplishing.

It is important to remember that not all behavioral changes patients want to make are in their best psychological interest, no matter how desirable these changes are from other points of view, including, for example, cardiovascular fitness. For example, patients who believe, "I'm worthless unless I'm perfect" often embark on extremely demanding self-improvement programs, including exercise, diet, and psychological self-control. In fact, the model of cognitive therapy, which proposes that negative mood can be eliminated if irrational thinking is corrected, can seem to support these patients' pathological wishes never to experience any negative moods or other psychological imperfections of any sort. Another person who frequently strives for behavioral changes that are not in her best interest is the individual who believes, "I must do what is expected of me by others in order to gain the approval, acceptance and love I need."

Both types of patients are usually quite unaware that the behavioral changes they seek (and, not surprisingly, have difficulty making) are not in their interest, and in fact reinforce their pathological irrational beliefs. It is the therapist's responsibility to point this out.

The opposite problem can also occur. That is, the patient is not dating, for example, and disavows any interest in meeting men. Rather than accepting this at face value, the therapist has a responsibility to examine the lack of usual interest from the point of view of the patient's underlying beliefs. Things that patients say they don't want can be things they are afraid of. Again, it is the therapist's responsibility to raise these types of questions.

The therapist can assess the utility of a particular behavioral change for a patient by examining that patient's underlying beliefs carefully and asking, "Is this activity supportive of the irrational belief? Does it reinforce the irrational belief or does it challenge it?" Another way of getting at this question is to ask the patient the reasons for wishing to make the behavioral change being proposed. If the response is an automatic thought, particularly one that is derivative of the underlying belief, this indicates that the change sought will reinforce the irrational belief, not challenge it. For example, a computer programmer who wished to begin a daily weight-lifting program stated, "I want to do this because otherwise women will reject me." Although it is true that many women prefer physically fit men, the therapist's job is to help the patient see, first, that it is not true that if he does not do the exercises no woman will have him, and second, that if he pursues this weight-lifting regime it is likely to exercise and strengthen his irrational beliefs. An alternative homework plan might involve his initiating interactions with women, to test out his idea that if he does this before he becomes fit no one will have him. If the patient refuses to give up his weight-lifting, the therapist might work to keep the regime within safe and healthy limits; often programs pursued for irrational reasons are excessive.

The process of teaching the case formulation approach to behavioral problems was described in greater detail in the last chapter, but is emphasized here once again before the remaining behavioral interventions are presented. The process of examining the relationship between the proposed behavioral change and the underlying belief is best done as a joint, collaborative exercise, so the patient can learn for himself what the nature of his underlying pathological belief is, how his behavior reinforces it, and how to evaluate whether a given behavioral plan is productive or counterproductive in helping him reach his goals.

If a careful examination of the irrational beliefs indicates that a proposed behavioral change is a good one, the following behavioral strategies can be used to bring it about. These new behaviors might be described as "anti-belief" behaviors—behaviors that attack, contradict, or provide evidence against the irrational beliefs underlying the patient's problems.

REWARDS AND PUNISHMENTS

Rewards and punishments have powerful effects on behavior, and can be used in many ways in therapy. The use of rewards and punishments to accomplish behavior change has its origins in operant learning theory. Thorndike's (1935) Law of Effect states that behaviors that are followed by satisfaction are likely to be repeated, whereas those followed by discomfort are not likely to be repeated.

Rewards (positive reinforcement)

Six academics who faced upcoming tenure decisions but found themselves unable to write served as subjects in a behavioral treatment program designed and studied by Boice (1982). Boice showed that, although several treatment components appeared helpful in encouraging writing, an external reinforcer was required to produce reliable writing behavior. Each subject contracted for his/her own, individualized reinforcer; in one case, a daily shower, and in another, all reading activities, including newspapers, were allowed only when the agreed-upon number of pages for that day had been written.

Shaping

In the case of one of Boice's writers, who was unable to write even a single manuscript page, a variant of positive reinforcement was used. Shaping, or successive approximations, was required. This procedure rewards behaviors that are an approximation to the desired ones. Using this procedure, Boice's writer was reinforced in the first stage of treatment for writing and sending reprint request cards and for answering simple letters. In the second stage of treatment, she was reinforced for writing ideas on index cards, then for writing outlines, then for filling them in, and so on; finally, she was reinforced only for complete manuscript pages. This type of strategy is particularly helpful for the patient who is inactive because of automatic thoughts like, "I have to do the whole thing in order to feel I have accomplished anything." Such types of patients often have an underlying idea along the lines, "I'm incompetent; I can't be successful at anything."

Reinforcement strategies I used to write this book

Throughout the most productive period of writing this book, I used rewards to get the job done. I set myself a goal of writing one single-spaced page of manuscript each workday (Monday through Friday). I found that if I expected more, I avoided writing altogether. If I had trouble getting started on even this small task, I broke it into even smaller parts: e.g., turning on the computer, bringing the current chapter up on the screen, and so on. After I wrote my page, I rewarded myself by crossing off the item on my list of things to do that day and patting myself on the back. I made a point of telling my husband or a friend that I did my writing quota for the day, so others would pat me on the back too. I scheduled writing before everything else (unless a patient was scheduled for first thing in the day); in this way, I rewarded myself for writing with the opportunity to do the other things on my list. I reward myself for finishing a chapter by crossing off the chapter on my table of contents, sending the completed chapter off to my editor, telling my husband and my friends that I'd finished a chapter, and buying some clothes or a toy for the baby.

The case of the forgotten reinforcers

A father who was faced with the task of completing a financial aid form for his son's college procrastinated on the task, viewing it as an unpleasant thing he didn't want to do. He had the thoughts, "It's just a pain in the neck — I won't get anything out of doing this task." When we talked about the problem, he realized there were some important rewards for completing the form that he seemed to have forgotten — notably, that he was likely to get a financial award if he completed it and certain to get none if he did not. When he thought about it this way, he was able to complete it easily. This intervention might be viewed as a cognitive inter-vention or as a strategy using reinforcement principles; in this case, all that was needed was to make the reinforcers that were actually present in the situation more salient.

Application to depression

Lewinsohn's (1985) behavioral theory of depression states that de-pressed patients suffer from a reduced number of response-contingent reinforcers. As a result, their rate of responding is reduced and they experience dysphoria. Lewinsohn emphasizes the importance of social reinforcement and hypothesizes that depression-prone individuals are deficient in social skills and therefore receive lower levels of social reinforcement. Lewinsohn, Muñoz, Youngren, and Zeiss (1979) have developed a behavioral treatment for depression based directly on the theory. A major component of the treatment involves increasing the number of pleasant events experienced by the depressed person.

Several empirical studies (reviewed by Blaney, 1977) support Lewinsohn's hypothesis that pleasant activities are associated with improved mood (although some studies, cf. Hammen & Glass, 1975, do not). The causal relationship between behavior and mood described by the theory has not been convincingly demonstrated (does behavior cause mood or the other way around?). However, this is not a problem for the clinician, for two reasons. First, it is much more difficult to manipulate mood than to manipulate activity; therefore, treatment interventions tend to focus on behavior rather than on mood. Second, the interdependency of the mood-behavior-cognitive cycle described in Chapter 1 suggests that any intervention that has a positive effect on behavior is likely to produce an increase in mood.

To work on increasing pleasant events, the therapist can ask the patient to complete the Pleasant Events Schedule published in Lewinsohn et al.'s (1978) book, or to devise a personalized list of pleasant events and work to increase their number. This could be done by giving a homework assignment of completing a certain number of pleasant events on a daily or weekly basis, and working with the patient to overcome any obstacles to completing this task that may arise. This intervention is closely related to the scheduling intervention described in Chapter 4.

Punishment

Punishers are stimuli that decrease the probability of the behavior they follow. An easily understood example of a punisher is a spanking given to a child who runs into the street. Punishers are more effective if they are intense, occur immediately after the response, and if the contingency between the response and the punishment is 100% (Schwartz, 1984).

A clinical example of a rather benign punishment procedure is a strategy useful with patients who come late to sessions, make inappropriate telephone calls outside sessions, fail to pay the bill promptly, or engage in other types of behaviors that interfere with therapy (and can make the therapist furious!) (Linehan, 1987). When one of these therapy-interfering behaviors occurs, it becomes the first item on the agenda for the next therapy session. This strategy makes good therapeutic sense for two reasons. First, a problem-solving discussion of the problematic behavior can teach the patient the skills she needs to prevent it from happening in the future. Second, this discussion is probably perceived by the patient as a punishment (she would probably prefer to be discussing other problems than the fact that she came five minutes late to the session). If so, this discussion will reduce the frequency of the behavior in question.

When using punishment to eliminate a behavior, it is important to remember that the behavior is presumably occurring because it is positively reinforced. For example, exhibitionistic behavior is reinforced by sexual gratification. Punishment to remove the behavior will not be very effective unless the therapist also teaches the patient alternative behaviors that will lead to gratification.

Aversion therapy

Aversion therapy refers to treatment procedures that involve aversive stimuli or negative reinforcers. Negative reinforcers increase the probability of a given behavior by imposing a penalty in its absence. Traffic tickets are a negative reinforcer of lawful driving. A clinical example of negative reinforcement is the use of penalties for failing to live up to an agreed-upon behavior. For example, one of Boice's (1982) writers placed $250 in the hands of a colleague and agreed that, if the scheduled amount of writing for the week was not completed, the money would be sent to a group whose aims she hated (e.g., an anti-abortion group).

Aversive stimuli can also be used as punishers, to decrease the probability of certain behaviors; rowdy behavior is reduced by confining a child to his room when he is rowdy. Although these examples utilize the operant model, a Pavlovian conditioning model can also be used to explain many aversive procedures.

In aversion therapy, undesirable stimulus situations or behaviors are paired with aversive stimulation. Aversion therapy for alcoholics, for example, pairs alcohol and nausea; the alcoholic is given a drink of his favorite alcohol, to which an emetic agent has been added (Cannon & Baker, 1981). A variant of this procedure, rapid smoking, is used to help smokers break the habit. Rapid smoking capitalizes on the fact that rapid smoking of several cigarettes in an airless room, in a group, in a brief period of time, spontaneously produces many noxious physiological and psychological symptoms. Rapid smoking is currently one of the most effective known smoking cessation procedures (Hall, Sachs & Hall, 1979; Hall, Sachs, Hall & Benowitz, 1984); however, aversion therapy has not so far been shown to be a particularly effective treatment of alcohol problems (reviewed by Wilson, 1978). Aversive stimulation has also been used to treat sexual problems; for example, an electric shock, for example, is administered in the presence of a fetish object. Studies of the efficacy of these treatments have shown mixed results (reviewed by Rachman & Wilson, 1980; Wilson, 1978).

Aversion treatments have been improved by evidence from the study of taste aversions showing that some associations are much more readily learned than others. This phenomenon is illustrated naturally by the readiness with which organisms learn to associate a taste with symptoms of nausea; after one such pairing, the taste is often avoided for the rest of the organism's life. In contrast, an association between a taste and a loud noise is much more difficult to learn (Garcia & Koelling, 1966). Garcia and Koelling also showed that an association between a loud noise and a painful electric shock is much easier to learn than an association between a loud noise and nausea. Thus, some stimuli are more readily paired than others; taste goes with illness, sights and sounds to external pain. This particular pairing of cues makes good evolutionary sense, as Seligman (1970) pointed out. Organisms in the wild will find it extremely useful to learn that illness was preceded by eating a certain flavor (perhaps a poison). Behavior therapists can make use of these principles by pairing stimuli involving taste or smell (alcohol, smoking) with nausea rather than with another type of aversive stimulus or reinforcer.

Guidelines to the therapist in the use of aversive stimuli

The use of aversive stimuli presents personal, legal, and ethical dilemmas for therapists. Many, if not most, therapists find the use of aversive stimuli distasteful, and some applications of aversive stimulation may even be illegal in some states.

There are three primary psychological disadvantages of aversive stimulation. First, aversive stimulation can produce the negative side effect of fear, which is unpleasant and can become a problem in itself. Aversive stimulation can disrupt even unpunished responses, perhaps via a generalized sense of fear or discomfort. Finally, the use of punishment, especially with children, can provide an unfortunate model: if you don't like what someone else is doing, then hurt them to make them stop.

Despite the unattractiveness and many disadvantages of the use of aversive stimulation, these strategies cannot be discarded, because they offer hope for certain patients who need it desperately. Punishment is the most rapid procedure for removing undesirable behaviors (Schwartz, 1978), and in the case of an autistic child who batters herself, or a professional person whose exhibitionism threatens his personal and professional life with ruin, time is of the essence. As Stewart Nixon (personal communication, May, 1985) points out, one important protection for the therapist using aversive stimuli is to set up the procedure in such a way that the patient — not the therapist — administers the aversive stimulation.

Covert reinforcement

The treatments described so far use actual aversive and rewarding stimuli. Cautela (1967, 1970) developed a set of procedures he called covert reinforcement. The term covert refers to the fact that the response and reinforcement are presented in imagination, as in the following example of a covert aversive stimulus used to treat alcohol abuse:

> You are walking into a bar. You decide to have a beer. You are now walking toward the bar. As you are approaching the bar you have a funny feeling in the pit of your stomach. Your stomach feels all queasy and nauseous. Some liquid comes up your throat and it is very sour. You try to swallow it back down, but as you do this, food particles start coming up your throat to your mouth. You are now reaching the bar and you order a beer. As the bartender is pouring the beer, puke comes up into your mouth. You try to keep your mouth closed and swallow it down. You reach for the glass of beer to wash it down. As soon as your hand touches the glass, you can't hold it down any longer. You have to open your mouth and you puke. It goes all over your hand, all over the glass and the beer. You can see it floating around in the beer. Snots and mucus come out of your nose. Your shirt and pants are all full of vomit. The bartender has some on his shirt. You notice people looking at you. You get sick again and you vomit some more and more. You turn away from the beer and immediately you start to feel better. As you run out of the bar, you start to feel better and better. When you get out into clean fresh air you feel wonderful. You go home and clean yourself up.

To use this covert stimulus in treatment, the patient can be asked to imagine going into a bar and having a drink, and then to immediately imagine the covert aversive image in all its gory detail. This procedure must be repeated many times to be effective.

I used a variation of covert reinforcement when writing this book: I "patted myself on the back" whenever I finished my writing quota for the day.

Guidelines to the therapist in the use
of rewards and punishments

Of course, intrinsically rewarding objects or activities (food, sex) or aversive ones (giving away money to a hated cause, setting a $20 bill on fire) are obvious choices. However, sometimes choices are not so obvious. What's important is the meaning of the reinforcer *to the patient*. For example, a businessman planned to reward himself for sales calls with new clothes; this was ineffective, however, because he did not enjoy buying new clothes — in fact, buying new clothes made him anxious and uncomfortable!

Thus, reinforcers are not *intrinsically* reinforcing; their reinforcement value is determined by their meaning to the patient. Premack (1962) showed that high frequency behaviors can be used as reinforcers for low frequency behaviors. Using this idea, the therapist can look for reinforcers by finding out what behaviors the patient frequently engages in. Thus, one patient may reinforce herself for jogging by going shopping for clothes, while another may reinforce herself for going shopping for clothes by jogging.

Reinforcers are more effective if they immediately follow the behavior they reinforce. And the reinforcers must be certain — not dependent on other people's plans, the weather, or other events outside the patient's control.

The therapist as reinforcer

The therapist can play a powerful role as a reinforcer of the patient's behavior; in fact, the therapist plays this role at all times whether or not he is aware of doing so. For example, in every session, the therapist makes dozens of decisions about which remarks and topics raised by the patient are likely to lead to progress, and which are not. By responding to some remarks and not others, the therapist reinforces the patient for focusing and working on these topics and not others.

An example is provided by the case of an elderly patient who complained incessantly of severe and unremitting depression, hopelessness and anxiety, saying at least three dozen times in each therapy session, "I have to get rid of the anxiety or I'll die," "My life is nothing but unremitting pain and suffering," "I feel as if I've been condemned to eternal suffering," and so on. In contrast to her anxious, helpless mood during this litany of dramatic statements, the patient showed excitement and enjoyment when she discussed her work as a travel agent.

After attempting, without success, to demonstrate to the patient the maladaptive nature of her catastrophic thoughts so that she might make a choice to eliminate them, the therapist simply adopted the strategy of ignoring the "disaster" cognitions and working instead to elicit and attend to cognitions focusing on the patient's work. The number of work-oriented cognitions quickly increased and the number of disaster cognitions decreased. Although many other problems remained, the patient reported leaving these therapy sessions feeling much better than when she arrived. In addition, she bought herself some new clothes for the first time in months, initiated treatment of several medical problems she'd been ignoring, and began making efforts to expand her business.

Another example is provided by the case of patient who, when asked to work actively in her treatment, typically became frightened, resistant, helpless, and uncooperative. For example, she often responded to the therapist's statement, "What would you like to put on the agenda for today?" with a symptom, "I can't think — my head is spinning." This was a recurrent pattern in all her relationships; a common strategy for asking for comfort and support for her husband was to complain of suicidal thoughts and wishes. The therapist using reinforcement to guide his intervention would be ill-advised to reinforce this maladaptive behavior by responding to it (e.g., "How long have you been feeling this way?"). Instead, a more helpful rejoinder would be, "Let's wait a moment until your head stops spinning and then work on an agenda." That is, the therapist works to remove the reinforcer (attention, empathy) for the maladaptive behavior. In addition, it will be important to reinforce the patient for productive behaviors.

Difficulties

Difficulties in the use of rewards and punishments can arise for many reasons. Failure may occur because the patient and therapist do not have a correct understanding of the contingencies operating in the situation (that is, the case formulation is inaccurate). For example, a student attempted to reward himself for working on his dissertation by reminding himself why he chose to attend graduate school in the first place (reminding himself of rewards he had forgotten). This strategy was ineffective because his procrastination was due to a fear of failure, not forgotten reinforcers. In addition, his list of reasons included items like, "I'll prove to my father that I can succeed in spite of him," and reviewing this list made him feel angry and upset.

Sometimes a treatment intervention based on reinforcement principles fails because the wrong behavior is reinforced. For example, an undergraduate student who had difficulty writing a term paper decided to reward herself for time spent on the term paper; for every two hours she worked on the paper, she allowed herself a half hour with her friends. This procedure did lead to an increase in the time spent on the term paper, but it didn't lead to a written term paper, because she spent many hours reading but continued to avoid the thing she was most afraid of: the actual writing. To address this issue, we made the reward contingent on written pages.

Sometimes a treatment plan focused on increasing pleasant activities fails because the patient does not undertake the activities. The therapist can address this problem by first finding out why this happened, beginning with an examination of the antecedents and consequences of the problematic behavior, including cognitions and moods. If, for example, the patient didn't go to the movies because he didn't believe he would enjoy it, the pleasure-predicting exercise (Chapter 4) may be helpful. Sometimes patients who do carry out the scheduled activities report they didn't enjoy them. Again, the therapist will need to find out what interfered with the enjoyment. Often patients report negative thoughts that rob them of pleasure: "These people are just being nice — they don't really like me," "I should have done this months ago," and so on. Correcting the distortions in these negative cognitions can make the activities more rewarding.

BREAKING TASKS INTO SMALL PARTS

Common antecedents of undone tasks include automatic thoughts like, "It's too difficult," "I won't be able to do it," and "It will take forever." These automatic thoughts are derivatives of underlying beliefs like, "I'm incompetent," "I'm weak and fragile," and "I can't tolerate stress of any kind." The strategy of breaking tasks into small parts can be used to address this problem, which can interfere with both large, demanding tasks, like doing income taxes or writing a dissertation, and apparently small tasks like getting out of bed.

PATIENT   My income taxes are not done, but whenever I think of doing them, I get overwhelmed.

THERAPIST   I see. Well, let's find out how overwhelmed you get. When you say to yourself, "This weekend I'm going to do my taxes," how overwhelmed do you feel, on a scale of 0 to 100?

PATIENT   100!

THERAPIST   And does feeling overwhelmed help you do your income taxes?

PATIENT   No!

THERAPIST   Let's see if we can find a way to make the taxes less overwhelming. Any ideas?

PATIENT   No, not really.

THERAPIST   Well, let me ask you this: what's the first thing you need to do to start your income taxes?

PATIENT   I need to get all my papers together.

THERAPIST   If you say to yourself, "I'm going to start by getting all my papers together," how overwhelmed do you feel?

PATIENT   I still feel pretty overwhelmed. Whenever I sit down at my desk, I get overwhelmed by how many things I have to do. Maybe what I need to do is get my desk organized first.

THERAPIST   This sounds like an avoidance activity to me. What do you think?

PATIENT   You're probably right.

THERAPIST   Let's stay on the track of the income taxes. When you sit down at your desk, what's the single first thing you have to do to start on your taxes?

PATIENT   Find the envelope where I've been saving all my dividend statements.

THERAPIST   Great. Let's make a list (handing the patient a piece of paper) Number one, find the envelope. OK, what's next?

PATIENT   Look in the envelope to see if anything's missing.

THERAPIST   OK, write that down as number 2. What's number 3.

PATIENT   Look for any papers that are missing.

THERAPIST   OK, what's number 4?

PATIENT   Find the income tax forms. Then I need to start filling them out.

THERAPIST   Before we go on, let me ask you how long it will take to do everything we've talked about so far.

PATIENT   About an hour.

THERAPIST   I would suggest it's time to stop.

PATIENT   OK.

THERAPIST   There's one more thing to do before you stop. What I would suggest is that you make a list just like the one we made here of what you're going to do the next time you sit down to work on your taxes.

PATIENT   OK, that's a good idea.

THERAPIST   Now, when would you like to sit down and do the things on the first list?

PATIENT   I can do it this afternoon.

THERAPIST   Terrific. Let me know next time how it went.

EXPOSURE

Exposure to the feared object or situation is widely viewed as the active ingredient of a variety of behavioral treatments for fears and phobias, including systematic desensitization, flooding, and exposure and response prevention (Barlow & Waddell, 1985; Foa & Kozak, 1986; Marks, 1981).[1] Because these treatments have been described in detail elsewhere, detailed descriptions are not provided here.[2] Instead, this section describes the way in which exposure affects a patient's underlying pathological beliefs, and offers three simple rules for the effective use of the exposure principle in treating fears and phobias.

Exposure treatments correct underlying beliefs

Foa and Kozak (1986) offered a cognitive model of the efficacy of exposure treatments that is similar to the case formulation model offered here. When patients are avoiding feared situations (behavior), experiencing anxiety (mood), and reporting irrational fears (cognitions), they tend to have central underlying beliefs along the lines, "I must avoid these types of situations or something terrible will happen and I won't be able to cope." Often the irrational beliefs described by Beck et al. (1985) as typical of anxious patients are applicable here, particularly the belief, "I'm a weak and vulnerable person, and I can't cope with stress." Exposure treatment is effective because it provides the patient with evidence that contradicts these central underlying beliefs. Thus, the patient who fears driving on bridges for fear she'll have a heart attack and die will find, if she exposes herself to the situation, that she does not have a heart attack and die. Nor does her anxiety cause her to lose control of the car, another of her fears. Thus, effective exposure is a way of chipping away at pathological automatic thoughts and irrational beliefs.

Successful exposure

Figure 5.1 illustrates the results of an effective exposure treatment; each separate curve corresponds to one exposure session, and the number of the curve corresponds to the number of the session. These curves were obtained from records I kept of a patient treated with imaginal exposure for a fear of death (Persons, 1986a). Two effects can be seen: within-

[1] In spite of the widespread use of the exposure principle to account for the effectiveness of these varied treatments, few direct tests of the exposure principle have been done, and results have not always been positive (cf. Jannoun, Munby, Catalan, & Gelder, 1980).
[2] Detailed descriptions of systematic desensitization are found in Wolpe (1973). Steketee and Foa (1985) describe exposure and response prevention for obsessive-compulsives.

Figure 5.1   Fear ratings over the course of repeated flooding sessions (odd-numbered sessions only).

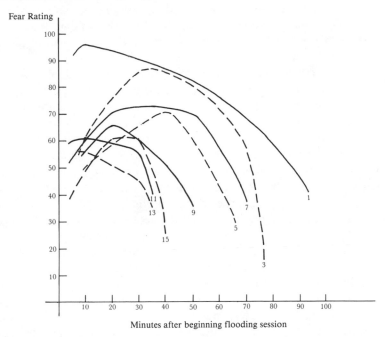

Minutes after beginning flooding session

session habituation and between-session habituation (Foa & Kozak, 1986). Within-session habituation is the drop in fear that occurs within an exposure session. For each session (each curve), anxiety decreases as duration of exposure to the feared situation increases. Between-session habituation is the drop in fear that occurs between exposure sessions. As the patient repeatedly exposes himself to his feared situation, the maximum fear level he experiences drops. The between-session habituation effect is represented by the drop in maximum fear level over the series of curves in the figure. Foa and Kozak (1986) argue that between-session habituation occurs only if within-session habituation occurs.

Presenting exposure to patients

The "old plan/new plan" strategy (Chapter 4) can be used to explain the need and purpose of exposure to patients. Or the therapist can ask, "Imagine you take your child horseback riding, and the child falls off the horse and is frightened. How would you handle this situation?" Most patients give an answer that involves exposure: "I'd put him back on the horse," and "I'd stay with him and gradually bring him over to pat the horse," are two common answers. These answers reflect an intuitive understanding of the exposure principle and the therapist can draw on this understanding to teach the patient how to work effectively on his own fear.

A few patients, once they understand the exposure principle, can use it to overcome their fear—they simply start doing the things they've been avoiding. Most, however, need some assistance and structure from the therapist. Help from the therapist can occur in a formal, intense treatment program, such as a series of flooding sessions, or in a less formal way, in which the therapist helps the patient develop a hierarchy to guide exposure exercises outside the sessions, works to help the patient over rough spots, cheers him on to continue working, and teaches cognitive strategies, relaxation, and other coping techniques. Work with spouses and other members of the family may be necessary as well, to be certain they understand and are working to increase, not prevent, exposure.

Effective exposure can be done gradually or intensely, in imagination or in vivo, individually or in groups. Although there is some evidence that in vivo exposure is superior to imaginal exposure, particularly for certain problems, such as agoraphobia and obsessive-compulsive disorder (Foa & Kozak, 1986), in general these factors do not relate to the effectiveness of the exposure procedure. For patients wishing a gradual exposure experience, the use of a hierarchy like the one described in Chapter 4 is helpful.

Three rules of effective exposure

Three factors determine the effectiveness of exposure: duration, frequency, and comprehensiveness.

DURATION. Effective exposure is prolonged. That is, the patient remains in the fear situation until a substantial decrement in fear level occurs. Each curve in Figure 5.1 illustrates the pattern of fear responding expected during a successful exposure session. If the patient exits the situation before a decrement occurs, no benefit is expected. One way to think about this is to remember that unless the person remains in the situation until the fear drops, the person's nervous system retains the knowledge that to be in this situation is to be afraid and uncomfortable. Unless the anxious person stays in the situation until some amount of relief is experienced, the nervous system never learns that it is possible to be in this situation and feel at ease. Several studies (reviewed by Foa & Kozak,

1986) demonstrate that prolonged exposure is more effective than brief in reducing fear.

FREQUENCY. Effective exposure is frequent. This idea can again be conveyed with a question: "Suppose you had a fear of speaking in meetings, and you took a new job that required you to speak in meetings on a daily basis. What would happen to your fear?" When asked this question, most patients quickly understand that repeated exposure to the feared situation leads to a reduction in fear. Because this is so, daily practice is the most effective way of overcoming fear. To encourage repeated practice, the therapist can ask the patient to keep a daily log in which she records her exposure experiences and to bring the log to the therapy session for review.

COMPREHENSIVENESS. Effective exposure is comprehensive. That is, exposure to all aspects of the feared situation is carried out. Some evidence indicates that if exposure is not comprehensive, relapse may be more likely. For example, Foa and her colleagues treated two groups of obsessive-compulsives: one received exposure only to the feared objects and situations; the other also received exposure (in imagination) to the patient's "disastrous consequences" — for example, "If I touch this dirt, I'll poison my family." The two groups did not differ at the end of treatment, but the first group relapsed more frequently than the second. For this reason, the therapist's job is to push for a complete understanding of all aspects of the patient's fear and to expose the patient to them all.

To achieve comprehensive exposure, it is important to be aware of all of the mood, cognitive, and behavioral components of the patient's fear, and of the core irrational beliefs that appear to underlie the fear. Unless these beliefs are disconfirmed by the exposure situation, treatment is incomplete. In addition, external stimulus situations are important as well. The therapist can work to expose the patient to all aspects of the stimulus situation that are frightening. Often this must be done in imagination, as in the case of a patient who was afraid of death and thought of it as involving coldness, terrible loneliness, no thoughts or feelings, and so on. To expose the patient to behavioral and physiological aspects of the fear, the therapist can help the patient focus her attention on the physiological sensations, palpitations, sweaty palms, and so on, during exposure. To expose her to the cognitive components of the fear, the therapist may need to probe the meaning of the fear to the patient, consequences the patient fears, and so on. For example, an agoraphobic might fear, "If I overcome my problems, I'll want to leave my husband, and he'll fall apart." Unless this aspect of the fear is addressed, treatment is not likely to be completely successful; in fact, the phobic patient may be unable to follow through with a good exposure program.

Difficulties

Some anxious patients refuse exposure, directly or indirectly. When this happens, the therapist's task is to find out why and to work to remove the obstacle if possible.

Sometimes patients avoid because they find the frightening situation and their anxiety response so aversive that they are unwilling to tolerate it. A more gradual exposure procedure can be helpful here. Patients may be more willing to expose themselves if they have some coping strategies they can use in an active way; to provide these, the therapist can teach relaxation or cognitive strategies. Sometimes patients' families reinforce avoidance and block the patient's effort to expose herself and to overcome her fears; when this happens, work with family members is necessary.

Some patients agree to the therapist's treatment program but then manage to not carry it out. A hysterical, dramatic agoraphobic continually came to sessions upset, panicky, rambling disjointedly, and evading my attempts to focus her attention and work systematically on any issue for more than five minutes at a time. Not surprisingly, therapy was not successful, and in fact the patient became worse—more anxious and more depressed. This therapy went nowhere until I conceptualized the patient's behavior during the session as avoidance behavior, made a contract with the patient to work to reduce it, and continually brought the patient back to the original treatment plan, which involved daily exposure to feared situations outside the house.

Two important factors that inhibit patients' willingness to expose themselves and may also prevent exposure from being effective are "overvalued ideation," and depression (Foa & Kozak, 1986). Most phobics perceive that their fears are irrational ("I know elevators aren't dangerous, but I panic when I get in one."). A few aren't so sure ("I actually might die during the panic attack."). Those with overvalued ideation are less successfully treated. To assess overvalued ideation, the therapist might ask the patient, "How probable is it that you will die during the panic attack?"

In the case of depression, some evidence indicates that depressed patients are less successful in exposure treatments, whereas other studies show no difference (see Foa & Kozak, 1986). Depression may interfere because the belief that things are hopeless or the passive behaviors associated with depressive cognitions may interfere with the patient's willingness to undertake exposure.

STIMULUS CONTROL

Reward and punishment strategies are based on the knowledge that consequences control behavior. Stimulus control strategies drawn the fact that stimuli also exert control over behavior. Therefore, to change behavior, change the controlling stimuli in the environment.

For example, the person who wishes to control his eating might do so by not buying fattening foods or not leaving them out in plain sight. The person who wants to stop drinking might stop going to bars and parties and spending time with friends who drink. The person who is under doctors' orders to stop smoking might avoid buying cigarettes, get up from the table immediately after eating, and stop drinking coffee, because these stimuli all elicit smoking behavior.

Although these types of stimulus control procedures are often helpful, especially in the beginning stages of eliminating problematic behaviors, the difficulty with them is that we do not always have complete control over our environment, and on occasion we will be exposed to the stimulus situation that elicits our problematic behavior. We cannot always get up from the table immediately. In situations where this can't be done, the person relying on stimulus control alone is vulnerable to smoking. To address this issue, extinction is necessary. That is, the connection between the eliciting stimulus (sitting at the table after dinner) and the problematic behavior (smoking) must be extinguished. To do this, exposure is needed. This procedure involves the *opposite* of stimulus control: instead of avoiding sitting at the table after dinner, the person must purposely do it, and not smoke. Shaping might be helpful here, with the person gradually extending the length of time he can sit at the table after a meal. Smoking treatment procedures using the extinction model ask patients to carry an opened pack of cigarettes with them at all times!

Thus, the use of stimulus control to eliminate problematic behaviors by avoiding cues that elicit those behaviors is sometimes problematic. Another use of stimulus control, creating new stimulus-behavior connections, does not seem to have this problem.

For example, a person who wishes to eat less might make a rule that no eating is done in the car; this rule, if strictly enforced, will control eating by breaking the connection between being in the car and eating, and may forge new connections between being in the car and not eating. A variant of stimulus control is involved in the plan one patient made of scheduling his exercise class immediately after the therapy session; he knew that attending the therapy session would "set the stage" for going directly on to the exercise class. I use stimulus control to help write this book by scheduling writing before all other activities for the day. By scheduling the writing first, lots of cues become associated with writing: walking into the office first thing in the morning, my morning cup of coffee, and so on. After these associations have been built up, they all help push me in the direction of beginning writing when I come into my office and have a cup of coffee in the morning.

EXERCISE

Many patients report that physical exercise relieves anxiety and depression, and these statements are supported by some evidence (Simons, Epstein, McGowan, Kupfer, & Robertson, 1985). Many patients spontaneously wish to begin treatment by increasing their exercise, and for some exercise can be a key component of treatment throughout. Especially at the beginning of treatment, exercise can be helpful because it is concrete, does not require complex cognitive processes that can be difficult to muster when anxiety and depression are severe, can be done in small doses, and is immediately gratifying.

Difficulties

Sometimes patients who report that exercise is helpful also report quite a lot of difficulty in getting themselves to do it. For patients who don't exercise because their schedule is chaotic and they do not make plans, scheduling (see Chapter 4) can be helpful. Sometimes patients have irrational ideas that block them from exercising, and these can be addressed directly: "other people will laugh at me when I jog," "the aerobics instructor will ask me why I stopped coming six months ago," "if I start exercising, I'll get overinvolved and obsessive about it again."

For some patients, exercise is more of a problem than a solution. This is true both for those who do too little exercise and those who do too much. In the case of the exercise avoider, prescribing exercise is not likely to be helpful in overcoming depression, anxiety or other problems, because exercise is a problem in itself. Other patients do too much exercise, and the therapist's task is to pick up on this and not reinforce it by prescribing more exercise when less would be better.

CHAPTER 6

Dysfunctional thinking

This chapter and the next one focus on dysfunctional thinking. This chapter describes, in detail, common cognitive difficulties and the process of eliciting these cognitive problems in therapy sessions. The next chapter outlines strategies the therapist can use to bring about cognitive change.

This chapter focuses on the cognitive component of the problems on the patient's problem list. In the case formulation model outlined in Chapter 1, this is the "cognition" node of the patient's overt difficulties. In his theory of depression, Beck (1972) labelled these thoughts "automatic thoughts" because they seem to arise spontaneously and automatically, without effort.

THREE TYPES OF DYSFUNCTIONAL THOUGHTS

Three types of problematic cognitions are described here: derivatives of the underlying irrational beliefs, maladaptive thoughts, and distorted thoughts. Derivatives of the irrational beliefs are automatic thoughts that are close restatements of the patient's underlying irrational beliefs. Maladaptive thoughts seem accurate, logical, and realistic; however, they have negative effects on mood and functioning, and they reinforce the underlying irrational beliefs. Distorted thoughts present an unrealistic view of reality or involve illogical reasoning.

These three types of automatic thoughts are not mutually exclusive; a given thought can — and usually does — fall into more than one category (more about this later). Each type of thought is described in detail below.

DERIVATIVES OF THE UNDERLYING BELIEFS

Derivatives of the irrational beliefs are simply that: they are automatic thoughts that are close restatements of the underlying beliefs. For example, a young man who held the irrational belief, "Until I correct all my defects, I will not be accepted or loved," reported, over the course of therapy, the following automatic thoughts: "I don't belong on this nature hike; when the others find out how little I know about nature, they'll ignore me"; "When my friends visit from out of town, I should know all the historical information about Philadelphia they want to know, or they'll think I'm dumb"; "If I want girls to like me, I have to become a better conversationalist": "Unless I do a good job of my cognitive therapy homework, Jackie will think I'm a bad patient and want to stop seeing me." We can understand this type of thinking if we view the patient's underlying irrational belief as a type of "template" he places over his ongoing experience in order to understand it and make choices about how to handle problems or choices. Beck, et al. (1979) also used the word "schema" to describe the way in which the underlying beliefs organize ongoing experience, the view of the world, and the self.

Because of their close relationship with the underlying beliefs, which are generally quite irrational, the derivatives are generally irrational as well. Derivatives are also maladaptive because they are consistent with and support other irrational and maladaptive automatic thoughts, they strengthen behaviors that lead to and are produced by those thoughts, and they are consistent with the patient's pathological world view and sense of self.

Many cognitions that do not appear to be dramatically distorted or clearly maladaptive can, if viewed from the vantage point of the underlying irrational beliefs, be perceived as problematic. Many of these thoughts seem trivial and unimportant and may escape the therapist's notice, but the strategy of looking for derivatives of the core irrational beliefs can shine a spotlight on them. For example, a patient whose central irrational belief was "I'm inadequate" came to the session saying, "I'll need to spend next week revising my vita so I can apply for the job that was listed in the paper on Sunday." Although this statement is not dramatically distorted or maladaptive, the tipoff to its problematic nature is its very close relationship to the patient's core cognitive beliefs about herself. A discussion of whether a complete overhaul of the vita is really necessary is indicated here.

An agoraphobic accountant, working with the therapist to schedule her practice driving sessions, stated, "I can't drive on the bridge after work — there's too much traffic." At first blush, this statement appears reasonable. The tipoff to the problematic nature of the thought comes from the observation that it is a close cousin of one of the patient's core irrational beliefs about herself ("I can't do anything right, I'm incompetent."). Another patient who believed, "I must be perfect in order to be accepted," stated, "I should review *Feeling Good* every evening, so I can learn not to make any errors in my thinking." In this example, another hint of a problem is the excessive nature of the activity.

Cognitive derivatives of the formulation can also be difficult for patients to perceive. They are often so tightly linked to a patient's world view and identity that he may resist the suggestion that they are problematic in any way. Thus, the agoraphobic who is unwilling to drive in heavy traffic may protest that this reluctance is perfectly rational — that there's no point driving when the traffic doesn't move. Although this argument appears rational, it is not. It is rational if the purpose of driving the bridge is to get somewhere; however in this case, a traffic jam improves the patient's opportunity for exposure to traffic situations she's afraid of. Even more important, this thought reinforces the patient's core belief that she is weak, vulnerable and incompetent, and supports her widespread avoidance behavior.

Careful attention to the patient's verbalizations typically reveals many derivatives of the formulation in each therapy session and across a wide range of problems discussed in the therapy. The patient who believed "I don't count" was terrified of a promotion interview, stating, "I won't be taken seriously." She was afraid to enter new social situations because of the thought, "No one will want to talk to me." She occasionally developed blocks in therapy sessions, unwilling to raise certain topics because of her concern that the therapist would find them boring. When she became suicidal, she was reluctant to ask her husband to remove his guns from the house, saying, "He won't understand. He thinks the idea of suicide is ridiculous."

A young lawyer had the repeated thought, "I don't belong here." She felt foreign and out of place at work, although she had been employed at the same firm for 10 years. She felt uncomfortable at home, where she lived with a roommate she hardly knew, and in social situations, where she believed she was less attractive and successful than everyone else. She felt uncomfortable with married people because she was single, and uncomfortable with singles at her health club because she was not interested in weight-lifting. The thought, "I don't belong here," appeared to be related to her core belief, "I'd better not attach myself much to this or something terrible will happen," in that it prevented her from developing strong attachments to anything — people, work, activities, or places.

This patient frequently placed herself in situations in which she did not really belong and *was* different from others present — she held on to the fringes of a social group she had belonged to for years although everyone else in the group was married and had children, and she was not. As a result, the thought, "I don't belong," was frequently true and always compelling. The therapist who is aware of the underlying belief reflected in these thoughts can point out and question these thoughts whenever they occur. Without an awareness that these thoughts are derivative of the formulation, the therapist might let them slip by unnoticed.

MALADAPTIVE THOUGHTS

Maladaptive thoughts[1] seem accurate, logical, and realistic; however, focusing on them causes negative mood, impairs behavioral functioning, impedes productive thinking about the situation, and reinforces underlying irrational beliefs. Therefore, they are maladaptive, counterproductive, dysfunctional, unhelpful.

For example, the writer sitting down to begin work for the day might have the thought, "This book will take months of hard work." This is a true statement. However, it is a counterproductive statement because it arouses anxiety, displaces thinking about the task at hand, and produces the impulse to walk away from the desk. If we assume that the irrational belief underlying this automatic thought is something like "I'm incompetent — I can't do it," we can see that the automatic thought, particularly when combined with its negative cognitive, behavioral, and emotional affects, subtly reinforces this belief. The writer who becomes anxious and experiences difficulty writing or even avoids writing altogether will collect evidence to support his belief that he is not equal to the task before him.

Another example is the student who repeats to herself, over and over, "I'm not prepared for the exam, I might fail the exam." The student is not, strictly speaking, distorting reality in any way. However, this pattern of thinking makes her upset and replaces, rather than promotes, effective preparation for the exam. It also reinforces her belief, "Unless I succeed at everything I try, I will not be accepted by others."

Most of the automatic thoughts described in this chapter are maladaptive. Derivatives are maladaptive by definition, because they support the

[1]This account of maladaptive thoughts draws heavily on discussions with Ricardo Muñoz.

underlying irrational belief. Most distorted thoughts are also maladaptive. For example, the young man who is thinking, "The fact that Linda turned me down means I'll never get a girl to go out with me" is likely to feel upset, and to find it harder to ask another girl for a date. This thought also reinforces his underlying belief about himself, which is that he is undesirable and will be alone for the rest of his life.

To determine whether a thought is maladaptive, the therapist can teach the patient to ask four questions: "Does this thought help my mood?" "Does this thought help me think productively about the situation?" "Does this thought help me behave appropriately?" "Does this thought reinforce my irrational beliefs?" Thus, maladaptive thoughts have counterproductive effects on the three components of overt behavior and on the underlying irrational beliefs.

Attention to the consequences of a stream of thoughts rather than the details of the thoughts themselves can uncover maladaptive thinking. For example, a bridge phobic decided to see a therapist. She reported a great deal of difficulty actually following through with her plan, however, because whenever she decided to call for an appointment she found herself overwhelmed by a string of thoughts invalidating her decision: "I should have solved this problem years ago," "I should be able to manage it on my own," "Therapy is too expensive," "I won't find anybody I like," "It won't help."

Rather than examining each of these thoughts individually to search for distortions, a task that is frequently overwhelming to both patient and therapist, the therapist can point out the overall pattern, which is that these thoughts block the patient from seeking treatment. The fact that such an overwhelming barrier of thoughts was necessary in this situation leads to the speculation that seeking treatment is anxiety-provoking for the patient. The therapist and patient can go on to explore why this situation is so frightening.

Another example is provided by a socially isolated young woman who wanted to begin dating. She pushed herself into situations where she would meet men, but as soon as she encountered one, she was flooded with a torrent of negative thoughts: "He's too tall, he's too short, he's wearing a pink T-shirt, he's too good-looking, he's not good-looking enough," and so on. The patient herself noticed an interchangeable quality about these thoughts: if he was wearing a pink T-shirt, she didn't want to know him for that reason; if his T-shirt was blue, she didn't want to know him for *that* reason. The interchangeableness of the thoughts suggests that their content is not particularly important. What's important is the role they serve; in this case, they promote the patient's avoidance of social interactions with men.

Thus, in both these cases, maladaptive thinking served as a barrier that prevented these young women from approaching anxiety-evoking situations. The young woman who wanted to meet men was able to see that her maladaptive thoughts did not make much sense. Sometimes, however, the thoughts provide so compelling a rationale that they effectively put up a smokescreen that blocks the patient from any awareness of the protective nature of his thoughts. Thus, a young assistant professor who was having difficulty submitting her articles to professional journals was blocked by a string of thoughts she believed to be true and reasonable ("The article has a methodological problem," "I didn't review the literature fully," "I need to revise it to meet the format of this journal," "I need to ask a colleague to review it."). These thoughts were so believable that the writer was unaware that she was frightened of sending out the articles for fear they would be rejected. The therapist can begin to break the pattern by pointing out the maladaptive nature of the thoughts.

Self-criticism

Self-criticism is a common pattern of maladaptive thinking. Many depressed individuals carry on a running commentary on every aspect of their performance, appearance, and experience, berating themselves dozens of times a day for any and all faults. Extremely self-critical individuals are often people whose central irrational belief is that they are inadequate. They were often reared by demanding parents whose continual criticism led the child to conclude he was inadequate. Self-critical individuals often also believe, "Unless I criticize myself for my defects, I'll become a mediocre person."

Poor coping

An anxious woman may repeat to herself, over and over, "I can't cope, This is too much for me, I won't be able to do it." These cognitions may occur so automatically that the patient is not aware of their presence. When they are pointed out, the patient may say, "Oh no, I didn't say that—and it's definitely not true." A few moments later, the thoughts return in full force once more.

These thoughts are maladaptive because they produce anxiety and impair coping. The thoughts become a self-fulfilling prophesy. In this case, the thoughts are also a direct statement of the patient's underlying belief, "I can't cope."

Another example of maladaptive thinking is provided by the graduate student working on his dissertation who repeatedly tells himself: "This project is boring and superficial; I should make a theoretical contribution, not just draw on established work." Not surprisingly, he has difficulty sitting down to work on the project. Similarly, the writer who returns to work on his book after several months of procrastination criticizes himself with the thoughts, "I should have done this years ago, The book is out of date. Someone else will publish on this topic before me."

Rumination

Ruminating — repetitive, intrusive, unproductive thinking, usually negative, and often about a situation that occurred in the past and cannot be changed — is another type of maladaptive thinking. A lawyer who lost a case reviewed the situation over and over, thinking, "I should have handled that deposition differently," "I should have hired a better expert witness," "I didn't take the right approach in the brief," "Everyone will think less of me because I lost this case," and so on. Some of these thoughts are distorted, and some are simply maladaptive, but the repetitive pattern of thinking itself is unproductive and maladaptive.

Patients often believe that ruminating helps them solve problems. A young woman who had experienced many unsuccessful relationships with men believed that if she ruminated about these failures, they would be less likely to occur again. To test this hypothesis, I asked her to rate, after each bout of rumination, how helpful it was in solving her problems and preventing a recurrence. This experiment convinced her that ruminating about past failures was not helpful.

In fact, rumination tends to block productive problem-solving. Rumination about a past negative event often has the theme, "This shouldn't have happened" (Emery, 1982). This nonaccepting stance, of course, blocks thinking along the lines, "This *did* happen, and I'm very unhappy about it. Now, is there anything I can do at this point to repair the damage? What can I do to ensure that in a similar situation in the future I won't make the same mistakes?"

Cognitive avoidance

The most easily spotted type of maladaptive thinking involves overattention to problems and deficits, too much energy given to unproductive, unprofitable lines of thinking. However, *too little* thinking can also have devastating effects, as in the case of the executive who avoids recognizing that she drinks too much.

Patients frequently alternate between maladaptive thinking and cognitive avoidance. A 39-year-old woman who wanted a relationship and a child spent most of her waking hours avoiding thinking about the issue. She tended to ruminate about the issue when lying in bed in the morning before getting up. During these times, she berated herself mercilessly for not having solved her problems and accomplished her goals long ago. Because this type of thinking was so painful and upsetting, she tended to bail out as soon as possible, returning to her avoidance once more. She alternated between these two unproductive modes of thinking about her problem for years. Needless to say, she made very little progress in solving it.

Another type of cognitive avoidance appeared in a lawyer who was quite anxious about her relationship difficulties. Avoidance was a dominant coping strategy. Avoidance also appeared in a fascinating way in her speech: she failed to complete half the sentences she started when discussing her interpersonal problems. She also came late to sessions, made notes about things to discuss in therapy but forgot to bring them, was too busy in her work to do therapy homework, and so on.

Another young woman avoided her problems in an even more dramatic way. This is a patient who sought treatment for panic attacks and anxiety, and reports she is particularly uncomfortable when thinking about her children, but has no idea why this is. She states she wants to leave her husband because he is an alcoholic—in fact, he was drunk all day every day last week—but feels unable to leave because she depends on him to take care of their two-year-old child while she goes to school. This woman is completely unaware (not quite completely—she is anxious) that she has a serious problem needing immediate action. We might speculate that this pattern of avoidance has its basis in irrational thoughts like, "There's no way out of this situation—I can't do anything to solve it."

The awareness that many people cope by avoiding reminds the therapist that it is unwise to accept the patient's description of problems at face value, assuming that if the patient doesn't bring it up, it is not important. A careful formulation can help the therapist raise important issues the patient does not.

IRRATIONAL THOUGHTS

Distorted thoughts present an unrealistic view of reality or involve illogical reasoning. Most distorted thoughts are also maladaptive. This fact is particularly useful when patient and therapist disagree as to whether a cognition is distorted. The patient may insist that the thought, "My boss is planning to fire me," is realistic. Instead of struggling to convince the patient of the irrationality of this thought, the therapist can simply move to a discussion of the maladaptive nature of the thought.

Common cognitive distortions are labeled and described here. This discussion draws heavily on Beck, et al. (1979) and Burns (1980). Often a distorted thought can be given more than one name. For example, the thought, "I'll always be depressed" might be viewed as emotional reasoning, catastrophizing, or predicting the future. Although the labels offered here are overlapping and categories are loosely defined, they are useful in helping both therapists and patients pinpoint problematic cognitions and begin to change them.

Emotional reasoning

In emotional reasoning, a person makes an inference about himself, the world, or the future on the basis of an emotional experience. For example, a suicidal housewife might reason, "I *feel* hopeless. Therefore, I *am* hopeless and things will never improve for me." A bridge phobic might say, "I feel very anxious when I'm on the bridge. This means that something bad is going to happen there." Other examples of emotional reasoning include: "Because I feel guilty I must have done something wrong," "Because I feel anxious about starting my business, this means it will fail"; "Because I'm feeling incompetent and inadequate, I must be doing a poor job"; "Because he's angry with me, I must have done something wrong." In the last case, the irrational inference is made on the basis of someone else's feeling, not one's own.

To counter emotional reasoning, which can be quite compelling, remember that *feelings are not facts* (Burns, 1980). The fact that a phobic feels anxious in an elevator is not good evidence that elevators are dangerous.

The therapist can also give a short lesson about the mood-state dependent nature of thinking. When a person is in a negative mood, he has a bias to recall negative thoughts and memories and to forget positive ones. In fact, we know (Miranda & Persons, 1988; Miranda, Persons, and Byers, 1988) that individuals are more likely to report irrational beliefs if they are in a negative mood state when they are questioned. Bower (1981) suggested that this is because memories associated with any particular mood state are linked to each other as in an electrical circuit, in such a way that activation of thoughts and memories associated with a particular mood state activates other thoughts and memories associated with that mood state.

Mood-state dependent thinking is illustrated in Figure 6.1, which

Figure 6.1   Schematic of mood-state dependent thinking

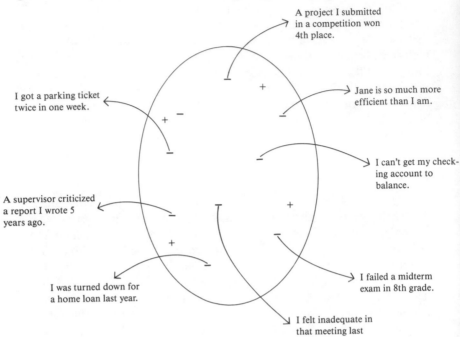

A project I submitted
in a competition won
4th place.

I got a parking ticket
twice in one week.

Jane is so much more
efficient than I am.

I can't get my check-
ing account to
balance.

A supervisor criticized
a report I wrote 5
years ago.

I was turned down for
a home loan last year.

I failed a midterm
exam in 8th grade.

I felt inadequate in
that meeting last
week.

shows the "mind" of a person experiencing a powerful negative mood. A large number of negative ideas, thoughts, memories, and moods are activated, but positive thoughts, moods and memories have faded into the background and are difficult to retrieve. One of my patients, looking at this diagram, said, "I see that when this happens, I'm not getting the full picture." The statement, "I'm not getting the full picture," became a useful watchword for her when she saw herself slipping into depression.

Overgeneralization

The depressed man who is turned down for a date might conclude, "This means I'll never find a date for Saturday, This means Lisa doesn't like me, This means I'll never get a date, This means I'll never find a satisfying relationship." All these conclusions are overgeneralizations of the available evidence. The evidence at hand only indicates that he won't be going out with Lisa next Saturday night. Overgeneralization involves using a single piece of evidence or an isolated experience to draw an unwarranted conclusion that far overreaches the evidence at hand. For example,

THERAPIST: Let's go back to your statement "Lots of women have turned me down." Tell me the names of these women.

PATIENT   Well, I don't really remember.

THERAPIST   Well, let's try to remember. If you want to conclude from these experiences that you can't get a date with a woman ever, it's important to remember who all these women are who turned you down, isn't it?

PATIENT   I guess so . . . (pause). Well, last week Joan turned me down.

THERAPIST   OK, who else?

PATIENT   (pause) Well, a woman named Susan that I didn't know very well.

THERAPIST   And when was that?

PATIENT   I can't really remember—a long time ago.

THERAPIST   I see. Anyone else?

PATIENT   I really can't remember.

THERAPIST   I see (pause). Now what do you make of this?

PATIENT   It really doesn't sound like very many women, does it?

THERAPIST   No, it doesn't. In fact, it sounds like your problem is not that you're getting a lot of turn-downs; it sounds like your problem is that you're not asking very many women out. Is that possible?

PATIENT   Yes, that's probably right.

THERAPIST   OK, let's think about it: How many women would you need to be turned down by before you would want to conclude that you could never get a date?

PATIENT   Well, I don't know. Maybe 10 or 20.

THERAPIST   (teasing a little) Twenty sounds good to me. Let's come back to this discussion after you've asked out twenty women. How many do you want to ask out this week?

Illogical thinking

Illogical thinking, or arbitrary inference, involves unwarranted connections between ideas that are unrelated or related in a much different way. For example, a dieter who lost five pounds became anxious, thinking, "Now that I've lost five pounds, I'll have to lose 15 more." A lesbian had the thought, "The fact that my relationships with men aren't successful shows there's something wrong with me." An unemployed computer programmer had difficulty looking for a job because of the idea, "If I'm offered a job, I'll have to accept it even if it's not right for me." A young woman became upset when the therapist described her problems as agoraphobia, because she had the thought, "If what I have is a disease, this means I can't do anything on my own to control it." After three sessions of treatment, a patient concluded, "If I haven't shown substantial improvement by now, I'll never get well."

All-or-nothing thinking

An example of all-or-nothing thinking is provided by the patient who has completed only part of her homework assignment and comes to the therapy session saying, "I didn't do my homework." Other examples include: "Unless I win the Nobel Prize, my work is valueless." "Unless I do it perfectly, it's not worth doing at all." "I made a mistake with that patient; I'm a failure as a therapist." The all-or-nothing thinker sees things as all black or all white, but never gray. Statements that include terms like *always*, *never*, *completely*, *totally*, and *perfectly* generally involve all-or-nothing thinking. Less distorted statements include terms like *sometimes*, *usually*, *frequently*, *partially*, *generally*, *often*, *somewhat*, and *occasionally*.

Should

Although "should" statements appear innocuous, they are distorted and maladaptive in several ways. The person who insists, "My boss *shouldn't* hit me with last-minute projects," has a distorted perception of reality. In this man's view, his boss should behave the way *he* (the employee) thinks is best. The difficulty with this view is that it is not an accurate picture of how the boss *does* behave. Similarly, the jogger who complains, "It shouldn't rain so much in California," is demanding that weather conditions suit *his* convenience. To point this out, the therapist can respond, "Let's draw up a schedule for your boss and indicate when you would like him to be doing what," or, "Let's make a schedule of when, from your point of view, rain would be desirable." When I said this to my patient the jogger, he responded, with a smile, "Oh, I guess you're telling me I'm being a spoiled brat!"

Similarly, the person who says, "The Viet Nam war should not have occurred," is struggling to change reality. However, reality is not malleable in this way. As Gary Emery (1982) points out, the person's real choice is to accept or refuse to accept reality, but not to change it. An acceptance of reality is expressed in the statement, "The Viet Nam war *did occur*. I don't like it, but it happened." When offered this solution, many people reject it because they confuse acceptance with endorsement. However, these two are quite different. To accept the fact that the Viet Nam war occurred is to not endorse it as a good idea.

Fear often lies behind a should statement. To demonstrate this, the jogger's therapist can ask, "If it rains too much, what would happen? Why would this be a problem?"

PATIENT   If it rains all the time, I won't be able to exercise: I can't run, and it's a drag to swim in an outdoor pool, and there isn't an indoor one nearby.

THERAPIST   And if you can't exercise, why would this be upsetting?

PATIENT   If I can't exercise, it means I can't do something I really enjoy that's important to me, and it means I might get more depressed, because exercise is one way I fight depression.

THERAPIST   And if you get more depressed, why would this be upsetting?

PATIENT   I might relapse completely.

THERAPIST   And if that happened, why would that be upsetting?

PATIENT   Because I'd be miserable and I'd have no way of getting out of it.

THERAPIST   OK, well, it looks as though what we have here is a situation where your ability to be free of depression depends on the weather.

PATIENT   (laughs)

THERAPIST   Well, isn't that what you're saying?

PATIENT   I guess it is.

THERAPIST   Do you really believe that your ability to be free of depression depends on the weather?

PATIENT   No, I guess I don't.

THERAPIST   OK, good. Now let's imagine it rains every day for a month. Now what can you do to work on your depression?

PATIENT   (silent)

THERAPIST   Let's brainstorm. Let's list as many ideas as we can, no matter how nutty.

PATIENT   (pause) Well, I could take aerobics classes.

THERAPIST   Good. What else?

The person who insists that things go his way can benefit from a detailed understanding of why they do not. This point was made by David Burns (1980) in his excellent discussion of "should" statements. Burns suggests that a good solution to the "should" trap is empathy — understanding the other person's point of view. In the earlier example, the employee needs a clear understanding of why his boss behaves the way he does (contingencies governing his current and past behavior, his history, his personality, and so on) — and a convincing explanation of why, as a result of these factors, the boss *should* behave the way he does.

In addition to providing a distorted view of reality, should statements are highly maladaptive. They elicit negative emotional and behavioral reactions. To understand this, repeat emphatically to yourself a should statement like, "I *should* keep detailed tax records," or, "I *should* exercise three times a week!" Now, how do you feel? Many people feel coerced, pushed around, irritated, and annoyed. The behavioral response to these statements often involves passive resistance or the urge to do something else.

Should statements often lead to anger: "He *shouldn't* treat me like that!" The person who does this type of thinking adds a second problem to the one he started with: in addition to the discomfort of being treated poorly, he now has unpleasant angry feelings. These two are not inextricably linked; the angry feelings come from the "should," not from the boss' behavior.

Should statements are also maladaptive because the nonacceptance of a problematic situation blocks problem-solving efforts. Instead, the patient attempts to "solve" the problem by ruling it out of order: "I shouldn't be having this problem." I noticed this when, as a postdoctoral psychology intern in Philadelphia, the hospital in which I was working stopped providing heat to my office in the dead of winter. Repeated calls to the maintenance staff were unavailing. I felt furious, and I was locked into the view, "The hospital *should* provide heat for my office!" After weeks of struggling with this issue, I finally developed a detailed explanation for the failure to provide heat for my office: there was a possiblity that the unit would be closed shortly, so the hospital was unwilling to undertake the major repairs that would have been required to fix the problem. It didn't make sense for the hospital to spend thousands of dollars to repair a system they might not need next winter. Once I clearly understood this, I was able to move from nonacceptance ("The hospital *should* provide heat for my office") to acceptance ("The hospital is not going to provide heat for my office. It's very uncomfortable for me, but that's how it is. Now, what am I going to do about it?"). At that point, I bought a space heater.

One final note about should statements. As my colleague Charles Garrigues points out, not all should statements contain the word "should." Sometimes we express our dissatisfaction with reality in the form of a question: "Why is he always late for appointments?" "Why didn't my son call me on Mother's Day?" These "questions" are easily translated into should statements.

Predicting the future

Predicting the future, which David Burns (1980) also labels "fortune-telling," is self-explanatory. The student who didn't understand the material the first time she read it predicts, "I'll never understand it." The depressed patient who has not recovered completely after three sessions of therapy concludes, "I'll always be depressed. This therapy won't help me." The socially anxious young man looks into his crystal ball and observes, "If I ask her to go bike-riding, she'll turn me down." In the case of the depressed patient who fears she won't benefit from therapy, this type of statement can serve as a self-fulfilling prophecy, because it can prevent the patient from making the commitment necessary to give the treatment a good chance of success. A more adaptive stance involves an attitude like, "It's possible this therapy won't help me. The only way I can find out is to give it a try. Let me ask my therapist how many sessions I need to commit to in order to give the therapy a good trial."

Mind-reading

"He thinks I'm lazy for quitting the class." "She thinks less of me because of my divorce." "My therapist feels disappointed that I'm not improving faster." "My boss is planning to fire me."

To address these thinking errors, the therapist can ask, "What's the evidence?" The fact is that until some important scientific advances are made in the field of mental telepathy, it is simply not possible to read others' minds. The therapist can ask, "What evidence do you have that the boss is planning to fire you?" One patient's response to this question was, "I don't really have any. In fact, the boss gave me a top rating on my performance review three weeks ago!"

Another way of handling this error is to ask, "Let's assume your boss is planning to fire you. Why would that be upsetting to you?" Although the patient (and therapist) may be unwilling to confront the feared situation, usually when it *is* confronted, it is much less frightening than anticipated. For example, the patient may acknowledge that he dislikes his job and would like to leave the firm.

Another way of tackling mind-reading is to examine the possibility that the patient's mind-reading involves projection. The thoughts patients believe others are having about them are usually the very thoughts they arc having about themselves.

Selective negative focus

In selective negative focus, the individual focuses on the negative aspects of a situation and ignores the positive ones. For example, the student who gets an A on the written part of an exam and a D on the oral part reports, "I really messed up the exam." A lawyer who settles an important case worries, "I should have been able to get a better deal." The patient who completes her homework assignment of sewing for an hour berates herself for not having finished the outfit. The shy young man who finally manages to invite a girl to dinner feels like a failure when she refuses. All these individuals focus on the negative aspects of a situation, ignoring the positive ones.

One way to fall into this trap is to confuse one's own behavior, e.g., asking for a date, which is a positive behavior, with the outcome of the action, which in this young man's case was negative. Because the outcome was negative, the young man views his behavior as negative, and criticizes it. However, the fact that the outcome was negative doesn't mean the behavior was negative or inadequate in any way. In addition to providing a distorted perception of the situation, this thinking error is maladaptive, because the patient punishes himself for adaptive, positive behavior, which decreases its frequency.

Disqualifying the positive

In selective negative focus, the individual *ignores* the positive aspects of a situation. In disqualifying the positive, the individual *actively invalidates* the positives. For example, the student who got an A on the written part, and a D on the oral part of an exam might explain, "The written part doesn't really count — I always do well on written exams — it's the oral exam that really matters to me." The student invalidates the score on the written exam precisely *because* she always does well on written exams! This logic can make a therapist's head hurt!

Magnification and minimization

In magnification, the patient makes too much of something; in minimization, he makes too little. The harried psychologist who thinks, "I lost my keys today. I'm incompetent at everything!" is magnifying, or overemphasizing, the meaning of the lost keys. The anxious musician who did well in rehearsals who thinks, "I did well today, but this doesn't mean anything about how I'll do tomorrow," is minimizing the meaning of the good rehearsal performance.

Catastrophizing

"The failure of this relationship is the end of all happiness to me!" "If I don't get rid of this lower back pain, I'll be miserable for the rest of my life!" "Being fired from this job is a financial disaster!" "If I can't have a baby, I'll never be happy!"

Although these statements can be quite convincing, they are nevertheless distorted. For example: Is it true that all patients with lower back pain are unhappy all the time? Are all women who want a child but don't have one miserable for the rest of their lives?

Personalization

Personalization occurs when a person interprets an event or situation as indicative of something about himself — usually something negative. A graduate student felt socially inadequate; whenever a social interaction went poorly, he concluded, "This proves I'm a social dud." A hospital social worker felt inferior because of her career choice; whenever she found herself doing a particularly dull and routine task, she felt her self-esteem and mood take a plunge as a result of the thought, "The fact that I'm doing this routine job proves that I'm a stupid person incapable of taking on a challenging position."

Labeling

In labeling, a behavior or characteristic of a person or situation is made definitive of the person or situation, often with terms that are derogatory and emotionally loaded. The person who spends long hours at work is a "workaholic," the one who jumps the red light is a "jerk," the one who makes a mistake is an "idiot," the one who drinks too much on his birthday is a "drunk," and so on. The alternative to this distortion is to view a person's objectionable behaviors as *behaviors*, not intrinsic to the nature of the person. Thus, the person who makes a mistake is someone who did something wrong, not an inferior human being.

Labeling is maladaptive because it produces negative feelings; the man who calls his boss a dumbo adds fuel to the fire of his anger toward the man. The person who calls himself a jerk increases self-hate and reduces self-esteem. Similarly, a public speaker who makes a flub in a public lecture and responds with self-abuse ("What an idiot!") is likely to make more mistakes. A more adapative alternative is, "I made a mistake, probably because I wasn't concentrating enough. I can work on my concentration and improve my performance."

Labeling also inhibits problem-solving. Thus, I tell my patient who labels himself a loser when he fails an exam that this attitude is a cop-out. It lets him off the hook of examining why he failed the exam and what he could do to solve the problem. Similarly, if the overeater has a behavioral problem, we can look for the causes and mechanisms controlling the behavior and work to change it, whereas if the person is a "pig," little can be done.

ELICITING AUTOMATIC THOUGHTS

Many automatic thoughts require no effort to retrieve—they occur spontaneously and frequently in the patient's speech. Often the patient is completely unaware of them; they are so much a part of his view of himself and the world that they do not appear distorted or problematic. It is the therapist's responsibility to be aware of the problematic nature of these thoughts and to point them out. For example, the agoraphobic who says, "I don't want to drive on the bridge when there's a lot of traffic" is not experiencing an emotional upset, nor is she aware of any behavioral problem. However, this thought is maladaptive, and the therapist who is listening carefully, with the formulation in mind, will perceive this statement as an automatic thought.

Sometimes conscious, focused effort is required to retrieve automatic thoughts, particularly if the thoughts connected to a particular situation, mood state, or behavioral problem are sought. The patient may come to the session saying, "I can't clean my apartment," or "I've been feeling lousy ever since the staff meeting." Information about the automatic thoughts occurring in these situations will provide useful clues to understanding and working on the problem.

In these situations, automatic thoughts are frequently readily obtained in response to a direct question about them. Thus, the therapist working to help the patient clean up his apartment or feel better can ask, "When you think about cleaning up your apartment, what thoughts do you get?" or, "When you think about the staff meeting, what thoughts do you have that make you feel lousy?"

Difficulties eliciting automatic thoughts

Some patients are unable to report feelings and/or cognitions when the therapist asks for them. Some patients have no experience in monitoring their mental processes. They may be having many thoughts, but they are completely unaware of them. For these patients, the process of monitoring their thinking is foreign and incomprehensible. Several strategies for obtaining thoughts are suggested here.

First, the case formulation model suggests that the therapist can address this problem by focusing on the other components (mood, behavior) of the problem. In this example, the therapist teaches the patient something about his "missing" feelings by focusing on behaviors.

PATIENT   I feel scared about the trip—but it's silly to feel scared!
THERAPIST   And how do you feel when you tell yourself that idea: "It's silly to feel scared!"

PATIENT   (after a long silence) I don't know how I feel – I don't feel anything.

THERAPIST   Well, try this. Imagine you told your friend Susan that you felt scared about the trip, and she said, "Angela, it's silly to feel scared!" How would you feel?

PATIENT   (long silence) I don't know.

THERAPIST   Well, what would you *say*?

PATIENT   (a long silence)

THERAPIST   Well, maybe you'd say, "Well, go jump in the river!"

PATIENT   No, I'd say something stronger than that! I'd say, "Screw you! You don't know what it's like!"

THERAPIST   I see. How do you feel when you say that?

PATIENT   I feel angry.

THERAPIST   Do you see why you feel angry?

PATIENT   Because she's not listening to me.

THERAPIST   Right. When you feel not listened to, you feel angry. Do you see that this is what you are doing to yourself when you tell yourself, "It's silly to feel scared"?

PATIENT   So I'm making myself feel angry and inferior because I'm not listening to myself and my own feelings.

Because cognitive therapy offers a way to reduce or eliminate negative feelings, patients often interpret this therapeutic approach as carrying the message, "I shouldn't have negative feelings." This idea then leads to ideas like, "I shouldn't feel scared." As this dialogue demonstrates, this is a distorted, maladaptive thought.

The therapist can also get at the automatic thoughts by focusing on feelings. For example, in response to the question, "What thoughts do you have when you sit down to work," the procrastinator may say, "I don't have any thoughts, I just feel fuzzy and paralyzed." The therapist might ask for more information about the feelings themselves, including information about physiological sensations. When asked to describe feelings and sensations in greater detail, thoughts often emerge. For example, in response to a probe for more feelings, the procrastinator may respond, "I feel I won't do a good job." Even if thoughts do not emerge, the therapist can use the feelings to probe for the thoughts. In this case, the therapist can point out that these feelings are symptoms of anxiety and ask the patient what he is frightened of.

A second strategy for obtaining automatic thoughts involves asking the patient to provide images, instead of words: "Do any pictures come to mind?" The images themselves may reveal the cognitive component of the problem, or may lead to verbal expressions of it.

Third, to improve the accessibility of the automatic thoughts, the therapist might ask the patient to vividly imagine the situation: what furniture was in the room? Who was there? What were they wearing? What was happening? How did you feel? "Now, if you imagine all that, what thoughts come to mind?"

The therapist might also say, "Try making something up!" Or, "What thought would another person have in this situation?" The patient's response may reveal something about his own experience.

Finally, the therapist might make some suggestions about what the patient's automatic thoughts are likely to be. These suggestions might be based on the therapist's own experience (imagine being in the patient's place — what thoughts would come to mind?). Even better, they might be based on the patient's central underlying irrational beliefs. For example, a housewife who is puzzled by her failure to distribute a neighborhood petition on an issue she's quite concerned about and unable to report automatic thoughts about her procrastination, holds a central irrational belief along the lines, "No one will pay any attention to me; no one will listen to me or take me seriously." In this case, the therapist might suggest, "Perhaps you were having the thought, 'There's no point in doing this, no one will pay any attention to me — they'll slam the door in my face!'"

Some patients resist all attempts to obtain their automatic thoughts. They grasp the cognitive model quite readily, but state that it does not apply to them. *Their* feelings are not accompanied by thoughts. This notion has a certain amount of validity, and we all probably have this experience at times. Rachman (1981), Zajonc (1980), and others have discussed this fascinating issue at length. With these patients, the therapist may wish simply to focus on behavioral strategies and indirect cognitive interventions.

Sometimes the patient's refusal to retrieve automatic thoughts is founded in cognitive distortions. For example, the patient who says, in an aggressive tone, "Thoughts may precede moods for some people, but not for me," is probably not discussing the common experience described by Rachman (1981) and Zajonc (1980). This patient may feel he is not being taken seriously, may feel coerced by the therapist or frightened about failing. The therapist might form a hypothesis about this by consulting the case formulation and test out the hypothesis by asking the patient about the details of his reaction. Sometimes the patient's insistence that no thoughts precede his feelings is due to a thought like, "I shouldn't be feeling like this; if I do, I'm out of control," which causes him to avoid his own feelings and thoughts. Again, if the therapist can use empathy and careful questioning to elicit this irrational idea, it can be worked on directly.

CHAPTER 7

Changing dysfunctional thinking

This chapter presents a set of strategies useful in helping patients make cognitive changes. The chapter begins with a brief discussion of the role of the case formulation in planning cognitive interventions and a description of two general strategies useful in challenging all types of dysfunctional thinking. Next, strategies for challenging derivatives of the irrational beliefs, maladaptive thoughts, and irrational cognitions are described in turn. A final section discusses common difficulties that arise in the process of changing dysfunctional thinking.

USING THE CASE FORMULATION TO PLAN COGNITIVE INTERVENTIONS

The goal of treatment is not to eliminate all of the patient's irrational, maladaptive thinking. The goal is to help the patient solve her chief problems in life. Thus, work on dysfunctional thinking is best done with those problems in mind, not by attacking all the cognitive distortions that appear.

If not all dysfunctional cognitions require attention, which ones ought the therapist to work on? The case formulation, particularly the underlying belief, provides the answer to this question. For example, a depressed, withdrawn patient who has been working in therapy to be more socially active comes to her therapy session saying, "I want to work on being able to go to see my third cousin Rose in Los Angeles—she keeps calling and wants me to come see her. When I think about going, I feel guilty and upset, because I have the thoughts, 'It's too big a trip for me, I just don't have the energy, and if I see her, she'll see how depressed I am, and it will bring her down.'" Without the case formulation, the therapist might jump in to help the patient overcome the belief that she is too fragile to make the visit. However, an awareness that this patient's key problem is the idea, "In order to get my needs met, I must first meet others' needs," suggests that it would be more helpful to find out whether the patient *wants* to visit cousin Rose (does the visit meet any of *her* needs?), and if not, to explore how she might assertively refuse the requests for a visit without feeling guilty.

When the therapist has made a decision to work on a particular dysfunctional thought or group of thoughts, the strategies described below can be used.

TWO GENERAL STRATEGIES

Whether working on derivatives of the underlying beliefs, maladaptive thoughts, or irrational thoughts, two general approaches to working toward cognitive change are useful in enhancing the work.

Use questions

Use questions to get your points across. This recommendation was made by Beck (Beck et al., 1979) and long before by Socrates. Questions are preferable to statements, proclamations, and lectures for several reasons: First, questions allow the therapist to keep track of the patient's progress in making a cognitive change, so that, if the patient gets "stuck" at a certain point, the therapist can stop there, too, and work to understand the source of the halt in progress. Second, there is rarely a single "right" solution to a problem. The therapist's job is not to point out the "right" answer, but to ask questions that help the patient find an answer that works for her. Third, questions help the patient integrate new ideas. If the therapist presents a large number of well-reasoned arguments that present a conception of the problematic situation that is very different from the patient's view, the patient is unlikely to be able to integrate this into his own thinking.

Fourth, in responding to questions, the *patient* is doing most of the work, whereas in listening to statements from the therapist, the patient becomes a passive recipient. Finally, if the therapist talks too much, the patient may feel lectured to, criticized, or treated in a condescending or patronizing way.

Work on specific situations

Therapeutic work that focused on cognitions that arise in specific situations is much more helpful than work focused on general, abstract views of the world (Beck et al., 1979). For example, the therapist can focus the session on the student's angry reaction to being pushed in the bus station and his thoughts, "He shouldn't have pushed me," "I always get pushed around," and so on, rather than on his abstract cognitions about people in general, "People should be more considerate of others." Discussions of specific situations are much more likely to be charged with affect than abstract discussions, and good therapeutic work seems to require a minimum level of affective charge (Safran & Greenberg, 1986). General, abstract discussions tend to bog down in unproductive, philosophical discussions with little or no impact on the patient's emotional responses to troublesome situations in his life. These discussions can even deteriorate into an apparently irreconcilable philosophical difference between the patient and therapist that is harmful to the therapeutic relationship.

Thus, effective therapeutic work directed at making changes in thinking addresses specific situations in which the cognitive problems arise. Patients' irrational and maladaptive patterns of thinking tend to recur over and over again, the same theme arising repeatedly in different situations. Although both patient and therapist may feel frustrated by the fact that it is necessary to work on the same issue again and again, there does not appear to be any substitute for this kind of work. Lessons learned only in the abstract are not lessons learned.

With these two general strategies in mind, let us turn to the detailed strategies for challenging derivatives of the irrational beliefs, maladaptive thinking, and distorted, irrational thoughts provided below. Although the strategies are divided into the three types of dysfunction described in Chapter 6 (derivatives, maladaptive thoughts, irrational thoughts), because of the great overlap among the categories the therapist will frequently use strategies from more than one category in an attempt to dislodge the patient's dysfunctional point of view.

CHALLENGING DERIVATIVES OF
THE UNDERLYING BELIEFS

This section describes four techniques for pointing out and working on dysfunctional thoughts that are derivatives of the underlying beliefs. First, the therapist can teach the patient the relationship between his automatic thoughts and his underlying irrational belief. Second, the therapist points out, over and over, derivatives of the irrational belief the patient is unaware of. The third strategy is the old view/new view technique for generating alternatives to the automatic thoughts and the irrational beliefs, while the fourth involves teaching the patient the origins of his irrational belief.

Teaching the relationship between automatic thoughts and underlying beliefs

To teach the relationship between automatic thoughts and underlying beliefs, the therapist's first task is to teach the patient the nature of his own irrational beliefs. The case formulation, of course, provides the therapist with a beginning hypothesis about the nature of those beliefs. Several strategies for obtaining a hypothesis about the nature of the patient's chief underlying beliefs were described in Chapter 3.

In addition, cognitive strategies can be used to discover the nature of the patient's underlying beliefs. The downward arrow technique devised by David Burns (1980) is particularly helpful. Here the therapist begins with the patient's automatic thoughts about a particular situation and asks, about each one, "If that were true, why would that be upsetting?" This can be done repeatedly, as in the following dialogue. This simple exercise is designed to lead "downward" to the irrational idea underlying the automatic thoughts. For example, a young man is feeling anxious about his girlfriend's loss of interest in sex. He has the thought, "This means she's losing interest in me."

THERAPIST   Well, let's assume for a moment this thought is true. Let's assume Julie's losing interest in you. If this were true, why would it be upsetting to you?
PATIENT   Because it would mean that she doesn't like me!
THERAPIST   OK, right. And if that were true, why would that be upsetting?
PATIENT   Because it would mean she's pulling away from me.
THERAPIST   And if that were true, why would that be upsetting?

PATIENT   Because she'll break off with me.

THERAPIST   Imagine she breaks off with you. Why would that be upsetting?

PATIENT   Because then I'll be alone!

THERAPIST   And what does that mean to you?

PATIENT   I'll always be alone!

THERAPIST   I see. It sounds like you have the idea, "When anyone gets to know me better, they won't like me, and they'll leave, and I'll be alone."

PATIENT   Right!

Another cognitive approach to teaching the patient about his central fear is to keep a running list of derivatives of the irrational belief as they occur in the session. After a short list has been obtained, the therapist can ask the patient to point out the common theme in the thoughts. An examination of the topics discussed across a series of therapy sessions will often reveal a common theme as well, and this theme is likely to be closely related to the patient's central irrational belief.

Pointing out derivatives

When the patient learns the nature of his irrational beliefs, and the way they are reflected in his thoughts, behavior, and mood, he will not experience a complete recovery, of course. His derivative automatic thoughts will not disappear. The therapist will need repeatedly to point out the way his irrational beliefs dominate his thinking. For example, when a patient who holds the irrational belief, "I'm a fragile and vulnerable person" says, "I can't do it today — I have a cold," the therapist might point out, "That kind of statement sounds familiar to me. What idea does that remind you of?"

A running list, perhaps with the irrational belief at the bottom of the page, can be used to point out the derivatives and the irrational beliefs. Additional derivatives can be added as they appear in the session or in later sessions.

"Old view/new view"

Often when the patient sees the underlying pattern, she sees the thinking distortion and can see what type of a correction is needed. Sometimes, however, the patient has difficulty generating an alternative to the old view of things. In this case, the old view/new view strategy is helpful.

The "old view/new view" strategy is analogous to the "old plan/new plan" intervention for behaviors (Chapter 4). The "view" strategy focuses on cognitions, whereas the "plan" approach focuses on behaviors, but the interventions are essentially the same and the best approach is to focus on both, as this example illustrates.

A college student felt uncomfortable at a meeting to assist local Democratic office-seekers in the fall election. He had the automatic thoughts, "I don't belong here — I'm not fully informed on the issues and the candidates," and "Others will discover this and reject me." These thoughts were accompanied by the urge to stop going to the meetings and by a plan to read up on the issues and candidates. This pattern of moods, cognitions, and behaviors was grounded in his underlying irrational belief, "I must be perfect or I'll be rejected."

The downward arrow method and a series of questions can be used to point out to this patient the close relationships among his negative mood, cognitions, and behavioral reactions in this situation, and the way all these parts of the problem reflect his underlying belief. The therapist might draw the diagram shown in Figure 7.1 as part of this exercise.

After pointing out the current pattern, the search for alternatives begins. As they are generated, the therapist might add them to the diagram, as shown in Figure 7.1. To initiate the search for alternatives, the therapist might propose:

THERAPIST   Imagine a person who feels comfortable in this situation
      (writing "comfortable" in the "New View" part of the figure). What
      kind of thoughts is this person having? He's probably not thinking,
      "I don't belong here." What's he thinking instead?
PATIENT   (pause)
THERAPIST   I know it must be hard for you to see things from such a
      different point of view. But let's try it. Imagine you're in a situation
      where you feel perfectly comfortable. What are you thinking?
PATIENT   I'm probably not thinking much.
THERAPIST   Well, you're definitely not thinking, "I don't belong here."
      Suppose someone came up to you and said, "You don't belong
      here." What would you say?
PATIENT   I'd say, "Yes, I do."
THERAPIST   OK, now try to use that in this situation. Imagine you're at
      the campaign meeting. Instead of thinking, "I don't belong here,"
      what can you think?
PATIENT   I can think, "I belong. It's OK for me to be here."

Figure 7.1   "Old view"/"New view" intervention

OLD VIEW

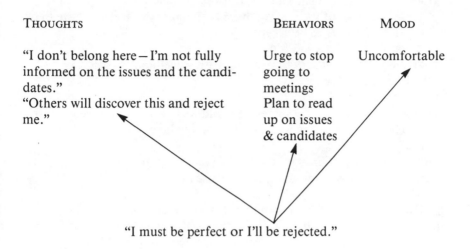

THOUGHTS   BEHAVIORS   MOOD

"I don't belong here—I'm not fully   Urge to stop   Uncomfortable
informed on the issues and the candi-   going to
dates."   meetings
"Others will discover this and reject   Plan to read
me."   up on issues
                                            & candidates

"I must be perfect or I'll be rejected."

NEW VIEW

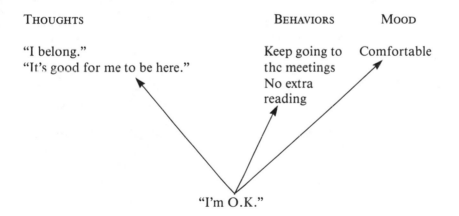

THOUGHTS   BEHAVIORS   MOOD

"I belong."   Keep going to   Comfortable
"It's good for me to be here."   the meetings
                                            No extra
                                            reading

"I'm O.K."

THERAPIST   Fine. And what would you be doing? Would you feel you
    needed to do a lot of reading on the issues?
PATIENT   (pause). . . . No, I guess not.
THERAPIST   Right. What kind of irrational belief might this person
    have, instead of the one you have that makes you feel you have to be
    perfect in order to be accepted?
PATIENT   I don't have any idea.
THERAPIST   Well, let's try to come up with something. We need an
    alternative, don't we?
PATIENT   I guess so.
THERAPIST   Well, just try something, and we'll work on it if we need to.
    (The patient's perfectionism is interfering here, too.)
PATIENT   I'm OK.
THERAPIST   That sounds pretty good to me. What do you think?
PATIENT   . . . It sounds great, but not like me!

Patients frequently complain that new automatic thoughts, and particularly new underlying beliefs about themselves, feel strange and foreign
and are difficult to believe. This is expected, as the old beliefs have
dominated the patient's experience for years (more about this later).

Teaching the origins of irrational beliefs

When an irrational belief has been exposed, the therapist can ask,
"How did you learn that idea?" An exploration of the patient's family
history, particularly his interactions with parents, usually yields this information. For example, the young man who believed, "I must be perfect
or I'll be rejected" was reared by a man who continually punished and
criticized the patient for every fault and flaw in his behavior and appearance. Patients who believe, "I must meet others' needs in order to be
accepted or loved," were often raised by needy and demanding parents
who required their children to meet *their* emotional and other needs and
were unable to meet their children's needs. The patient who believes, "If I
make a mistake, a disaster will occur," may have been raised by perfectionistic parents who created a crisis whenever the patient did something
wrong or by disorganized, inept parents who, as a result of their inept-
ness, experienced a series of reverses and catastrophes. Neglected children
may have learned, "I don't count. No one cares about me."

Obtaining information about the origins of the irrational beliefs can
be helpful in at least three ways. First, particularly when patients have

difficulty extricating themselves from these powerful beliefs, an under-standing of where and how they learned these ideas can remind them that these are *learned* beliefs about themselves that can be unlearned, not facts about themselves or the world. Second, patients often maintain the old, destructive relationships with their parents that produced these be-liefs and continue to support them. Efforts to make changes in these interactions can be quite powerful in challenging the beliefs. Third, even when patients no longer have contact with their parents, role-play interac-tions that involve a new, productive, "counter-belief" way of relating can be extremely powerful in teaching patients that things can be different after all. The therapeutic relationship can also be used as a testing ground for new types of interactions with an important figure.

The reader may be surprised that more direct strategies for attacking underlying irrational beliefs are not presented. The reason for this has to do with the abstract/specific issue raised earlier. Underlying irrational be-liefs are usually expressed in somewhat abstract terms (e.g., "Unless I'm loved, I'm worthless"). The top-down approach here proposes that the most powerful work on the irrational beliefs is done by working on the specific situations, cognitions, behaviors, and moods in which the irration-al beliefs play themselves out, including the therapeutic relationship.

CHALLENGING MALADAPTIVE THOUGHTS

Maladaptive thoughts are flushed out by asking the patient, "Is this thought helping you in this situation?" If the answer is no, the thought is maladaptive. Maladaptive thoughts can be counterproductive in many ways: they produce negative mood, behavioral problems, and cognitive problems, and they reinforce underlying irrational beliefs. Usually they are simultaneously maladaptive in all these ways.

When patients have difficulty seeing that their thoughts are causing them problems, the therapist can use the Thought Record to teach this. The Thought Record (Figure 7.2) can be used to provide a structure for pointing out maladaptive thinking and generating alternatives. It in-cludes spaces for describing the problematic situation, problem behav-iors, and negative moods. Next comes a place for automatic thoughts, and finally, for responses to the automatic thoughts. The Thought Rec-ord is modeled on Beck's Daily Record of Dysfunctional Thoughts (Beck et al., 1979), but differs from that record in the addition of a column for behavior. The addition of the "behavior" column emphasizes the point that cognitions play a role in behavioral problems in addition to

Figure 7.2 Thought Record

DATE	SITUATION (Event, memory, attempt to do something, etc.)	EMOTION(s) (Rate intensity, from 1–100, before & after responding)	BEHAVIOR(s)	THOUGHTS (Rate degree of belief, 0–100, before and after responding)	RESPONSES (Rate degree of belief, 0–100).

their well-known role in contributing to depression and other negative moods.

To fill in the mood, behavior, and cognition sections, and to teach the relationships among them, the therapist asks a series of questions, as in the following example of a lawyer who is having difficulty writing a letter to a potential employer.

THERAPIST   What thoughts do you have about writing the letter?
PATIENT   I keep telling myself, "I *have* to write the letter!"
THERAPIST   I see. Does that thought help you write the letter?
PATIENT   If I didn't tell myself that, I'd *never* write the letter!
THERAPIST   I know that's how it seems to you, but let me ask you this: have you written the letter?
PATIENT   No, I haven't!
THERAPIST   So perhaps that thought doesn't help after all. Let's find out. Try saying to yourself, "I *have* to write the letter." Now, on a scale of 0 to 100, how much do you feel like writing the letter?
PATIENT   Zero. I don't want to do it. In fact, I feel angry, like someone is pushing me around and making me do something I don't want to do.
THERAPIST   That's a good observation, and that's exactly what I'm trying to point out. It seems to you that the thought, "I *have* to write the letter" makes it easier to write the letter, but it looks like it actually makes it harder.

To work toward alternatives to the maladaptive thinking, the therapist can ask, "How could you think about this situation in a way that would help you?" In the case of the lawyer who's having trouble writing the letter, the therapist can ask,

THERAPIST   If the thought "I *should* write the letter" is not helping you write the letter, what thought could you have that *would* help you write the letter?
PATIENT   (long pause)
THERAPIST   Any ideas?
PATIENT   No.
THERAPIST   Let's just start with any idea you have, and go from there.
PATIENT   I could say, "I'll spend 10 minutes on the letter."
THERAPIST   Let's try it out. Imagine going home, sitting down at your desk, and saying, "I'll spend 10 minutes on the letter." How does it feel?

PATIENT   It feels OK. It feels like I can do it.
THERAPIST   That sounds good. Would you like to try it?

Patients often have difficulty generating alternatives to their maladaptive thinking. When this happens, the therapist can generate several possibilities, and the patient can "try them on for size" until he finds one that suits. The patient may complain that the new approach won't help. In response, the therapist can suggest an experiment: one day of the old approach, and one day of the new, to compare the effectiveness of the two.

CHALLENGING IRRATIONAL THINKING

This section describes several strategies for challenging irrational, distorted, unrealistic, illogical thinking.

Thought Record

The Thought Record is also useful in challenging irrational thinking, as in this example of a young woman who comes to the therapy session saying, "I'm upset about the unemployment hearing that's scheduled for Friday." Here, the patient has already described the problematic situation and her negative emotional reaction, and this provides a good start to a session focused on the Thought Record.

PATIENT   I'm upset about the unemployment hearing that's scheduled for Friday.
THERAPIST   (writing on the Thought Record) Let's use the Thought Record to work on this. The situation is the unemployment hearing on Friday, and it sounds like you're feeling upset. Any other feelings?
PATIENT   (pause) Well, nervous, I guess.
THERAPIST   OK (writing that down). Anything else?
PATIENT   Not that I know of.
THERAPIST   Let's see if we can catch some of the thoughts. What thoughts are you having that are causing you to feel upset and nervous?
PATIENT   I don't really know.
THERAPIST   Try imagining the unemployment hearing. Where will it be held?
PATIENT   In City Hall.

THERAPIST   OK, do you know what room?
PATIENT   No.
THERAPIST   Do you know how many people will be there?
PATIENT   I think three or four.
THERAPIST   Now, imagine it's Friday morning, you're sitting in the
    meeting room in City Hall, and three or four people are there, and
    they're going to ask you questions. Try to imagine that as vividly as
    you can. Try to feel the nervous, upset feeling. Now, let me ask you:
    what thoughts are you having in this situation?
PATIENT   I won't know what to say.
THERAPIST   (writing this down in the "automatic thoughts" column).
    OK, any other thoughts?
PATIENT   They won't believe me.
THERAPIST   OK (writing this down). Any other thoughts?
PATIENT   I'll get turned down.
THERAPIST   (writing this down). Any other thoughts?
PATIENT   I'm letting my husband down.

At this point, after eliciting three or four or five automatic thoughts, it's
often useful to move to working on finding the distortions and responding
to them; strategies for doing this are presented in the next sections. Even
before this work begins, however, patients often experience some relief
from the simple activity of structuring the problem and gaining some
distance from the thoughts ("these are thoughts, not reality").

To quantify the work done on the Thought Record, patients can be
asked to rate on a scale from 0 to 100 the degree of belief in their
automatic thoughts, the intensity of their negative moods, and the intensity of their urges to carry out or avoid problematic behaviors. Rating
these things before and after working on them quantifies the effectiveness
of the therapeutic work. This is particularly helpful when the patient
brings the therapist a Thought Record completed outside the session. A
Thought Record in which anxiety about working on the dissertation was
rated at 100 at the beginning of the work and 50 at the end demonstrates a
clear success. In an even clearer instance of success in this case, a patient
completed the Thought Record and went on to spend an hour working on
the dissertation.

Name the distortion

To teach patients to identify cognitive distortions, ask them to read
Chapter 6 of this book or Chapter 3 of *Feeling Good* to learn the defini-

tions of the various types of thinking errors. Patients usually like doing this, because it gives them a concrete way to begin using the therapy.

When the patient is familiar with these types of thinking errors, the therapist can point out an error and take a first step toward working on it by asking, "What kind of distortion is going on here, would you say?"

Then, one more step can be taken as well. Ask the patient to use what he knows about the type of thinking error he's making to generate a rational response: "If the problem is mind-reading, how can you eliminate the mind-reading? What can you say to yourself instead of saying, 'She hates me'"? (Answer: "I don't know what she thinks of me. Even if she does hate me, why is that a problem for me?")

Ask for the evidence

A powerful strategy for bringing patients back to reality is the question, "What evidence do you have for that idea?" This is one of the questions most frequently asked by cognitive therapists. For example:

PATIENT   I feel very anxious. I'm worried my girfriend is getting bored with me and wants to end the relationship.

THERAPIST   What's going on that makes you think she's planning to end the relationship?

PATIENT   Well, she seems to be less interested in sex lately.

THERAPIST   I see. Any other evidence?

PATIENT   Well, I asked her to spend the weekend with me, and she said she could only see me on Saturday, not the whole weekend.

THERAPIST   I see, and why was that?

PATIENT   Well, she has a big presentation to make on Monday morning, and she wants to spend Sunday preparing for it.

THERAPIST   I see. Now, what do you think? Is Julie avoiding you, or is she genuinely concerned about her presentation?

PATIENT   (a little sheepish) I actually think she's genuinely concerned about her presentation.

THERAPIST   Is there any other evidence to support your idea that she's planning to end the relationship?

PATIENT   Well, I don't think I really have any.

THERAPIST   So it sounds like you get the idea that she wants to end the relationship because she's less interested in sex and she wants to spend Sunday preparing for her presentation. Let's think about why she might be less interested in sex.

PATIENT   Well, she's been having migraine headaches.

THERAPIST And does she tend to be less interested in sex when she has
    migraines?
PATIENT Yes.
THERAPIST This has happened before?
PATIENT Yes.
THERAPIST And did it mean the end of your relationship?
PATIENT No.
THERAPIST Does it sound like you're having an overreaction here?
PATIENT Yes, I think so.
THERAPIST Why is that? Why are you getting concerned about her
    breaking off?
PATIENT (pause) I think it's because our relationship has been going
    better lately, and we've even talked about marriage. Whenever we
    get closer, I get anxious that she'll want to break off.
THERAPIST Yes, we've seen that before. So if we think about it this way,
    it sounds like the relationship has been getting closer, not more
    distant, and that's what's making you anxious. That sounds like it
    has to do with your irrational belief, "If I get close to someone, I'll
    get hurt."
PATIENT Yes, I think that's it.

In this dialogue, the therapist's strategies include asking for the evidence, seeking alternative explanations of the evidence, and pointing to
the underlying belief.

Look for alternative explanations

Here the therapist's strategy is to look for alternative explanations of
evidence the patient offers as supporting his automatic thoughts. These
are not usually hard to come by, as in the dialogue above, and the patient
and therapist can make a list of alternative explanations. This strategy
points out to the patient that he tends to believe one explanation of the
evidence while ignoring all others. Sometimes this strategy is not very
powerful, and the patient clings to his foregone conclusion; when this
happens, the therapist will need to try other strategies. However, sometimes reviewing alternative explanations can be quite powerful, particularly when one the patient has ignored fits the evidence perfectly.

The reader may be worrying, "Suppose the patient *does* have good
evidence to support his point of view? What if the girlfriend *doesn't* have
a good reason for being less interested in sex and wanting to see him less?
Then what?" If this happens, the therapist can ask, "Suppose your

girlfriend loses interest in you and decides to leave the relationship? Why would this be upsetting?" The anxious young man will probably answer with several automatic thoughts, such as, "This means I'm a loser," "I can never be successful in a relationship," "I'll never be happy without her," and so on. Probing may reveal his central belief that he cannot be happy unless he has love and approval from an attractive woman. Plenty of good therapeutic work can be done when this idea is exposed.

Ask about another person

Patients who condemn themselves mercilessly for a failure—say, being fired from their job—are often remarkably accepting of exactly the same "failure" in another person. To point this out and to give patients some room to change, the therapist can ask a series of questions:

PATIENT   Being fired from this job makes me a failure. It means there's something wrong with me.
THERAPIST   Do you have any friends who ever got fired?
PATIENT   No, I don't think so.
THERAPIST   Well, take a minute and think. Anybody you know ever get fired? (If the therapist was ever fired, this might be the time to take advantage of it.)
PATIENT   (pause) Well, my sister Jane got fired once.
THERAPIST   Did you think she was a failure because of it?
PATIENT   No, I didn't.
THERAPIST   What did you think?
PATIENT   I thought it was a lousy deal.
THERAPIST   And did you give up your relationship with her because of it?
PATIENT   Of course not. I tried to stand by her and do what I could.

When using this strategy, it's important to discuss particular individuals. Ask for the name of a particular individual, rather than the vaguer, "my friends." Otherwise, the patient may slip into generalities that support his distorted view, for example, "All my friends who are divorced are miserable." To counter this, the therapist can ask for the name of a particular individual and get the details of that person's misery, alternative explanations for the misery, and so on.

For even greater power, the therapist can use this strategy to examine the patient's beliefs about a famous person he admires. The therapist can ask, "Did you lose respect for Cary Grant when he got divorced the first time? How about when he got divorced the second time?"

Make the abstract concrete

Working to get the details regarding any irrational statement the patient makes is usually quite helpful in revealing distortions, as in the preceding example discussing the use of the double standard for oneself and others. Another example:

PATIENT   I can't handle this new job. I'll fall apart.
THERAPIST   I see. Well, let's talk about what you mean by the term "fall apart."
PATIENT   Well, I don't know, I'll just fall apart.
THERAPIST   Right, but what will that involve exactly? Will you just stay in bed all the time? Will you start drinking heavily? Will you have to be hospitalized?
PATIENT   No, I'll just feel anxious all the time.
THERAPIST   OK, let's imagine you're right, and that you do feel anxious all the time for a while. Can you handle that?
PATIENT   (long pause) Yes, I guess I can.

Use the therapeutic relationship

When there is a strong, positive therapeutic relationship, the therapist can take advantage of this to challenge the patient's irrational ideas. For example,

PATIENT   I made a mistake in the report I wrote last week – I'm afraid my boss is going to fire me for it.
THERAPIST   Well, I see I'd better not make any mistakes in my sessions with you – I might get fired for it!
PATIENT   Oh no, I wouldn't fire you!
THERAPIST   Why not?
PATIENT   Because making a few mistakes is normal – overall, you're doing a great job!
THERAPIST   So if I make a few mistakes, that might still mean that overall I was doing a good job? What about you? Is it possible that you might make a few mistakes and still be doing a good job?

Although the general strategy of helping patients correct distortions by asking questions is a good one, sometimes the therapist can make a powerful statement by simply contradicting the patient. This strategy makes powerful use of a strong, positive therapeutic relationship. For example, a salesman may come to his therapy session describing an unproductive week, saying, "I'm just a lazy bum." The therapist can speak up to contradict this, saying, "I don't think you're a lazy bum."

If the therapist doesn't speak up when patients make these derogatory, cruel statements about themselves, the therapist may appear to endorse the patient's negative view about himself. In addition, the therapist's behavior can serve as a model for how the patient might treat himself.

Exaggeration and humor

The perfectionistic lawyer who feels upset with herself for locking her keys in her car may say, "I'm *always* doing dumb things like that!" The therapist can respond, "Oh, so everytime you drive your car you lock your keys inside?" The overdependent housewife may say, "If my husband dies, I'll fall apart." The therapist can respond, "Oh, do you think the men in white coats will come to take you away?" The self-critical student may say, "I never get anything done! The therapist can respond, "Oh, you didn't make it to your therapy session today?"

Another type of exaggeration involves simply following the patient's line of thinking to its logical, but extreme conclusion. The distortion in the thought, "I should never have gone out with him," can be exposed by the therapist's exaggerated restatement: "Oh, so you feel you should have known in advance that he was going to have a car accident that night?"

The use of humor may not be a good idea for the patient who is so extremely fragile and vulnerable that he feels ridiculed or criticized by the therapist's humorous or sarcastic remarks.

DIFFICULTIES

Difficulties often arise in the process of work on dysfunctional thoughts. Common difficulties include the patient's complaint that the cognitive responses make sense intellectually but do not have an emotional impact; the patient's insistence that her thoughts are true, not distorted; and patients who, despite repeated interventions, do not show cognitive change. Following a brief discussion of a general strategy useful in coping with difficulties, each of these particular problems is discussed in turn.

A general strategy

A good rule of thumb when working with difficulties is: "use the formulation." That is, obstacles to change in therapy can be viewed as a problem like the patient's other problems. This vantage point allows the therapist to take a problem-solving approach to the difficulty, rather than feeling thwarted, attacked, or defensive. If a problem arises, the therapist can state the problem, bring up a situation in which it occurs, and ask, "What automatic thoughts come up in this situation that create the problem?" In this way, collaborative productive work can take place.

The case formulation view is also helpful because it suggests that the mechanisms underlying the problem may be the same mechanisms underlying all of the patient's other problems: the central irrational beliefs. Thus, for example, a young lady who was extremely depressed, passive, and socially isolated appeared to have the central irrational belief, "I'm incompetent; I can't be successful at anything." Not surprisingly, she responded to the therapist's suggestions about cognitive and behavioral changes she might make with the automatic thought, "I can't do that."

Cognitive responses make intellectual but not emotional sense

Patients who learn responses to their irrational, maladaptive thoughts sometimes complain that these thoughts make rational, intellectual sense, but they do not make emotional sense. They don't "feel" right.

This problem is readily understood from the point of view of the case formulation model. The patient's current emotional experience is based on a large set of thoughts, behaviors, and moods, many of which are generated by irrational beliefs. Current life situations may support and reinforce all these components. New ideas that attack the "old plan" are quite likely to seem foreign, to "not fit," and to "feel wrong." New plans that chip away at the old plan are bound to feel wrong. In fact, from the point of view of this model, their feeling wrong does not invalidate them; rather, it supports the notion that they contradict the old, pathological view.

From this point of view, the solution to the problem of "feeling wrong" is simply the process of gradually, over time, accumulating more thoughts, behaviors, moods, underlying beliefs about the self, and life experiences and situations that reinforce, support, and are consistent with the new, rational, but strange-seeming cognitions. Thus, the fact that new ideas and behaviors "feel wrong" does not mean that they are not helpful. In fact, if change is a goal of therapy (it generally is), the fact that things feel strange and unfamiliar might be viewed as a positive sign that this goal is being achieved.

My thoughts aren't irrational — that's how it is!

Empathy is an excellent first response to this difficulty. Sometimes the patient's claim that her thoughts are not irrational arises from a feeling of not being listened to or not being taken seriously, and empathy can break through these perceptions. The patient may feel that the therapist is not taking seriously the negative realities of her life. The therapist must be sensitive to this complaint, particularly in view of recent arguments by theorists (Krantz, 1985) that the cognitive model of depression does not fully consider the effect of the patient's actual hardships.

Although the patient's view may be clearly (to the therapist) irrational, unless the therapist begins with some acceptance and understanding of it, the patient may be unable to change. In the following example, the patient begins with the belief, "I should visit my parents." To the patient, this idea seems *true*, not distorted. To break through this, the therapist begins by accepting the idea that the patient should visit her parents, and then asks why she does not.

PATIENT   I haven't visited my parents in more than a year, and I feel terrible about it. I keep telling myself, "I *should* go to see them."

THERAPIST   And how do you feel when you say that to yourself?

PATIENT   Terrible.

THERAPIST   Well, what kind of distortion is going on that makes you feel so terrible?

PATIENT   There *is* no distortion. It's true — I *should* visit my parents. They're old and ill, and if I don't go soon, I might not see them again.

THERAPIST   Well, if you're telling yourself you *should* go, but you don't there must be some reason you don't go. Let's think about why you don't visit them.

PATIENT   (reluctantly, feeling anxious) Well, there are lots of reasons.

THERAPIST   OK, let's think about them. What are the reasons?

PATIENT   Well, I'd have to take time off from work. It's expensive to fly to Boston. But I can do all that. The main reason is that when I spend time around my parents I feel awful. That's *terrible* — I *shouldn't* feel awful around my *parents*!

THERAPIST   OK, let's think about it. If you feel so bad, there must be reasons for it. Why do you feel awful around your parents?

PATIENT   (pause) Well, for one thing, my mother criticizes me all the time. She says just *awful* things. She'll say, "Joan, you look like a *pig* when you wear your hair like that." Or, "The reason your husband drinks is because *you're* fat!" (Patient is crying anxiously.)

THERAPIST   That sounds very painful. And your father?

PATIENT   Oh, he ignores me.

THERAPIST   So when you go to visit them, your mother criticizes and abuses you, and your father ignores you.

PATIENT   (nods)

THERAPIST   Well, if a person goes home, and her parents criticize her and neglect her, how *should* she feel?

PATIENT   Terrible.

THERAPIST   That makes sense to me. And how do *you* feel?

PATIENT   Terrible.

THERAPIST   Right. And how *should* you feel?

PATIENT   Terrible.

THERAPIST   Right. OK, now, can you explain to me why you *should* want to visit your parents as infrequently as possible.

Similarly, many patients have difficulty seeing that the thought, "I shouldn't feel upset," is distorted and problematic. They insist, "It's *true!*" To address this, the therapist can do the following:

PATIENT   I shouldn't feel upset about such a small thing!

THERAPIST   What kind of a distortion is that?

PATIENT   It's not distorted—it's true. I shouldn't be so upset about such a small thing.

THERAPIST   Well, try this. First focus on how upset you feel about this small problem. How upset do you feel?

PATIENT   Oh, about 60.

THERAPIST   OK, now say to yourself, "I shouldn't be so upset about this small problem." Now how upset do you feel?

PATIENT   A little more, I guess.

THERAPIST   That's what I would expect. Do you see why?

PATIENT   Not really.

THERAPIST   When you say to yourself, "I *shouldn't* be so upset about this," you double your trouble. Now you have two problems instead of one. The first problem is how upset you feel over the small thing. The second problem is how angry you feel with yourself for having the first problem. I'm suggesting you work on the second problem, and try to buy out of the idea, "I *shouldn't* feel so upset over the small thing." If you can do that, you'll have solved half of your problem, and then we can work on the first problem.

The patient who insists her thoughts are *true* may believe that if the therapist does not feel as hopeless and upset as she does, then the therapist does not really understand or does not truly wish to help. Another possibility is that, to the patient, the alternative to her irrational idea is even more frightening than the "reality" that she insists on. For example, the patient may insist, "I'm stuck in this job. That's reality for me — there's nothing distorted about it!" We can understand the patient's clinging to this idea if we realize that to see things differently may mean confronting her fear of looking for another job (she may fear that no one would hire her).

Although many patients are able to see that their irrational beliefs are irrational, and to catch some glimpse of alternatives, some cannot. These patients seem to have only one fixed, extremely negative sense of themselves. As a result, the search for alternatives comes up empty. In this case, the therapist's task becomes one of generating some alternatives, beginning with attempts to promote some automatic thoughts, behaviors, and cognitions that are consistent with a healthier sense of self.

Failure to change

Sometimes, despite repeated interventions, irrational, maladaptive views of the world simply do not budge. Sometimes a power struggle develops: the therapist pushes the patient hard to change, the patient digs in his heels and does not. Entire books could be written about this topic. Several brief suggestions are offered here. First, the therapist might do well to study the diagnosis and case formulation. A different way of understanding the patient's problems might lead to a more productive way of working on it. Second, the therapist can raise the problem as a problem to be addressed as any other, working with the patient to understand the problem and generate solutions. Third, and related, the therapist can focus on empathy, attempting to understand the patient rather than pushing him to change. Fourth, the therapist can ask himself, "Do I *need* this patient to change?" If the therapist can buy out of this stance, the patient may be able to move. Fifth, it is possible, as Guidano and Liotti (1983) suggested, that the resistance to change may be due to the prominent role in the patient's sense of self that these cognitions play. The patient is reluctant to change these thoughts because to do so would require surrendering his identity. In this case, the patient may need to learn some new, more positive things about himself before he will be ready to give up the old, comfortable view.

CHAPTER 8

Homework

This chapter begins with a brief discussion of the rationale for using homework in formulation-based cognitive behavior therapy and a review of empirical evidence supporting its importance. The remainder of the chapter illustrates the use of the case formulation in making effective homework assignments, anticipating obstacles to completing assignments, and understanding and managing difficulties, particularly the failure to complete homework.

RATIONALE FOR THE USE OF HOMEWORK

Homework plays a central role in formulation-based cognitive behavior therapy. No matter how many insights and changes occur during the session, patients will not solve the problems on their problem list or make significant changes in their underlying irrational beliefs unless they make behavioral and cognitive changes outside the session.

Homework assignments allow the patient to work on problems when they are "live" and particularly meaningful (Burns, Adams, & Anastopoulos, 1985). By the time of his regularly scheduled therapy session, the patient may have difficulty retrieving an upsetting situation he experienced some days ago. Situations that arouse powerful affect probably involve the patient's key underlying ideas, and the ability to work on these when they are activated offers a potent opportunity for change that would be missed if all therapeutic work took place during therapy sessions.

The "top-down" model proposed here suggests that in order to change underlying irrational beliefs, many cognitive and behavior changes in everyday life are required. Homework promotes continued practice of new ideas, new views of the self and the world, and new behaviors and plans for action.

Homework also teaches the patient that his recovery is the product of his own efforts rather than those of the therapist. For this reason, it is particularly important in the treatment of patients who are inclined to become overly dependent on the therapist, particularly those who hold irrational beliefs like, "I can't cope on my own." When the patient claims, "I won't make it without you during your vacation," the therapist can remind the patient that, through homework assignments, he has practiced coping with problems that arise when the therapist is not available. Homework may also shorten the treatment, because it teaches the patient to solve his own problems, rather than depending on the therapist to solve them for him.

Homework provides a structure in which the patient can practice skills learned in therapy sessions outside the sessions. Homework practice may prevent relapses because it teaches the patient to identify and solve problems before they lead to a full-blown clinical episode. Simons et al. (1986) suggest this may be one of the mechanisms accounting for lower relapse rates among patients treated with cognitive therapy than patients treated with antidepressant medication.

Finally, homework transactions present important opportunities for "in vivo" work. For example, the patient who procrastinates on completing time sheets at work is likely to also have difficulty completing homework assignments. There is likely to be a common mechanism underlying these two problems, perhaps a resistance to requests from others for fear her own interests will be pushed aside. Work on the homework problem is a powerful way of working on this underlying problem as it arises "in vivo" — that is, "in real life," in the therapy session.

EMPIRICAL EVIDENCE

Although several compelling arguments for the central role of homework in formulation-based cognitive and behavioral treatments can be given, few empirical studies examine the question of whether homework has a positive impact on outcome. As yet, studies examining the relationship between cognitive and behavioral homework activities and changes in underlying beliefs have not been carried out.

Persons, Burns, and Perloff (1989), in a study of depressed patients treated in the first two authors' private practice, found that, for depressed patients who completed treatment, those who did homework outside of therapy sessions improved more than those who did not. The benefits of homework were much greater for patients who were severely depressed at the beginning of treatment than for those who were less depressed. Maultsby (1971), in a study of rational emotive therapy, showed that patients who reported they did more homework were rated by their therapist as having a more successful outcome than patients who did less homework. These two studies both have the weakness that patients were not randomly assigned to homework and no-homework conditions, and ratings of outcome were not independent of ratings of homework. In a study which did randomly assign patients to homework and no-homework groups, Kazdin and Mascitelli (1982) found that patients who practiced assertive behavior outside of therapy sessions made greater gains at post-treatment assessment and eight-month follow-up than patients who did not.

Kornblith, Rehm, O'Hara, and Lamparski (1983) found that self-control therapy for depression was *not* more effective when it included homework assignments than when it did not. However, several of the patients in the no-homework condition carried out homework assignments they devised for themselves. Thus, it is not clear that the homework and no-homework conditions differed substantially in the amount of homework that patients actually carried out.

USING THE FORMULATION TO MAKE AN EFFECTIVE ASSIGNMENT

The case formulation indicates the types of behavioral and cognitive homework activities that might be therapeutic for any particular patient. For example, the young man described earlier who felt uncomfortable attending political campaign meetings had the central irrational belief "I must be perfect or I'll be rejected." He had the automatic thought, "I'm not fully informed on the issues and the candidates and when others discover this they will reject me," and he came to the therapy session with a plan to spend several hours reading up on the issues. It would be easy for the therapist to assign the campaign reading as homework. However, from the viewpoint of the case formulation model, this plan would be counter-therapeutic. Why?

The fact that the patient's reading plan is prompted by a set of automatic thoughts that are close derivatives of the formulation tells the therapist that the reading is consistent with and reinforces the underlying belief. Thus, doing the reading would reinforce the patient's idea that if he is uninformed he will be rejected. Instead, a better homework assignment would be to do a Thought Record to talk back to the automatic thoughts that are making him uncomfortable in the meeting, and to interact with several people during the meeting to test out his idea that he'll be rejected.

Another example is provided by the common problem of a socially isolated person who wants to begin dating. When the impulse to find a partner is driven by the idea, "Unless I have a partner, I'm a failure in life," dating may actually be exactly the wrong thing to do, as Burns (1985) points out. In this case, dating reinforces and supports the person's pathological views about himself. In addition, attempts in this direction may not be particularly successful, as potential mates are likely to be repelled by the neediness they perceive in the patient. Instead, homework assignments designed to generate some evidence contradicting the pathological belief will be more helpful. For example, the person could keep a log of activities alone and with others and rate the predicted and actual enjoyment obtained from each in order to test out his idea, "I'm happier when I'm with others than when I'm alone."

Thus, the homework assignment is a helpful one if it involves an activity that works to provide some evidence against the patient's automatic thoughts and central underlying beliefs. If the activity is consistent with the underlying beliefs, it will strengthen those beliefs, and therefore is counter-therapeutic.

In addition, a homework assignment is useful if the patient perceives it as relevant to his difficulties and likely to help in solving them. To make the assignment relevant to a current problem, the therapist can try to link the homework assignment directly to the material discussed in the session. Patients often come to therapy sessions to discuss a task they have been avoiding or nccd to practice. Dozens of examples could be provided: telephoning a girl for a date, going swimming, buying clothes, having a discussion with a spouse about his drinking, requesting that the family participate in an activity the patient wants to do, etc. When this happens, the session can be spent uncovering the automatic thoughts that prevent the patient from tackling the problem (e.g, "When I call up for the schedule of swimming classes, the receptionist will be rude to me. Then I'll feel worse.") and working on responses to them. Next, the task itself (making the telephone call) can be the homework assignment.

Although the injunction to the therapist to make a "counter-irrational belief" assignment that seems relevant and useful to the patient may appear quite demanding, in practice this is not always so, primarily because the patient can be asked to play a major role in planning the assignment. Frequently, patients have excellent ideas about what behavior changes or cognitive exercises would be helpful to them. If not, the therapist can suggest several possible tasks and let the patient choose among them. If the patient makes a poor choice, the process of pointing this out and negotiating a change can be used to do some important teaching, as illustrated in the next section.

USING THE FORMULATION TO ANTICIPATE OBSTACLES

Many obstacles interfere with the successful completion of assignments. The case formulation model suggests that the problems patients have that prevent them from carrying out homework assignments are likely to be the same problems that prevent them from doing other things in their lives and that produce many of the other difficulties that bring them to therapy. If this hypothesis is correct, the therapist can make good use of the formulation to anticipate—and work to remove—obstacles to completing homework assignments.

To use the formulation in this way, the therapist asks himself the questions, "What is this patient's key underlying belief? How might it interfere with carrying out this homework assignment?" Another good question is, "What are the typical behavior patterns and automatic thoughts that are likely to arise when the patient confronts this homework task?" This section of the chapter describes several common obstacles, stated in terms of patients' central problems, and suggests strategies for managing them.

Perfectionism

Many depressed and anxious patients have beliefs along the lines, "Unless it's done perfectly and completely, it's not worth doing," and "Unless I do a superhuman amount, I will never accomplish anything." These patients typically set themselves unreasonable and unattainable homework tasks, which cause them to feel overwhelmed and inadequate. As a result, little or nothing is accomplished. This failure reinforces the patient's idea that unless he does a superhuman amount, nothing will be accomplished. To get out of this cycle, the therapist can help the patient set small, manageable goals. A valuable guideline for the therapist's use in determining how much homework to assign is the motto, "Start where you are, not where you want to be." Thus, if the patient has not jogged for two months, a homework assignment of daily jogging during the next week is unrealistic — once or twice makes more sense. Similarly, it is unwise to assign as homework a task the patient found too difficult, even with the therapist's help, to complete during the session.

When the patient insists on setting unreasonable goals, the therapist can work to point this out to the patient and to negotiate some change, as illustrated here.

PATIENT   I want to work on making sales calls.

THERAPIST   All right, let's think about it. What thoughts do you have about your sales calls?

PATIENT   I *should* be making 10 calls a day. Actually, I should be making 20 a day, but I'd settle for 10 right now.

THERAPIST   I see, so you're telling yourself, "I should be making 10 calls a day." Well, let me ask you this: how many calls, on average, are you actually making right now?

PATIENT   Well, last Thursday I made 14, but I haven't made any since then.

THERAPIST   It sounds like, on average, you're making about 2 calls per day — one day with 14 calls, but no calls on the other days.

PATIENT   Right.

THERAPIST   OK, so you're making two calls a day right now. So if you wanted to set a goal for yourself about how many calls a day you'd like to make next week, what goal would you set?

PATIENT   I should be making 10 a day. Actually, I *should* be making 20. If I can't do at least 10 a day, my territory will go down the tubes!

THERAPIST   Well, it sounds like one way you try to get yourself to make sales calls is to say to yourself, "I have to make 10 calls a day."

PATIENT   Right.

THERAPIST   And how long have you been using this approach, would you say?

PATIENT   (ruefully) Years!

THERAPIST   And how well does this approach work?

PATIENT   Not very well!

THERAPIST   Right. Do you see why? When you tell yourself, "I have to make 10 — or 20 — calls a day," the result is usually zero calls. Do you see why?

PATIENT   I guess I get overwhelmed and hopeless.

THERAPIST   That's what it sounds like, doesn't it? Now, how can you solve this problem?

PATIENT   I don't know.

THERAPIST   Well, I have an idea about it, but you're not going to like it. Are you willing to try it?

PATIENT   I'll try anything!

THERAPIST   Terrific. OK, now how can you make a plan for making sales calls that doesn't cause you to feel overwhelmed?

PATIENT   I could start with five calls a day.

THERAPIST   OK, let's try it. Say to yourself, "Today I'm going to make five calls." How does that feel?

PATIENT   A little overwhelming.

THERAPIST   OK, what does that tell you?

PATIENT   I need to set a smaller goal.

THERAPIST   Right. What goal do you want to set?

PATIENT   Two calls a day.

THERAPIST   OK, let's try it out. Say to yourself, "Today I'm going to make two calls." Do you feel overwhelmed?

PATIENT   No, I don't think so. But if I do two calls a day, I'll never get *anything* done!

THERAPIST   (facetiously) I see, so if you make two calls a day next week, at the end of the week you'll have made a total of zero calls.

PATIENT   (speechless, smiles)

THERAPIST   OK, if you make two calls a day, how many calls will you make next week?

PATIENT   Ten.

THERAPIST   And how many did you make this week?

PATIENT   Zero, so far.

THERAPIST   OK, so it sounds like if you followed this approach you'd be ahead of this week's tally.

PATIENT   I guess so.

THERAPIST   What do you think? Do you want to try it?

PATIENT   (reluctantly) I'll try it.

THERAPIST   I told you you weren't going to like this approach.

PATIENT   You're right!

THERAPIST   Well, if you want you can go back to your old approach. What do you think?

PATIENT   I guess it's time to try something new.

THERAPIST   OK, that sounds good. This can be an experiment. If it helps you, great. If not, we can try something else. Are you ready to try something new?

PATIENT   Yes.

THERAPIST   OK, here's an index card you can use to write down the

number of calls you make each day. I've written down each day of
the week. Can you do that?

PATIENT   Yes, I can do it.

The patient may insist that a goal of 10 sales calls is the only goal that
will work for him. If this happens, the therapist can accept the patient's
goal but suggest that the patient's performance during the week can be
used to evaluate whether this strategy really works. If the patient has
another week of poor performance, he may begin to see that his strategy
needs revision.

Fear of failure

Closely related to perfectionism are ideas like, "If I fail, I'm worthless,
and it proves I'll never accomplish anything," and, "If I fail, I'll be rejected." The patient who fears rejection may fear that the therapist will
reject him if he fails to complete his assignment, and he may even have
the impulse to drop out of treatment in order to avoid this calamity. Or,
the patient may do the homework but forget to bring it to the session so
he won't have to show it to the therapist. His fear may be reflected in
automatic thoughts like, "My spelling is so bad that when she sees it she
won't want to have anything to do with me."

The salesman described above can be used again to illustrate work on
this problem. What if the salesman doesn't make the two sales calls a day
he agreed to? He may become demoralized ("I should be doing 10 calls,
and I can't even do two!") and have the impulse to drop out of therapy. To
prevent this, the therapist can work with the patient to plan strategies for
coping with failure before it happens, as in the following example.

THERAPIST   Let's think about how you'd like to handle it if you have a
day, or several days, when you don't make any sales calls.

PATIENT   (waits, looks blank)

THERAPIST   Well, suppose you miss one day. How would you handle it?

PATIENT   I don't know.

THERAPIST   Well, what do you think about the idea of setting yourself a
goal of four calls the next day, so you can stay on schedule?

PATIENT   That sounds good to me.

THERAPIST   Yes, I thought it would. That's why I'm raising it. But I'm
going to try to convince you it's not a good idea. Do you see why?

PATIENT   I might just get demoralized. Then the next day I might have
to do six, and I'd be in a hole again.

THERAPIST   Exactly. So what does that tell you?

PATIENT   Well, if I don't make my goal on one day, I should still go for two calls the next day.

THERAPIST   Great. OK, now what else can you do?

PATIENT   I don't know.

THERAPIST   Well, what would you usually do?

PATIENT   Well, I might just get busy with things around the house, and not think about it.

THERAPIST   I see — you'd try to just put it out of your mind.

PATIENT   Right.

THERAPIST   That seems to be a pattern for you.

PATIENT   Yes, it is.

THERAPIST   And does it pay off for you?

PATIENT   No, absolutely not!

THERAPIST   OK, let's see if we can come up with another approach. (pensively) OK, now imagine the day has passed, you didn't make any sales calls; now what can you do?

PATIENT   (blank)

THERAPIST   OK, now, I have two ideas. First, it's the end of the day, so it's time to fill out the log, so you need to write down "zero" for the number of sales calls for the day.

PATIENT   Ouch!

THERAPIST   Right, it hurts, but what we're working on now is how not to push the whole problem to the side and avoid it, and keeping the log is part of facing up to things. Does that make sense to you?

PATIENT   Yes, it does.

THERAPIST   OK, now the other idea I have is about tomorrow. Is there anything you can do that will increase your chances of keeping your goal tomorrow?

PATIENT   I can promise myself I'll keep my goal tomorrow.

THERAPIST   Yes, and that's fine, but I think you might need a little more structure than that. What do you think about planning out exactly which two calls you're going to make, and writing them down?

PATIENT   That sounds good.

THERAPIST   OK, how about if we make that the homework: two sales calls a day, and a log of how many calls you make each day. If you don't meet your quota on any given day, try writing down the plan for the next day. How does that sound?

PATIENT   Fine, I can do that.

THERAPIST   I think you can do it too. But I think it's a good idea to think about what might happen if you don't do it. If the week doesn't go well for you, you might get the idea, "I didn't make many sales calls, I didn't do a good job with my log, I might as well just quit this therapy!" Then I'm thinking you might have the urge to call and cancel your session. What do you think? (The patient has cancelled sessions before when things haven't gone well.)

PATIENT   (quickly) I wouldn't do that.

THERAPIST   Well, I hope not. But it seems like this kind of thing has happened before. Do you remember the time you cancelled when you had a bad weekend?

PATIENT   Yes, I guess so.

THERAPIST   If things don't go well, how can you handle it so you can come to therapy and work on it, instead of cancelling your session and avoiding the whole thing?

PATIENT   Well, I just need to come, I guess.

THERAPIST   Well, I think that's a good idea. Then, if something's not going well, we can pick up on it right away and work on it. How does that sound?

PATIENT   It sounds good.

Another way of addressing the fear of failure problem is to design the homework assignment so that it is impossible to fail at it. One example of a no-lose assignment might be a plan for the patient to do something he has been avoiding, and if he doesn't do it, to spend 15 minutes writing down the thoughts that kept him from doing it. This is (almost) a no-lose assignment, because if the patient completes the project, he wins, and if he doesn't do it, he learns something about what's keeping him from completing it. Of course, it's not completely a no-lose assignment because the patient could fail to do both. More about noncompliance later.

The therapist might also point out to the patient who suffers from a fear of failure that if he is not successful at his homework assignment he has an excellent opportunity to work on his fear of failure; he might do this by completing a Thought Record responding to his automatic thoughts about failure.

The therapist can also prevent problems arising from perfectionism and fear of failure by making clear, specific assignments. A vague, unstructured homework assignment creates a problem for the perfectionist because he may interpret it very differently from the therapist, and often in a way that makes it difficult or impossible to carry out. For example, the assignment, "Start cleaning the house," may be interpreted as, "Clean the entire house." This task may be so overwhelming to a depressed person that she may be unable to tackle it at all. A vague task creates a problem for the person who feels inadequate because it can increase his already high anxiety about doing the task imperfectly or incorrectly. Vagueness may also communicate to the patient that the therapist does not expect the patient to follow through with the assignment, does not believe the patient can do the assignment, does not feel the assignment will help, does not take the patient's difficulties seriously, or any number of similar demoralizing messages.

An additional problem is that a vague assignment makes it difficult for the therapist (and the patient) to determine whether the task was actually carried out. Some patients, for example, seem to insist on carrying out a different task from the one that was agreed upon in the therapy session. This behavior may be related to similar behaviors outside the therapy and to irrational beliefs like, "If I do what others expect of me, then they will control me." Thus, it's helpful to be aware when this type of noncompliance occurs. However, if the assignment is too vague, the patient's distorted reaction will be difficult to pick up on, and discuss.

The importance of the format and mechanical details of the homework assignment is illustrated by the case of a nurse who wanted to stop smoking. She was given the homework assignment of logging every cigarette she smoked. She returned with a log, on an $8^{1}/_{2}'' \times 11''$ sheet of paper, of her cigarette smoking for one morning, but reported that it was cumbersome to keep the log and that she often forgot to take it to work or use it when she smoked. Next, the therapist showed the patient how to insert a small sheet of paper between the cellophane and the cigarette packet, together with a miniature pencil. The following session, the patient brought a complete record of all the cigarettes she had smoked during the week.

Need to please others

The patient who has beliefs along the lines, "I must do what others expect of me or I'll be rejected," or "If I comply with others, they'll like me, and then they'll meet my needs," are likely to agree quickly to the therapist's homework plan, but they may have difficulty carrying it out. This type of patient is unable to make an assertive statement to the therapist like, "No, I don't want to do that," or "I've already tried that and it didn't help. I'd rather try a new approach." Instead, these individuals commonly respond to these types of dilemmas with passive resistance: forgetting, doing a different assignment, or simply coming to the session saying, "I didn't do it." If the patient feels a great deal of pressure from the therapist to comply, but has strong reasons not to, coupled with an inability to state these directly, the patient may respond by simply dropping out of treatment.

The therapist who is aware that a patient is vulnerable to these reactions can try to predict them and neutralize them before they are activated by the homework assignment. After making a homework assignment, the therapist might say, "Now you and I know that it's hard for you to say 'no.' Here we have a situation where I've just suggested you do a certain thing. You might want to say no to me. If you did, what would you say?" A role-play in which the patient refuses the assignment and patient and therapist negotiate a better one can be quite helpful here.

These patients may also report they are unable to allot time or energy to completing their homework because their resources are overwhelmed by responding to others' needs. The therapist can predict this and work to overcome it by saying, "Now, we know that often when you plan to do things for yourself, you never quite get around to them because you're so busy doing things for others. I'm thinking that pattern might interfere with your homework assignment. How can you cope with that?"

USING THE FORMULATION TO MANAGE DIFFICULTIES

Homework difficulties are a common bugaboo for both patients and therapists. Patients often have problems completing homework assignments; therapists often have problems making homework assignments and following up on them. This section of the chapter focuses on the use of the formulation in understanding and managing these and other homework difficulties.

Patients' difficulties

The case formulation model views the difficulties patients have with homework assignments, particularly difficulty completing assignments, as important for two reasons. One, homework is an important contributor to therapeutic progress. Therefore, solving these problems can improve the power and efficacy of the therapy. Second, consistent homework difficulties are likely to be related to the patient's other difficulties in life, his typical automatic thoughts and behavior patterns, his mood disturbance, and his central underlying irrational beliefs. Therefore, work on the homework problems addresses the problems for which the patient sought treatment. Difficulties with homework are viewed with the same problem-solving, nonpunitive stance as the patient's other difficulties, and the same strategies are used to understand and work with them.

FAILURE TO DO HOMEWORK. When the patient comes to the session without a completed homework assignment, the therapist can begin by asking the patient for her thoughts about this: "It sounds like the homework didn't get done. Let's think about what interfered." If the patient complains that this is not an important issue, that she has other more important things to discuss, the therapist may want to provide the rationale for the importance of discussing homework problems provided in the preceding paragraphs. If the therapist has difficulty following up on homework assignments, particularly unsuccessful ones, she might benefit from examining the automatic thoughts that make this difficult (more about this later).

When asked about the failure to do homework, patients' responses tend to reflect their central underlying problem in an almost uncanny way. For example, in the following dialogue, the patient's difficulty doing homework is due to one of his central problems, the inability to refuse a request from a person important to him. Therapeutic work on his homework problem addresses this problem, which interferes with his work as well as his therapy.

THERAPIST   How did your homework go? (The homework assignment was to make an assertive request of his boss.)
PATIENT   I forgot to do it.
THERAPIST   Well, let's think about what that's all about.
PATIENT   I just forgot.
THERAPIST   Well, that does happen sometimes. But I know you take your therapy very seriously, and you don't usually forget to do your homework.
PATIENT   (pause) Well, maybe I forgot because I didn't think the assignment you gave me would help. I've tried being assertive with my boss before, and it hasn't helped.
THERAPIST   It sounds like you felt I gave you an assignment to do something that you had already tried and found wasn't helpful.
PATIENT   Right.
THERAPIST   Well, let's think about that. How can you handle it if I give you a homework assignment that you feel is not going to help? How can you be assertive about it?
PATIENT   I guess I can speak up about it.
THERAPIST   OK, good. Now, let's imagine I just gave you a homework assignment you don't want to do. What can you say to me?

PATIENT   I guess I could just say, "I don't think that would help."
THERAPIST   OK, fine, let's see if we can think of something else that
     might be more helpful. Do you have any ideas about what might
     work with him?
PATIENT   Well, what I'd like to do is to be assertive enough to say "no"
     when he asks me to do something that is not really part of my job
     description and that I don't have time to do.
THERAPIST   Let's step out of this role play. How do you think you
     handled it when I gave you that homework assignment?
PATIENT   That was fine. I was more assertive.
THERAPIST   I agree.

Another underlying difficulty that can interfere with homework compliance is the fear that others need and require the patient to do things
that are not actually in the patient's best interest. This type of patient may
have been reared by needy, demanding parents. She may feel coerced by
the therapist and have the automatic thought, "I *have* to do the assignment," which may make completion of the assignment difficult or impossible. In response, the therapist can ask several questions: Does the patient *have* to do the assignment? Does she have a choice about it? If she
feels the assignment is not in her best interest, what is the best way for her
to handle this? Does the strategy of simply not doing the assignment pay
off? Are there other strategies that might be more productive? Is this
problem related to other problems in the patient's life?

Once this problem has arisen, the therapist can expect it to occur again
and probe for it when the next homework assignment is being given by
asking the patient, "Do you *want* to do homework? What can you do if,
after you get home, you realize you don't want to do it?"

Patients often come to the therapy session saying, "I didn't do my
homework," or "I didn't do a good job on my homework." Such statements bear close scrutiny, as they are often distorted. Depressed patients
typically discount or ignore their accomplishments and underestimate the
quantity and value of what they do. Direct observation of distortions in
the patient's report provides an excellent opportunity for the therapist to
observe, firsthand, the discrepancy between the patient's version of reality and a more objective version. This information can be valuable in
alerting the therapist to other distortions the patient may report as fact.

Thus, an attorney who had been procrastinating on writing a certain
business letter agreed that, as a homework assignment, he would tackle
the letter. We agreed he would spend 40 minutes on it. At his next session,
he reported, "I didn't do a very good job on my homework." Upon
careful investigation, it turned out that the patient had in fact spent two

hours on the letter but felt dissatisfied because, "It's only a draft. It's not finished yet." This information led to a very good session in which the patient was able to see that he irrationally evaluated his effort as inadequate even though he had spent three to four times more time on the project than he had agreed to do. He also observed, in a very direct way, his tendency to criticize everything he did unless it was perfect. He began to have a better understanding of the why he felt unable to initiate many professional and personal projects and why he didn't enjoy the things he did do.

Some patients have difficulty doing homework because their understanding of the process of psychotherapy, perhaps based on previous experience, does not include homework. These patients may hold beliefs like, "It's not my fault I have these problems, so I shouldn't have to do anything to get over them." Hard work may be required to break through these ideas. Consistent homework assignments in every session, beginning with the very first one, are a good idea.

TOO MUCH HOMEWORK. A few patients will insist on doing excessive amounts of homework. Although the therapist may at first feel gratified by the patient's degree of commitment to the therapy, an excessive, obsessive level of effort probably reflects irrational thinking.

For example, a college student who experienced a very painful episode of depression that lasted for nine months was spending over an hour a day on efforts to uncover and respond to his automatic thoughts. An exploration of this behavior revealed the irrational idea, "I must work hard on my therapy in order to be certain that I *never* have another episode of depression. If I have another episode, this will prove I'm a failure in life." An attorney spent two hours daily on intensive self-improvement efforts, spurred by the thoughts, "If I work very hard at my therapy, I can eliminate all of my negative feelings and moods; unless I am successful at doing this, I am a failure as a patient and as a person," "Unless I work extra-hard at my treatment, I will never recover and I'll always be depressed," "Unless I work extra-hard at my treatment, my therapist will not approve of me, and if I don't get my therapist's complete approval and endorsement, I will never get well and I'll always be miserable." In both these cases, work on the distortions underlying the excessive homework is indicated.

Therapists' difficulties

Therapists commonly have difficulties making homework assignments and following up on them. Strategies for understanding and managing these difficulties are outlined here.

DIFFICULTY MAKING HOMEWORK ASSIGNMENTS. Typical automatic thoughts reported by therapists who experience difficulty making homework assignments, and suggested responses, are provided here.

> **This patient isn't getting better, and this homework assignment won't help.**
> Here the therapist's hopelessness about the treatment translates into a passive treatment approach, which exacerbates the problem. If the patient is not doing well, more adaptive strategies include reviewing the formulation and treatment plan, consulting with a colleague, discussing the situation with the patient, or assigning *more* homework.

> **If I suggest a homework assignment, the patient will feel coerced and controlled.**
> More productive thoughts: "I'm working with the patient to *suggest* the assignment. I'm not coercing the patient — she's not *required* to do the homework. It is my responsibility to *recommend* homework I believe will be helpful. If the patient feels coerced and resentful, this is due to the *patient's* irrational thoughts, and we can work on them. I can tolerate it if she becomes angry at me. If this happened, it would provide a good opportunity to work on this problem."

> **If I suggest a homework assignment, the patient won't do it, and then I'll have a problem on my hands. It will mean I'm incompetent.**
> "I can't be sure the patient won't do the assignment; the only way to find out is to make the assignment. Even if the patient doesn't do the assignment, this does not mean I'm incompetent — it means the patient didn't do his assignment. If this happens, we can work together to find out why and to solve the problem."

DIFFICULTY FOLLOWING UP ON HOMEWORK ASSIGNMENTS. A very common therapeutic error, one probably closely related to noncompliance and other treatment difficulties, is the therapist's failure to follow up on the assignment. The therapist who makes a homework assignment but does not ask about it in the next session conveys to his patient that the homework was not important, that he doubts the patient did it anyway, that it is not worth his time to remember what the homework assignment was, that he has given up on the patient, or any of a variety of similar counter therapeutic messages. As a result, the patient may lose confidence in his therapist and the therapy, and is not likely to put much effort into any subsequent homework assignments.

Several types of automatic thoughts inhibit therapists from following up on homework assignments. Common ones include:

If I ask the patient about the homework, and she hasn't done it, she'll feel like a failure.

Although the patient's failure to do the assignment may make him *feel* like a failure, it does not make him a failure. However, the therapist who avoids making a homework assignment for this reason may have bought into the patient's irrational fear. If the patient is vulnerable to feeling like a failure, the therapist can work with the patient to understand this reaction and prevent it from occurring; this work can be quite therapeutic. However, avoiding homework in order to avoid this reaction in the patient is counter-therapeutic. If the patient perceives the avoidance, it may reinforce her fear, as she thinks, "My therapist is avoiding homework. She must think I can't do it." In addition, the therapist's avoiding of homework reinforces the therapist's irrational beliefs that the patient cannot do it and cannot cope with the inability to do it.

If I ask the patient about her homework, she'll feel coerced and controlled and punished by me.

Although the patient may have this reaction, it is irrational. The therapist is not being coercive, controlling or punishing. If the patient has this reaction to something that's a central part of her therapy, it would be better to work on this, rather than avoid it. This problem is probably related to her other problems too.

The therapist who is having difficulty following up on homework assignments might do well to look for these or other automatic thoughts and to develop some compelling responses to them. In addition, some behavior changes may be indicated.

The therapist might make a plan to review each patient's case before the session to make a note of the previous week's homework assignment, so he will have it in mind when the session begins. He might make a heading for homework at the top of the progress note for that session. In addition, a note at the bottom of the page will serve as a reminder to make another assignment at the end of the session.

CHAPTER 9

The therapeutic relationship

Until recently, the role of the therapeutic relationship in cognitive behavior therapy received relatively little attention. Traditionally, cognitive behavior therapists have viewed the technical interventions of the therapy (for example, eliciting and responding to distorted automatic thoughts or systematically exposing patients to items on a fear hierarchy) as the active ingredients of treatment. Relationship factors were minimized or ignored. This view contrasts with the widely held view (Frank, 1961; Strupp, 1973; Rogers, 1957; Truax & Carkhuff, 1967) that the relationship between patient and therapist is a central curative element in psychotherapy.

The behavior therapist's initial lack of interest in relationship factors contributed to a distorted perception of behavioral treatments as cold, mechanical, and manipulative. Recently, however, behavioral and cognitive therapists have begun to view relationship factors as an important aspect of treatment. That view is reflected here.

The chapter begins with a brief review of some of the empirical evidence relating the therapeutic relationship to outcome in cognitive behavior therapy. Following a brief description of an alternative view of the therapeutic relationship (the relationship serves as the basis for the technical interventions of the therapy), the use of the case formulation approach to the therapeutic relationship is described in detail and illustrated with clinical examples.

EMPIRICAL FINDINGS: THERAPEUTIC RELATIONSHIP AND OUTCOME

Many studies have shown that the patient-therapist relationship affects the outcome of cognitive and behavioral treatments. A few are described here; comprehensive reviews of this evidence are provided by DeVoge and Beck, 1978; Rachman and Wilson, 1980; Sweet, 1984; Wilson and Evans, 1977.

Morris and Suckerman (1974a, 1974b) showed that undergraduate snake phobics treated with systematic desensitization improved more if they were treated by a warm, rather than a cold, therapist. Crisp (1966) reported that the course of behavior therapy in 11 patients appeared to be related to the patient-therapist relationship. Alexander, Barton, Schiavo, and Parsons (1976) reported that therapists' relationship skills were highly predictive of outcome in a study of 21 families of delinquents treated with a systems-behavioral approach. Rabavilas, Boulougouris, and Perissaki (1979), in a retrospective study of patients treated with flooding, stated that "most variables concerning the therapist's style of conducting the treatment are significantly related to outcome" (p. 293). Ryan and Gizynski (1971), in another retrospective study, showed that, for 14 patients treated with behavior therapy, technical interventions were not related to outcome, but many aspects of the patient-therapist relationship were. Luborsky, McLellan, Woody, O'Brien, and Auerbach (1985) reported that the patient-therapist relationship, as rated early in treatment, was predictive of the outcome of treatment of male opiate dependent patients treated with cognitive behavior therapy, supportive-expressive therapy, or drug counseling. Ford (1978) showed that patients receiving assertiveness training who reported a positive perception of the therapeutic relationship were less likely to drop out of treatment and reported a more positive short-term (but not long-term) outcome than patients with a negative perception of the relationship.

Persons and Burns (1985) studied the contribution of the therapeutic relationship to mood change during sessions of cognitive therapy. Seventeen patients provided data during routine therapy sessions that were spent eliciting automatic thoughts and supplying rational responses to produce a mood change. Patients rated mood intensity and degree of belief in the automatic thoughts at the beginning and end of the session; they also completed (at the end of the session) a brief questionnaire assessing the quality of the therapeutic relationship. Results showed that both technical interventions (changes in automatic thoughts) and relationship factors made independent contributions to mood change during the session.

Thus, there is evidence to support the notion that a positive therapeutic relationship makes a significant contribution to the outcome of cognitive and behavioral treatments. Also relevant is the fact that investigators have had difficulty demonstrating the specific effects of technical interventions (cf. Zeiss, Lewinsohn, & Muñoz, 1979). This difficulty may be taken as indirect evidence of the contributions to outcome of "nonspecific" factors, including the patient–therapist relationship, that are common to all therapies (for another viewpoint, see Telch, 1981).

The next question is: are relationship factors the sole or central mechanism of change? Few studies have addressed this question directly. In one study of cognitive behavior therapy, Alexander et al. (1976) found that relationship skills alone were not sufficient to bring about therapeutic change. This is probably also what Beck means when he says a positive therapeutic relationship is "necessary but not sufficient" to successful therapy (Beck et al., 1979). A reasonable conclusion at this point appears to be that relationship factors affect outcome in an interactive or additive way with technical intervention factors (Beck et al., 1979; Sweet, 1984), but that relationship factors are not the sole mediator of therapeutic change. However, much more research in this area is needed.

If we accept the evidence that the therapeutic relationship is related to the outcome of treatment, the next question becomes: how can we use the relationship therapeutically?

THE RELATIONSHIP AS A BASIS FOR THE TECHNICAL INTERVENTIONS

A traditional behavioral view is that the therapist's task is to establish a comfortable, positive, trusting working relationship so that the other therapeutic work can go on. According to this view, a trusting relationship with the therapist allows the patient to use the technical interventions developed by cognitive behavior therapists to confront and work on difficult and painful problems.

This view has much to recommend it. For example, a hopeless and suicidal patient who has a strong, trusting relationship with the therapist is willing to put aside the idea of suicide and work actively to get better, and the patient's willingness to do this may be enhanced by the strong personal relationship with the therapist. In many other less dramatic situations, patients are willing to try something that doesn't make sense to them or is frightening to them because a therapist they trust recommends it — confronting phobic situations is a good example. A warm, trusting relationship is vital to many patients with severe fears and phobias who must confront those fears in order to overcome them. It makes good sense that patients make more progress when they have a good, warm, trusting relationship with their therapist than when they have a poor, ambivalent, untrusting, one.

How can the therapist create a good working relationship? Carl Rogers viewed empathy, genuineness, and nonpossessive warmth as key elements of a positive and helpful therapeutic relationship (1951), and these and similar dicta have been widely adopted (cf. Goldstein, 1975).

This view of the relationship, however, poses a problem.

Warmth, genuineness, and empathy do not guarantee smooth sailing. Warmth, for example, is not always therapeutic. DeVoge and Beck (1978) suggest that hostile or schizoid individuals may find warmth aversive and threatening. Beck et al. (1979) point out that depressed patients may have a negative response to warmth on the part of the therapist: " . . . the patient may think, 'I am undeserving of such caring,' or 'I am deceiving the therapist, because he appears to like me and I know I am worthless'" (p. 47).

Consider the case of an attorney who habitually comes late to therapy sessions and fails to pay for sessions on time. An increased dose of warmth, genuineness and empathy does not help the therapist or patient understand this behavior and is not likely to help the patient come on time. In fact, if his reason for coming late is a fear of becoming dependent on the therapist, warmth may even worsen the problem. Another difficulty is that, if the therapist redoubles his efforts to be warm and empathic but the patient's behavior doesn't change, the therapist may begin feeling resentful and angry ("I'm working extra-hard, and he can't even come on time"), and the therapeutic relationship may deteriorate.

THE CASE FORMULATION APPROACH

An alternative approach to the therapeutic relationship draws on the case formulation to help the therapist understand and work effectively with the patient's interactions with the therapist (Turkat & Brantley, 1981). The case formulation approach assumes that the patient's behavior with the therapist is similar to his behavior with others and that interactions with both the therapist and with others are driven by the patient's central underlying problem. Therefore, the case formulation can help the therapist and patient both understand the problem and work to correct it.

The case formulation model gives the therapist a powerful way of understanding and coping with difficulties in the therapeutic relationship — lateness, angry outbursts, passive resistance, and on and on — that can otherwise be baffling and frustrating. Sometimes it may even seem, especially to the traditionally trained behavior therapist, that unless the patient can change his behavior with the therapist, the treatment cannot go on. However, this way of understanding the situation places the patient in an untenable position — he has to solve his problems in order to be able to get some help with them.

In contrast, the case formulation approach views problems in the therapeutic relationship in the same light as all the others on the patient's problem list, and then uses the same strategies to understand and work on them.

In the case of the man who rescheduled and came late to sessions, it was easy to see that these problems occurred frequently outside the session as well. In fact, a chaotic, disorganized lifestyle was his chief presenting problem.

This young attorney was frequently late to work and to activities he scheduled with friends. He regularly bounced checks and failed to turn in time sheets to the office manager. He ignored the procedures for using computers and other special equipment at his office, simply taking what he needed and returning it at his convenience. The telephone and electricity in his apartment were turned off more than once due to his failure to pay the bills, and he was nearly evicted when, although he was not short of funds, he simply failed to pay rent when it was due. He ran out of gas because he ignored the gauge telling him the fuel tank was empty.

When asked how and why these things happened, he stated, "I just didn't have time to do it. Those things just didn't seem important at the time." He agreed that he behaved as though he believed, "The rules don't apply to me." This attitude seemed to have originated in his relationship with his mother, who was a demanding, rigid person who had insisted that the patient do what the *mother* needed him to do, not what the patient wanted to do or felt was in his best interest. As a result, if the patient's needs and priorities seemed to him to be at odds with a rule or expectation imposed by another, he simply said to himself, "I don't have time to follow that rule," and he ignored it.

This problem appeared in the therapy in the patient's lateness, and in other ways as well. He frequently bounced checks he wrote to the therapist, and he failed to pay at each session, as requested by the therapist. He never did homework and evaded any discussions of this issue by raising another topic that was more important to him.

To verify the supposition that the patient's difficulties in the relationship with the therapist were due to the resistance to following rules, whenever a problem arose the therapist reviewed with the patient the circumstances responsible for the problem. The theme, "It's not important to me — it's just something someone else is making me do," quickly arose. When this happened, the therapist explored with the patient the accuracy and potential consequences of this point of view. These types of discussions occurred over and over. Usually the patient was not even aware of the fact that he was thwarting the rules. One of the therapist's chief tasks was simply pointing this out to him and helping him think about what the consequences of his behavior might be.

Because the therapist made a point of raising difficulties in the patient-therapist relationship as soon as they arose, the patient learned that any failure on his part to stick to the rules of the therapy would lead to a discussion of the topic, and this encouraged him to play by the therapist's rules. After he bounced three checks, the therapist stated that if another check bounced, payment must be made in cash. Another check did bounce shortly thereafter; the patient then paid for his twice-weekly sessions in cash — a procedure that was quite inconvenient. This event provided an in vivo lesson about the negative consequences of the irrational belief. Over time, the patient's behavior in therapy sessions gradually improved, and his behavior outside sessions improved as well.

This example illustrates two points. First, it shows the way in which the patient's interactions with the therapist repeat interactions with others. Thus, careful observation of the patient's interactions with the therapist can shed valuable light on problems outside the session that may or may not be reported by the patient. The relationship with the therapist thereby serves as a powerful assessment tool and tool for understanding (cf. Goldfried & Davison, 1976).

Secondly, the example illustrates the way in which the therapeutic relationship can be used as an active tool for promoting change (Goldfried, 1985). The therapeutic work accomplished in the context of the therapeutic relationship can be particularly powerful because it is *in vivo* work, and usually highly emotionally charged (Goldfried, 1985; Safran & Greenberg, 1986).

A third point can be made as well. That is, the therapist's understanding of the patient's behavior with others and of the patient's central irrational belief can help the therapist predict the types of obstacles that might arise in the patient-therapist relationship. Each of these points is expanded upon below.

THE THERAPEUTIC RELATIONSHIP AS A ROUTE TO UNDERSTANDING

The patient's behavior in the therapy session can yield important clues about his behavior outside the session and about the nature of his underlying difficulties. For example, Beck (1983) has suggested that patients who have difficulty leaving the session on time are likely to have central problems of dependency. Patients who become angry with the therapist when the therapist does not accommodate the patient's every request are likely to have angry outbursts and disturbed interpersonal relationships outside the therapy as well. If the patient establishes a distant, ambivalent relationship with the therapist, his relationship with his long-term girlfriend probably also has these qualities.

By asking himself, "What kinds of difficulties and problems would a person who behaves this way be likely to have?" the therapist may be able to deduce problems the patient fails to report. Patients who are overly compliant or solicitous of the therapist are likely to have difficulties asserting themselves, may give too much of their time and energy to meeting others' needs, may be relatively unsuccessful themselves as a result, and may be resentful toward those they take care of and view as holding them back.

The therapist's feelings and behaviors in response to the patient can yield important information, both about the patient's effect on others and about the patient's underlying irrational beliefs. Imagine that one of your patients becomes furious when you cancel a therapy session because of a death in the family. You are likely to feel surprised and resentful. Awareness of these feelings is quite helpful in understanding how others who interact with the patient are likely to feel. The patient's reaction also indicates the presence of some powerful feelings of dependency and vulnerability, "I can't make it alone, without the people I'm counting on to help me, even for a few days," and perhaps some ideas about entitlement as well.

Of course, in order to be able to use his emotional reactions to understand the patient, the therapist must not be overwhelmed by them. In addition to participating in the relationship with the patient, the therapist must be in a position to observe the relationship as well. Without distance, the therapist risks becoming another player in the patient's drama.

Strategies for managing the therapist's emotional reactions to patients are provided in Chapter 11.

THE THERAPEUTIC RELATIONSHIP AS A TOOL FOR CHANGE

Setting up the relationship

The therapist's behavior toward the patient carries powerful nonverbal messages. The messages patients receive depend on the nature of their underlying vulnerabilities. Thus, if the therapist keeps the patient waiting, the patient may become anxious and angry, thinking, "My therapist doesn't care about me. He just wants to make money and do things at his convenience." Another patient who does not have this underlying vulnerability may respond to the lateness differently, thinking, particularly if it is an infrequent event, "It's impossible to be on time to everything. If the session is shorter, I can ask my therapist to reduce the fee."

The case formulation approach suggests that patients with different problems need different types of relationships with their therapists. Patients frightened of loss of autonomy need more interpersonal distance than those feeling unable to cope without support. Those who fear they will be rejected if they say the wrong thing need, at least at first, more structure and less open-ended time in the session than patients who feel the need to "just say what's on my mind." Those frightened of humiliation may be unable to tolerate any teasing or joking by the therapist, whereas others may find it a welcome relief. Warmth is important for most patients, but, as pointed out earlier, severely depressed patients, who feel worthless and unacceptable, may feel they are duping someone who seems to like and respect them.

This approach can be difficult to carry out, particularly at the very beginning of treatment, when the therapist must begin interacting with the patient in some way before she knows much about him. This difficulty may contribute to the fact that many patients drop out of therapy after only one session (Bloom, 1981), and it emphasizes the importance of obtaining a formulation as early as possible in the therapy process. Clues to the patient's problems can often be obtained with the first patient contact, including the telephone call to schedule the initial interview.

Ideally, the therapist can set up with the patient a relationship that contributes to the more explicit teaching and change that goes on via the technical interventions of the therapy. However, sometimes the interpersonal relationship aspects of the treatment and the explicit technical interactions of the therapy carry two different messages. This may happen because the therapist, without being aware of doing so and perhaps partly due to vulnerabilities of his own, becomes drawn into a mode of interacting with the patient that reinforces the patient's pathology. If this happens, the therapist can, by her behavior, reinforce a pathological set of beliefs that undermines the therapy.

For example, an extremely dependent patient, whose chief irrational idea was, "I can't survive on my own — I need tons of support and help from others, or I won't make it" appeared to work productively in therapy to overcome this idea. He was compliant in eliciting and responding to irrational thoughts on this topic, and did homework as requested. However, he also asked for lots of extra attention and support from the therapist. At times he asked her to call a cab to pick him up at her office, because he felt too weak to drive home or take public transportation, and he even felt too weak to make the telephone call. He frequently requested that his therapy sessions be rescheduled to accomodate his moods: "When I feel too bad, I can't get anything out of therapy." The therapist was warm and accommodating whenever possible.

This young man did not make good progress in therapy, and in fact became worse; after months of unsuccessful work, the therapy was declared a failure and ended. Reflection on this unsuccessful therapy suggested that, although the patient worked during therapy sessions on his irrational beliefs, the interpersonal interactions between the patient and therapist reinforced the patient's sense of himself as fragile and unable to cope independently.

Although this is a dramatic example of the way in which the therapist's interpersonal interactions with the patient can undermine the therapy, many more subtle examples could be given. For example, a young entrepreneur frequently telephoned his therapist a few minutes prior to the session to say, "I'm running really late today, and I don't have time to come to the office. I'd rather have the session on the phone." Although it was not inconvenient for the therapist to accommodate this request, it is an unusual request, a deviation from the norm, and therefore worth examining. A few minutes' discussion revealed that this behavior was part of a regular pattern in which the patient overcommitted himself and then failed to meet his commitments. He had lost several important clients and his business was failing as a result. When this became clear, the patient agreed to change his behavior with the therapist.

Another example is provided by the case of a young woman seeking treatment for depression and complaining of an unsatisfactory relationship with a drug-abusing boyfriend who was living with her although she wanted him to move out. She began treatment by asking the therapist to extend the session and to reduce the fee. Although the therapist agreed, the patient dropped out of treatment after one session. We might speculate that this patient's central irrational idea was something like, "If someone else needs me to do something, I should do it." When the therapist agreed to the patient's requests, the patient may have perceived that she would be unlikely to learn what she needed to learn from a therapist who seemed to have the same problem.

To protect against the unconscious reinforcement of pathological interaction patterns initiated by the patient, the therapist can set a clear, regular structure to the conduct of therapy sessions, and use the case formulation to guide decisions about special requests and exceptions. If a clear, regular structure is set up, the therapist is better prepared to notice deviance from this pattern and to use this information to learn about the various pushes and pulls being exerted by the patient. If the therapist regularly starts and ends sessions on time, rarely cancels or reschedules appointments, and so on, then irregularities that occur in these matters can be quite informative because they are likely to indicate something about the *patient's* way of operating—not the therapist's.

Managing difficulties

Difficulties in the therapeutic relationship are addressed in a nonpunitive, problem-solving way. Problems in the therapeutic relationship are viewed as analogous to the other problems on the patient's problem list, except that therapeutic relationship problems may have a higher priority than the other problems, because unless the relationship problems are solved, none of the others are likely to be solved—at least not by way of the therapy!

Work on the therapeutic relationship is also important because it is a powerful way of working on the psychological difficulties that are the basis of all the patient's problems.

Several examples of the case formulation approach to managing difficulties in the therapeutic relationship are provided below.

LATENESS. Cathy was a 30-year-old nurse who sought treatment for "stress on the job." One of her main problems was the idea, "If someone wants me to do something, I should do it. My needs don't count." As a result, she couldn't say no to anyone who made a request of her, she was constantly overburdened and behind schedule, and she felt overworked, underappreciated, and resentful.

This formulation tells the therapist (who is a professional woman about Cathy's age) that she can play an important therapeutic role by modeling assertiveness (particularly refusing requests, when appropriate) and professional behavior: starting on time, ending on time, not allowing interruptions to the therapy session, and so on.

In addition, direct work on this problem could be done when problems arose in the therapeutic relationship. Relationship issues arose because the patient's problem interfered with her treatment: Cathy was habitually late to therapy sessions, which were scheduled after work. She regularly found it necessary to stay late at the hospital to fulfill frequent last-minute requests from patients, physicians, and colleagues. Direct work on this problem was done when it occurred in the session, as in the following example.

PATIENT   I'm really sorry I'm late — just as I was about to walk out the door, Dr. Parks asked me to do an admission workup on his patient.

THERAPIST   Boy, that really put you in a spot.

PATIENT   Well, I didn't really have a choice. I had to do it.

THERAPIST   I know it must seem to you like you had to do it. Does this remind you of some of the other things we've worked on, where it seems to you that you have to do a lot of things for other people?

PATIENT   Yes.

THERAPIST   Well, shall we work on this one, or do you have something else pressing on your agenda?

PATIENT   No, I don't have anything else.

THERAPIST   OK, let's think about it. So you had the thought, "If Dr. Parks is asking me to do this, I have to do it."

PATIENT   Yes.

THERAPIST   And if you don't do it, what will happen?

PATIENT   She'll get angry.

THERAPIST   Who?

PATIENT   Dr. Parks.

THERAPIST   I see. But maybe you're also afraid that if you don't come on time, I'll get angry.

PATIENT   A little.

THERAPIST   So you have the idea, "I have to stay or Dr. P will get angry," and you have the idea, "I have to leave, or the other Dr. P. will get angry."

PATIENT   Yes, I guess that's about it!

THERAPIST   What's the way out?

PATIENT   I don't know. I stayed, and did the absolutely vital parts of the
  admission workup, then I raced over here!

THERAPIST   I see, so you did your best to please both of us.

PATIENT   Yes, I guess so.

THERAPIST   Is running around trying to please everyone else a strategy
  that usually works for you?

PATIENT   No, it doesn't.

THERAPIST   OK, let's try something else. Instead of focusing on what
  the Dr. P.'s want in this situation, let's focus on what you want.
  What is it that you want?

PATIENT   I want to leave on time.

THERAPIST   OK, and what's "on time."

PATIENT   5 p.m.

THERAPIST   OK, if what you want to do is leave at 5 p.m., how can you
  get it? You be Dr. Parks, and I'll be you.

PATIENT   Oh, Cathy, I have a new admission I need you to take care of.

THERAPIST   Oh, Dr. Parks, I'm very sorry, but I'm not going to be able
  to stay late tonight. I have an important appointment I can't
  change. I'll be happy to leave a message for Susan, so when she
  arrives in a few minutes she'll know to start with your patient.
  What's the patient's name? (Now the therapist steps out of role.)
  What do you think? Would that work?

PATIENT   It might.

THERAPIST   OK, now you try it. I'll be Dr. Parks, and you be you. . . .

ANGRY OUTBURSTS. Angry patients pose particularly difficult problems
for therapists. One reason is that the therapist can become anxious and
agitated, and these reactions are not particularly helpful in managing the
problem. Strategies for managing the therapist's discomfort in this situation are provided in Chapter 11.

A patient's angry reaction may indicate that the therapist has behaved
unreasonably in some way, and this possibility is always worth consider-
ing. In addition, the case formulation model suggests that the patient's
anger may reflect the patient's problems with others and her underlying
psychological difficulties. If so, then the therapist may be able to accomplish some important therapeutic work if she can address, in the session,
the patient's anger toward the therapist. This can be done using the usual
cognitive and behavioral strategies, as in this example.

A 46-year-old divorced woman, Mrs. C., sought treatment for recurrent depressive episodes. She had a new job as a saleswoman, but because
she was working on commission she had asked for and received an ad-

vance from her employer to see her through "until she got her feet on the ground." Her central problem appeared to be, "I deserve special treatment from others, because I was deprived as a child. Unless I get this special treatment, I won't survive." She suffered recurrent episodes of depression when she did not get the special treatment she believed she deserved, and when, as happened frequently, her relationships and financial status foundered.

After several weeks of therapy, the patient requested a fee reduction; she became very angry when the therapist was unwilling to accomodate her.

PATIENT   I feel really angry that you're not willing to reduce my fee. It's just not fair that because I can't afford it, I can't get the treatment I need!

THERAPIST   It sounds like you feel really angry about this.

PATIENT   I do!

THERAPIST   Would you like to work on it?

PATIENT   OK.

THERAPIST   Let's use the Thought Record. Now, the situation is that you've asked me for a fee reduction, and I'm unwilling to do it, and you feel angry. Now, what thoughts are you having that are making you so angry?

PATIENT   I get the thought, "All Jackie cares about is making money."

THERAPIST   OK, let's put that down. Any other thoughts?

PATIENT   "If she really cared about me, she would reduce the fee."

THERAPIST   (writing on the Thought Record) OK, other thoughts?

PATIENT   "If she doesn't really care about me, I won't get well."

With some work, the patient was able to volunteer a surprising number of responses to these ideas, including:

"Being a therapist is a business proposition like the job I do, and Jackie is entitled to expect to be paid"; "The fact that Jackie doesn't reduce my fee doesn't prove she doesn't care about me — I think she really does care"; Maybe she can't afford to reduce the fee more — she has bills to pay, too"; and "I don't really need a therapist who cares about me like a mother would care for a child — I just need a good professional therapist."

EXCESSIVE COMPLIANCE. Although the opportunity to do in vivo relationship work often arises most obviously when a conflict or problem arises in the therapeutic relationship, this kind of work can also be done when the patient is excessively compliant. The patient may insist on paying in advance for the therapy sessions for the month, may always agree to and carry out the homework assignments suggested by the therapist, without any suggestions of his own, or be excessively generous or accommodating in other ways. These types of behaviors may reflect irrational ideas like, "I must do what others expect of me or I'll be rejected," or "If I do exactly what the therapist asks of me, I'll be able to solve all of my problems."

PASSIVITY AND HELPLESSNESS. A 70-year-old retired plumber sought treatment for daily bouts of intense and prolonged anxiety. Whenever he found himself with unscheduled time or an unstructured situation that required a decision, he became intensely anxious and had the thought, "I don't know what to do." Leaving home to do an errand, for example, made him quite anxious because he feared he would be unable to negotiate the task of finding a parking place. These difficulties had their onset when Mr. Plumber retired after working for 30 years for a large firm in which he was given very little autonomy and was supervised carefully.

This man's central irrational idea appeared to be, "I'm helpless; I can't take care of myself; I can't make independent decisions about how to spend my time." He grew up in a wealthy family where servants were always available to take care of his daily needs; his wife was a strong, assertive type who managed many of his interactions with the outside world; at work, he had functioned well in situations in which little independent decision-making was required — when he was closely supervised or did routine work.

In therapy sessions, Mr. Plumber asked the therapist for assistance in planning his schedule, saying, "After I take my walk in the morning, I don't know what to do until lunch." The case formulation indicates that a response like, "Well, that would be a good time to work in the garden," is counter-therapeutic and reinforces the patient's sense that he cannot make this decision himself. Instead, the therapist would be better advised to teach the patient a strategy for solving this problem, show him how his fear of making a decision plays itself out in this situation, and challenge him to work to overcome the fear by making an independent decision.

This example illustrates a general question that arises when patients have very real and serious life difficulties. That is: how helpful and accommodating should the therapist be? The case formulation can be used as a guide to answering this question. The formulation helps the therapist judge whether the patient's problems and helplessness stem from his irrational beliefs or not, and what kind of help from the therapist would be most therapeutic. For example, one reason the therapist did

not give a fee reduction to the angry patient described above, who believed that others ought to take care of her, was because this accommoda-
tion would reinforce the patient's irrational and excessive expectations
from others.

REQUESTS TO COME MORE OR LESS FREQUENTLY. Patients frequently request
changes in the parameters of treatment. Sometimes these requests are
reasonable and unrelated to therapeutic issues. However, sometimes they
are not. The difference between these two situations can be difficult to
discern; when this happens, the case formulation can be an invaluable
guide.

To determine whether the patient's request is related to his psychological difficulties, the therapist can ask for more information about the
reasons for the request. The patient may state that she wants to come
more frequently because she's frightened that she's having a nervous
breakdown. If the patient's central irrational belief is the idea, "I'm weak
and vulnerable and unable to cope — I'll fall apart and be unable to function," the therapist can point out to the patient that her request is a
derivative of this irrational fear. Moreoever, the therapist's satisfying the
request might actually exacerbate the patient's fear, because it reinforces
the fear.

Thus, the therapist can get more information about the reasons for the
request, in order to answer the question, "Does this request relate to the
patient's irrational beliefs?" The answer to this question can be used to
guide the therapist's response, as in the following two examples.

An anxious, withdrawn young man had been working in therapy for
nearly a year, without much progress, to overcome his anxiety and depression. He was socially isolated, unemployed, and extremely passive.
The patient requested that instead of meeting weekly he telephone the
therapist to schedule a session when he had something he needed to work
on. He wished to do this because "coming to a session when I don't really
have anything to talk about is stressful for me." A glance at this young
man's problem list (his inactivity was a key problem) and at his irrational
beliefs helped the therapist understand his request and handle it therapeutically. This patient's key irrational belief was, "I'm a weak and vulnerable person, and I can tolerate only minimal amounts of stress." Given
this belief, the plan to come to therapy sessions only when needed appeared counter-therapeutic.

Another patient requested a decrease in the frequency of sessions after
about six months of weekly sessions. She had begun therapy with an
extensive problem list: she was clinically depressed, and so avoidant that

she neither worked nor went to school, but spent most of her time doing errands and taking care of her boyfriend and apartment. This pattern was more than a decade old.

At the six-month point in therapy, the patient stated that she would like to come every two weeks. At this point, the patient had overcome her clinical depression, but almost no work had been done on the other problems. The therapist understood the patient's request to decrease the frequency of therapy from two points of view. First, the patient was a champion avoider. Rather than take on the other difficulties on her problem list, she preferred to avoid them because of her fear, "I'm inadequate and I'll fail at whatever I try."

From the second point of view, the request to come less frequently was more difficult to evaluate. The patient's fear in the relationship arena was, "If I get involved, I'll have to do what the other person wants, and I'll get abused and taken advantage of." From the point of view of this irrational fear, the patient could best overcome this fear by sticking with the therapy and seeing that the therapist did not abuse her or take advantage of her. However, the patient might not see it this way. From her point of view, the therapist's adopting the position, "Do it weekly or not at all," would have confirmed the patient's belief that being in a relationship involved always doing what the other person wanted, and she might have responded to this requirement by dropping out of therapy.

In this case, the therapist pointed out the disadvantages of coming every other week, in terms very similar to those used here, but agreed to the arrangement if the patient really wanted it. The therapist continued to point out the patient's avoidance, and about three months later the patient stated that she wanted to resume her weekly sessions. Shortly thereafter, she took a part-time job for the first time in years.

Some months later, this patient again expressed the wish to come less frequently. She had recently begun attending college full-time, a big breakthrough for her. She came to the therapy session saying, "I am feeling good, and I have been for some time. I don't have much to talk about. I was thinking maybe I could stop coming so frequently."

THERAPIST   Well, let's talk about it. What do you think about it?
PATIENT   Well, I was thinking I would like to come less often, but then I
    had the thought, "If I stop coming, something bad might happen
    and I wouldn't be able to cope."

This irrational fear is a derivative of the patient's central fear of being inadequate and unable to cope. In view of this, and in view of the patient's good progress, the therapist encouraged the patient to follow through with her plan to come less frequently.

USING THE FORMULATION TO PREDICT DIFFICULTIES IN THE THERAPEUTIC RELATIONSHIP

The information the therapist has about the patient's relationships with others and about the patient's underlying irrational beliefs can help him predict the types of problems that are likely to arise in the therapeutic relationship. If the therapist can predict problems, he may be able to prevent them from occurring. If this is not possible, he can be prepared to handle problems effectively and therapeutically when they arise.

For example, a patient who believes, "I'm vulnerable and unable to cope on my own," is likely to become overly dependent on the therapist. She will be frightened and anxious about the therapist's vacation. If the therapist is aware of this, active work during therapy sessions before and after the vacation can focus directly on the patient's fears, experiments the patient can do to test out her fears of not coping, and so on.

The patient who reports that she is furious with everyone she is close to is likely to become furious at the therapist as well. If the therapist can point this out, indicate a willingness to work with the patient on the problem, and encourage the patient to try to do that rather than simply quit the therapy, he may be able to prevent a treatment failure.

If the patient's history and formulation reveal that she has the belief, "I must meet others' needs," it is likely that she will feel the need to please the therapist as well. Thus, if the therapist asks the patient to schedule a session during the next week, the patient may do so even though it is not convenient for her. She may cope later with this problem by "forgetting" the appointment, telephoning to leave a message to cancel, or even dropping out of therapy.

If the therapist is aware of this problem when he begins the discussion about scheduling, he can probe for it by saying, "Do you have the thought that you should schedule this appointment with me because I seem to want to do it, even though you might not want to?" The therapist can encourage the patient to schedule at *her* convenience, and he can talk with her about the best way to handle the situation if she changes her mind about the appointment after she leaves the office (telephone to cancel, giving 24 hours' notice, and asking the therapist to call her to reschedule).

Vacations and other disruptions, such as a maternity leave, can arouse many fears and negative reactions in patients, particularly overdependent and anxious ones. The case formulation can help the therapist predict these reactions. For example, a patient who is overdependent on the therapist, believing, "I can't survive on my own," is vulnerable to emotional upset upon learning that the therapist plans an absence. Before a vacation or other planned absence, the therapist can find it quite useful to review his cases to attempt to predict and plan for any difficulties his patients might have. A patient who is afraid of being abandoned or rejected by others may become anxious and depressed or even suicidal, as the therapist's vacation approaches. The therapist who anticipates this reaction will be in a much better position to handle it effectively than the therapist who is caught by surprise by a suicide gesture.

CHAPTER 10

Assessment and treatment of suicidality

This chapter focuses on case formulation and cognitive behavioral approaches to suicide, with a heavy clinical orientation and numerous examples; neither clinical nor research issues are treated exhaustively. A large body of research findings and more general clinical work has been provided by other workers; the interested reader might begin by consulting Beck, Resnick, and Lettieri (1986), Farberow (1974), Kreitman (1977), and Linehan (1981).

Many therapists avoid treating suicidal patients because working with them can be quite anxiety-provoking. The difficulty with this strategy is that a patient who is not suicidal when she begins treatment may become so later. For this reason, learning to work with suicidal behavior is more effective than avoiding it.

ASSESSMENT

Assessment of suicidality is often difficult because patients may be reluctant to provide information about suicidality, fearing (justifiably) that the therapist will pressure them to give up the suicide plan, force them to surrender the means of carrying it out, or insist on hospitalization. Or they may fear that the therapist will end the treatment, as some

176

therapists do when suicidality arises. For this reason, assessment must be done carefully. The therapist needs to be alert to the possibility that the patient is understating the problem or evading the therapist's questions.

Assessing current suicidality

The approach to assessing current suicidality described here involves (1) identifying the cognitions, moods, and behaviors making up the current problem, and (2) proposing a hypothesis about the psychological mechanisms underlying the problem. Each of these is discussed in turn. It is important to remember that assessment of current suicidality is not a one-time event; it must be repeated frequently.

Cognitions, behaviors, and moods

COGNITIONS. To begin the assessment of cognitions, the therapist can ask, "Are you having any thoughts about killing yourself or about dying?" If the patient reports suicidal thoughts, particularly if they are frequent or intense, additional information is needed. In particular, the therapist needs to find out whether there is any chance the patient will act on these thoughts. This question can be asked directly.

Many patients report that they are having suicidal thoughts but that they feel confident they will not act on these thoughts. Usually this statement can be trusted, but in certain cases — for example, if the patient has a history of impulsive behavior or drug and alcohol abuse — it cannot be trusted. In this case, the patient must be viewed as a serious suicide risk, and if the patient cannot be protected in any other way, hospitalization may be necessary.

If the patient states an intent to commit suicide, this statement must be taken seriously, because direct verbal statements of intent are associated with actual attempts (Kreitman, 1977; Pope, 1985). If a direct, clear intent is stated, the patient must be viewed as a serious suicidal risk, and hospitalization may be indicated.

Sometimes patients report cognitions that fall somewhere between the confidence that they will not act on suicidal thoughts and the clear intent to do so. A patient may report passive wishes to be dead, stating, for example, that he would feel relieved if he learned he had a diagnosis of terminal cancer. Active thoughts appear more dangerous than passive wishes to be dead, because active thoughts can lead to a plan to accomplish the goal. However, these two are not always clearly distinguished. For example, the patient may give an ambiguous statement of intent, saying he wishes he would get hit by a car or die in another type of accident. This type of statement may conceal a suicide plan.

Sometimes a patient states that she is confident she will not act on her suicidal thoughts, but this confidence is misplaced. For example, the patient with a history of several suicide attempts, all precipitated by binge drinking, states, when sober in the therapy session, that she knows she can control her suicidal thoughts and impulses; however, the situation may change dramatically when she is drunk. Even if suicide is not intended, drugs and alcohol can be more dangerous than patients realize and lead to an inadvertent suicide. Alcohol is a contributing factor in one third to one fourth of suicides (Pope, 1985).

Another extremely important cognitive aspect of suicidality, of course, is the presence of a plan. To assess this, the therapist can ask, "Have you planned a way of killing yourself?" If the answer is "yes," more information is needed. The more detailed and feasible the plan, the greater the risk it will be carried out. If the means of carrying out the plan are available, the risk is greater than if they are not. If the patient has a suicide plan but does not have the means to carry it out, it is important to find out how readily available the means are. For example, the therapist can ask, "If you decided to get (the gun, pills, whatever), how would you do it?" Obviously, the answers to all these questions bear directly on the therapist's choice of intervention strategies.

Other important cognitive components of suicidality include reasons to die and to live. If the patient has strong reasons to die, the therapist needs to know about these in order to intervene to alleviate the patient's suicidality. Common reasons to die include wishes to stop psychological pain or to ease the suffering of others perceived to be experiencing a hardship because of the patient's condition ("Everyone would be better off if I were dead").

Similarly, an understanding of the patient's reasons for living can suggest powerful therapeutic interventions. Even the process of assessing reasons for living can remind the patient of compelling factors that he or she may have forgotten. Or the therapist can work (see the Interventions section) to strengthen reasons to live that may be present but weak. Strengthening the patient's reasons to live is important for obvious reasons: patients who report strong reasons for living are probably less likely to kill themselves than patients who cannot report any reasons for living. It seems likely that the Catholic patient who believes it is a sin to kill herself is protected to some degree against doing so. Responsibilities to family often provide a powerful reason to live. A married person is less likely to commit suicide than an unmarried one, and the presence of children reduces the risk still further (Pope, 1985). It is important to remember that reasons for living can change (e.g., the patient's wife leaves him), or the patient can move from the idea, "I need to stay alive to take care of my family," to the idea, "I'm just a burden to them, and I should just kill myself."

BEHAVIORS. To assess behaviors, the therapist asks and observes whether the patient has begun carrying out any suicidal behavior, such as preparing or revising a will, giving away a pet, writing a suicide note, stockpiling pills, or obtaining ammunition for a gun. Detailed, comprehensive information is necessary here; it may be necessary to communicate with family members, the consulting psychiatrist, or other available sources, to be certain that complete information is available.

Sometimes patients volunteer information about suicidal behavior (e.g., writing a new will or drunk driving) without describing this behavior as suicidal; in this case, the therapist will need to make the connection.

MOOD. To assess mood, the therapist asks about severity of depression and other psychological discomfort and about hopelessness. Depressed patients hospitalized for medical problems have reported that psychological pain is much more painful than physical pain (Osmond, Mullaly & Bisbee, 1984), and many patients report that suicide is an attempt to escape this pain. For this reason, information about the severity of the patient's discomfort is quite important; patients will usually volunteer this information spontaneously.

Assessment of hopelessness is important because hopelessness has been shown to be a predictor of suicide (Minkoff, Bergman, Beck, & Beck, 1973). Many patients are willing to tolerate considerable discomfort if they have some hope that things will improve for them in the future, but if this hope is gone the patient may see no reason to live. The therapist can assess hopelessness by asking questions like, "Do you feel hopeless about the future?" or "Are there times when things look so bleak you don't feel you can go on?" and by listening carefully for spontaneous verbalizations that carry this message. Item 2 on the BDI also assesses hopelessness.

In addition to the interview assessment of suicide described here, scales developed by Beck and his colleagues to assess suicidal ideation (Beck, Kovacs, & Weissman, 1979) and suicidal intent (Beck, Schuyler, & Herman, 1979) have proven useful.

Underlying mechanisms

To obtain information about the mechanisms underlying suicidal behavior, three strategies are suggested here. First, careful attention to the
cognitive, behavioral, and mood components of the suicidal problem
often provides good clues to the nature of the underlying mechanisms.
Second, the mechanisms underlying the suicidal behavior are likely to be
the same mechanisms underlying the patient's other problems. Therefore,
examination of the case formulation is indicated. Third, a study of the
antecedents and consequences of suicidal behavior is likely to reveal important clues to the mechanisms driving the behavior.

COGNITIONS, BEHAVIORS, AND MOODS. Imagine a suicidal psychology
graduate student who is feeling depressed and suicidal because she was
not admitted to a graduate program in clinical psychology. Her automatic
thoughts include, "No matter how hard I try, I always fail," "I can't be a
psychologist if I get depressed," "I'm a loser," and "What's the point of
going on—I never succeed at what I want." This young woman's underlying irrational belief appears to be, "If I fail, I am a failure."

Another common pattern is the patient who was rejected by a lover or
friend, who feels suicidal and reports the thoughts, "Life is not worth
living without him," "I'll never be happy alone," "No one will ever want
me." This patient's automatic thoughts reflect a belief like, "Unless I'm
loved by someone I care about, life is not worth living." Assessment of
the patient's thoughts about her funeral can also provide helpful information about the interpersonal aspects of suicidality.

THE CASE FORMULATION. The central irrational belief underlying the patient's other problems probably also underlies suicidal behavior. For example, a patient with depression, anxiety, and family problems held the
irrational belief, "I can't do anything without help; I can't cope alone."
As a result of this belief, she was inactive, anxious, and depressed, and
family problems developed because she had a husband who worked full-
time, three children, and a large house, but felt unable to do the things
necessary to keep the household functioning. She also felt resentful toward others for not providing the help and support she felt she required.
Suicidal behavior was precipitated by situations in which she felt abandoned and unsupported by others: when her therapist cancelled an appointment because of illness, when her husband was out of town on a
business trip, when her internist refused to prescribe the medications she
felt she needed to sleep. At these times she made suicide attempts or

gestures both because she felt overwhelmed by demands she felt she could not meet and as a way of eliciting help and support from others.

ANTECEDENTS AND CONSEQUENCES. Information about antecedents and consequences is helpful in proposing a hypothesis about the underlying beliefs driving suicidal behavior. For example, in the case of the psychology graduate student described above, the fact that this young woman's depression was precipitated by her failure to gain admission to the schools she wanted to attend supports the hypothesis that her underlying vulnerability is a tendency to feel worthless if she is unsuccessful at accomplishing her goals.

Information about antecedents and consequences can be more directly helpful in planning interventions. For example, a patient reported that bouts of heavy drinking inevitably triggered impulses to commit suicide and occasionally even suicidal acts. Promoting sobriety is an obvious intervention.

ASSESSING PAST SUICIDAL BEHAVIOR

The greatest single predictor of suicidal behavior is past suicidal behavior (Linehan, 1981). Thus, assessment of past suicidal behavior is crucial in working with suicide-vulnerable patients. This information is best collected *before* a crisis occurs.

Past suicide attempts

First, and obviously, the therapist wants to know whether the patient has made a suicide attempt in the past. If so, more information is needed. It is important to find out about the antecedents and consequences of each attempt, the nature of the method used, the motive for the attempt, its lethality, and the reasons for its failure.

Information about the antecedents and consequences of suicidal behavior provides information about the types of situations that may precipitate or reinforce suicidal behavior in the future. For example, if Annie attempted suicide when her boyfriend left her, the therapist can use this information to offset the possibility of suicidal behavior if the current boyfriend leaves. Even better, the therapist may be able to work with Annie before a breakup occurs to develop some alternative coping strategies and prevent suicidal behavior altogether. Sometimes therapeutic work can focus on preventing situations that tend to precipitate suicidal behavior: e.g., drunken fights with the spouse or huge credit card bills.

Of course, situations in the world (e.g., breakups with boyfriends) do not elicit suicidal behavior. It's the *meaning* of these situations that produces the suicidal behavior. Therefore, many situations, including some that are quite dissimilar to the ones that elicited previous suicidal behavior, can precipitate suicidal behavior if the interpretation of those events is similar. For example, a young woman attempted suicide when she felt unable to break off with an alcoholic boyfriend. She had the thoughts, "I have a big problem. There's nothing I can do about it. Suicide is the only way out." Although the therapist might predict that if the patient later finds herself unable to break off another problematic relationship she may again feel suicidal, it is also important to be aware that other problems that overwhelm her and elicit this chain of thoughts may also precipitate suicidal behavior.

Information about the means used in the past attempt can help the therapist prevent future suicidal attempts, if the means can be removed from the patient's environment. Even if the means cannot be removed (e.g., the car), information about them prepares the therapist to ask questions about them if the patient becomes suicidal again.

It is useful to know whether the suicide attempts were a genuine attempt to die or were carried out for some other motive. A young woman described several suicide attempts she made as an adolescent, saying, "I didn't really want to die. I just really wanted things to be different." This statement suggests that teaching problem-solving methods is likely to reduce or eliminate this patient's suicidality (Linehan, Camper, Chiles, Strosahl, & Shearin, 1987).

Assessment of the lethality of the attempt and the reasons for its failure provides some information about whether the patient wished to die or if another motive was operating—an attempt to get a respite from pain, or an attempt to communicate something to another person, for example. If the attempt was planned in such a way that it was likely to be interrupted (e.g., a woman takes a dose of sleeping pills at the time her husband usually comes home from work), this may indicate that she was ambivalent about dying but wished to communicate something to her husband or to elicit help and support from him, for example. If so, the therapist may be able to work to prevent future suicidal behavior by teaching this woman more effective ways to obtain support from her husband. Of course, this won't be helpful if the woman really wanted to die, rather than to communicate something to her husband. Previous suicide attempts that involve highly lethal methods (e.g., hanging, jumping in front of a train, shooting) indicate a higher risk for future suicide than when less lethal (pills, wrist cutting) methods were used (Rosen, 1976).

Other past suicidal behavior

If the patient denies previous suicide attempts, additional questions about other types of suicidal behavior are necessary. Patients who have not made a suicide attempt may have experienced repeated bouts of suicidal thoughts and urges and may even have stockpiled some drugs or a weapon for future use. Unless the therapist asks about this sort of thing directly, it may slip by unnoticed.

For example, an anxious patient, not currently suicidal, had previously planned a suicide attempt with a gun. She stated that she was frightened by the fact that her husband kept guns in the house—she was frightened she'd kill herself in a bout of severe hopelessness and agitation, "even though most of the time, I don't really want to die." We agreed on a homework assignment that involved asking her husband to remove the guns from the house, and she was able to do this.

INTERVENTION

This section describes and illustrates several behavioral and cognitive interventions for suicide. These interventions draw directly on the behavioral and cognitive components of the problem described earlier and elicited in the assessment process. Before describing these behavioral and cognitive interventions, an introductory section describes the role of the case formulation—the hypothesis about the underlying mechanisms—in managing suicidal behavior.

ROLE OF THE CASE FORMULATION

In addition to its general guiding role, the case formulation is helpful in treating suicidality in two specific ways. First, it allows the therapist and patient to predict dangerous situations—situations that are likely to lead to suicidal ideation or behavior. Second, it allows the therapist to initiate work on the underlying mechanisms driving suicidal behavior even when the patient is not suicidal.

Predicting dangerous situations

The therapist can work backward from the case formulation to predict situations that may elicit suicidal behavior. The term "working backward" is used because originally the case formulation was developed by obtaining information about situations (antecedents and consequences) that were problematic for the patient (see Chapter 3). Once the formulation has been obtained, it can be used to predict other situations that may be particularly troubling to the patient. For example, a patient who has a history of suicidal behavior and who holds the irrational belief, "Unless I'm successful in my work, I'm worthless," may contemplate suicide if he experiences business reverses. Similarly, if a patient made a previous suicide attempt following a rejection by a lover, then a current rejection by a lover sets up a high-risk situation that may elicit another suicide attempt. If the therapist is aware of the danger of these situations, he can be prepared for suicidality before it arises and can work with the patient to develop alternative coping strategies even before suicidal urges arise.

In working with situations that precipitate suicidality, the therapist can work to change both the internal beliefs in the patient that make that situation dangerous and the situation itself. For example, a young secretary who believes, "Unless I'm loved, I'm worthless," and who recently broke up with her boyfriend may experience thoughts about suicide on Friday evenings after work and several drinks, when a long, empty weekend stretches ahead. A good first intervention in this case would involve getting a commitment from the patient not to drink, because alcohol and drugs are factors in large numbers of suicides. Next, the therapist could work with the patient to schedule some activities with others to occupy the weekend hours. Although of course the long-term goal is to bring about internal changes in the thoughts that cause those situations to be dangerous for the patient, in the short term controlling dangerous situations can be life-saving.

Another important environmental intervention might involve increasing the patient's social support. Suicide is more likely for a person living alone than for someone living with another person (Pope, 1985). This may be both because if the patient is living with someone else, this relationship may give him reasons to live, and because others can help the patient prevent and control dangerous situations that lead to suicide attempts. A spouse may call for help if she observes her husband is distraught, drinking heavily and taking pills, for example. In addition, many studies have shown that people who are socially isolated, belong to minority groups, are unmarried, and in other ways lack social support, are at greater risk for suicide and suicidal behavior (Kreitman, 1977; Linehan, 1981).

The therapist can work with the patient and his family or friends to arrange social contacts and supervision that may prevent a suicide attempt. More frequent contacts with the therapist, even daily sessions, can be helpful as well.

Working on suicide before it becomes a problem

The fact that the mechanisms underlying suicidal behavior are also expected to underlie many of the patient's other problems indicates that suicide prevention work can be done even before the patient becomes actively suicidal. Work on problems that do not involve suicidal behavior, but that do involve some of the same underlying mechanisms, would be expected to reduce suicidal behavior.

For example, the young woman who became suicidal when she had difficulty breaking off a relationship with her alcoholic boyfriend felt overwhelmed and helpless in response to many other types of situations as well. Whenever a serious problem arose, she thought, "I have a big problem. There's nothing I can do about it. Suicide is the only way out." Her response to small problems was similar, though it did not usually involve thoughts about suicide. For example, in therapy sessions when I asked her a question she couldn't immediately answer, she became paralyzed and passive because she had the thought, "I can't answer that question. I don't know what to say." She felt unable to attend social gatherings because of her thought, "I won't know what to say." She felt unable to cope with job interviews, because she had the thought, "I don't know what's expected of me—I can't do it." This type of problem recurred over and over. Nearly every therapy session involved active work to break through her passivity, and her belief, "I can't do it," and this work would be expected to address her problem with suicidality as well.

BEHAVIORAL INTERVENTIONS

Obtaining a no-suicide contract

This is a useful first intervention with nearly every suicidal patient. It is particularly important for patients who state an intent to commit suicide, saying, "I may act on my suicidal thoughts," or "I want very much to kill myself." These statements must be taken seriously, because direct verbal statements of intent are associated with actual attempts (Pope, 1985).

The therapist can ask the patient to give up his intent to commit suicide and make an agreement with the therapist not to engage in suicidal behavior. The process of obtaining this agreement is both an assessment tool and an intervention. If the patient agrees to make this commitment, this may indicate a less serious risk of suicidal behavior. In addition, the patient's agreement to the commitment works against the carrying out of an attempt.

In a few cases, the therapist may not be able to trust the patient to make a contract. Examples include patients with organic brain syndrome, those experiencing hallucinations commanding the patient to kill himself, and those with drug and alcohol problems. Obtaining an agreement not to commit suicide is useful in working with most other patients, including those who need hospitalization, because, unfortunately, hospitalization does not necessarily prevent a suicide attempt.

To obtain a commitment not to act on suicidal thoughts, the therapist can ask, "Are you willing to make a commitment to me not to make a suicide attempt?" As Linehan points out (1981), it is usually necessary to attach a time limit to the agreement, as suicidal patients are often unwilling to make a commitment for the indefinite future. The time limit might be as short as "between now and the next time we meet" or as long as three months, depending on the patient's willingness to make the commitment. Whatever the length, the therapist must be alert to the need for renewal when the limit expires, or the patient is likely to conclude that the commitment is meaningless, or even that the therapist does not care if the patient commits suicide. The agreement may be written or verbal. A written agreement, signed by the patient, has added weight. The therapist may wish to involve the patient's spouse or other family members in this discussion of the commitment as another way of adding to its meaning.

Patients sometimes complain that this commitment is meaningless, that if they decide to kill themselves a commitment to the therapist will not prevent them from doing so. Frequently this argument is offered by the patient who most resists making the commitment. I do not feel convinced by this complaint. If the commitment is so meaningless, why is the patient so reluctant to make it?

Nonetheless, some patients are reluctant to make the commitment, and active work is needed to overcome this reluctance:

THERAPIST   It sounds like you're thinking seriously about suicide.
PATIENT   Yes, I am.
THERAPIST   Well, let me ask you this. How would you describe your
    usual mood state these days?
PATIENT   Pretty bad.
THERAPIST   Yes, you've been feeling quite depressed, anxious, and
    hopeless for several weeks now. Would that be a fair statement?
PATIENT   Yes.

THERAPIST   And how rational is your thinking, would you say?

PATIENT   I probably have a lot of distortions in my thinking.

THERAPIST   Yes, I would agree with that. The cognitive therapy model we're using tells us that when your mood is negative, your thinking is distorted. Do you see where I'm going with this?

PATIENT   Almost. . . .

THERAPIST   Let me explain it. You've been feeling really bad these days. The cognitive therapy model tells us that when your mood is real negative, your thinking is real irrational. The point I'm driving at is that your decision to commit suicide is a product of that irrational thinking. Do you see what I mean?

PATIENT   I guess so.

THERAPIST   If the decision to commit suicide is the product of irrational thinking, what does that tell you?

PATIENT   (blank)

THERAPIST   What I'm suggesting is that it doesn't make sense to act on this decision. It doesn't make sense to make important life decisions when you're in a negative mood state and when your thinking is so irrational. Especially a decision like suicide, which is irrevocable. Do you follow what I'm saying?

PATIENT   Yes.

THERAPIST   Would you be willing to put aside your wish to commit suicide and work with me on feeling better and correcting your irrational thinking? Are you willing to do that?

PATIENT   I guess so, I'll try it for a while.

THERAPIST   Good. How long are you willing to try it? I'd like to get a commitment from you that you won't commit suicide during that period of time.

If, unlike this relatively compliant patient, the patient is unwilling to make a contract, saying, "But what if I never feel better?" the therapist can move to the cognitive interventions described below for working on hopelessness.

Intervening to interrupt the plan

Therapeutic work devoted to interrupting the suicide plan is indicated when the patient has a plan but has not started carrying it out. If the patient has begun to carry out the plan, e.g., to stockpile drugs, this indicates a dangerous degree of risk, and hospitalization may be indicated. Work to interrupt the patient's plan depends crucially on a good therapeutic relationship. If, for example, the patient reports that she has a plan but will not disclose what it is, then the therapist cannot work with her collaboratively to gain control over the suicide risk; again, hospitalization is indicated. If impulse control is impaired, especially if the situation is complicated by drug or alcohol abuse, work to interrupt the plan is probably not sufficient, and hospitalization may be indicated. Hospitalization may also be necessary if the risk seems great and the plan cannot practically be interrupted (e.g., the patient plans to jump off the bridge).

If the patient has a plan and the means to carry out the plan, the obvious intervention involves working with the patient to remove the means. The therapist can ask the patient to surrender the gun or pills to a member of the family, a friend, or to the therapist. An obvious means of committing suicide that is sometimes ignored by therapists is the antidepressant or other medications prescribed for the patient as part of his psychiatric care. These medications are frequently quite lethal. Suicidal patients should receive only small, nonlethal amounts of these medications at one time; the nonmedical therapist may need to consult with a physician to learn what the lethal doses of various medications are. Because of their lethality, antidepressant medications are contraindicated altogether for some suicidal patients.

Family members' participation in protecting a suicidal patient is often vital. Family members can be asked to protect the patient against suicide by locking medicines and other dangerous items away, by supervising the patient's medication-taking, and in dozens of other ways. If family members are not available, the therapist can work with the patient to find someone else to take on some of these roles or step in herself. A physician, for example, can prescribe only one week's dose of medication at a time.

A plan that is obviously beyond the reach of the patient (the patient who plans to shoot himself but does not own a gun and has no idea how to get one) is probably less dangerous than the patient who has the means to carry out his plan readily at hand. However, if the patient does not have the means to carry out his plan, this is by no means a guarantee, because plans can be changed, and alternative, readily available means can be used. A bottle of aspirin can serve. To be helpful here, the therapist can try not to fixate on only one plan. The therapist should make a point of remembering the means used in any previous suicide attempt, as these may very well be the means for a subsequent attempt.

Similarly, the fact that the means to carry out the plan are not now at hand does not mean that they cannot be readily obtained: "I'd just ask my brother to give back the gun of mine that he has." Interventions here might include asking for a commitment not to obtain the means or asking the patient to ask the brother to call the therapist and agree to hide the gun.

Old plan/new plan

As Linehan points out, suicidal individuals view suicidal behavior as a solution, not a problem (Linehan et al., 1987). That is, these individuals feel overwhelmed by depression and psychological pain that appears excruciating and never-ending or by external circumstances that appear unmanageable, and suicide appears to be the solution. To help the patient give up the plan to commit suicide, the therapist will need to help the patient generate and test alternative solutions to the problem at hand.

Sometimes the problem is simply psychological pain and distress. In this case, the therapist can work to suggest some other possible ways of handling this. The therapist can work with the patient to propose alternative ways of feeling better; often scheduling the patient's time from the time of the current therapy session until the next one is an important part of doing this. In the case of the patient who felt she needed to kill herself because she couldn't get rid of an alcoholic boyfriend, the therapist listed, with the patient, a set of strategies that might be useful in solving the problem and engaged the patient in an experiment to test them.

COGNITIVE INTERVENTIONS

Alleviating hopelessness

Therapeutic work to remove or reduce hopelessness can be quite powerful and have an important effect on suicidality. A few strategies are outlined here; others are described in Burns and Persons (1982). The therapist can begin with the usual strategy of asking for the evidence:

PATIENT   I'll never get better, so I might as well kill myself.

THERAPIST   So it seems to you that you'll never improve. What convinces you that you'll never improve? What's the evidence for this prediction?

PATIENT   Well, I've been in therapy for two weeks, and I'm still depressed.

THERAPIST   I see, so if you haven't improved in two weeks, this means you'll never improve — does that make logical sense to you?

PATIENT   No, I guess it doesn't.

THERAPIST   Well, let's imagine you work with me for three months — or even six months — and you don't improve. Would that mean that you'll never get better?

PATIENT   It might.

THERAPIST   I don't think so. Why not?

PATIENT   I don't know.

THERAPIST   Is it possible that cognitive therapy won't help you but that some other therapeutic approach might? Or that I can't help you but that some other therapist might?

PATIENT   I guess so.

THERAPIST   Good, I agree. And I want to point out one more thing to you. It sounds like the mind-set you have right now is, "If this therapy doesn't help me right away, I'm just going to kill myself."

PATIENT   (nods)

THERAPIST   OK, now does this mind-set help you get the most out of your therapy?

PATIENT   (blank)

THERAPIST   Do you see what I mean? Holding on to the option of suicide makes it difficult to make the kind of commitment to the therapy that would really give it a good chance of helping you.

Hopelessness is frequently the result of emotional reasoning:

PATIENT   What convinces me I'm hopeless is the way I *feel*.

THERAPIST   I see, that's what I thought. Do you see what's going on here? What kind of thinking error is that?

PATIENT   It's emotional reasoning.

THERAPIST   Right. Now let me ask you this. Did you ever feel hopeless before? Did you ever have the powerful feeling that things would never get better for you and that you should kill yourself?

PATIENT   Yes, I had it five years ago when I made a suicide attempt.

THERAPIST   Do you think emotional reasoning was going on then?

PATIENT   Yes, probably.

THERAPIST   And was your emotional reasoning correct? Was it true that things would never get better for you, and that you should commit suicide?

PATIENT   No, it wasn't. I've had four or so good years without depression.

THERAPIST   Right. So does that help you cope with the hopelessness now? Remember, the hopelessness is a *feeling*, not a fact. It's the way you're *feeling* about things, not a description of how things actually are.

Intervening with reasons to die

Many patients view suicide as a way of getting relief from physical or psychological pain. "I can't stand the pain, and I can't get relief any other way." This belief is irrational and maladaptive in several ways.

The statement "I can't stand the pain" is irrational; the patient often has been standing it for quite a long time. In addition, telling herself she can't stand it is unproductive because it makes it harder to tolerate. The thought, "I can't get relief any other way" is probably all-or-nothing thinking; other ways of getting relief have probably been discarded because they do not provide total, unending relief. In addition, as Linehan (1981) points out, there is no firm evidence that suicide does in fact provide the relief the patient seeks. Linehan likes to point out to patients, in an almost humorous way, that there is no evidence that the person's experience after death is more comfortable than when alive — in fact, many religions and cultures believe just the opposite — death leads to limbo, hell, eternal suffering, and so on. Does the patient have evidence that killing himself will remove the pain?

Some patients are motivated to kill themselves because they believe they are a burden to others: "I'm miserable, and I'm just making life miserable for others as well." The therapist can ask, "Who are you making life miserable for? Let's imagine you commit suicide? Will that person be happier?"

Sometimes patients wish to kill themselves in order to hurt another person. To elicit this wish, the therapist can ask, "What is your fantasy about how other people would react?" Often the patient's ideas are distorted; working to eliminate these distortions can eliminate the patient's wish to commit suicide. The therapist can also point out that the patient won't be around to experience any gratification or satisfaction about the pain the other person is feeling.

Patients frequently forget important negative consequences of their suicide. They fail to recognize or acknowledge the powerful emotional effect their suicide will have on others, particularly children and other family members. The therapist can help by pointing out and frequently reminding patients about these negative consequences.

The same is true for patients with homicidal impulses. A lawyer felt extremely angry at a former lover who had treated him badly, and experienced a powerful urge to beat the man up and seriously hurt him. I worked with the patient to examine reasons this might not be a good idea. I pointed out that the act he contemplated was illegal, and if he were prosecuted he might lose his right to practice law, but this fact was not meaningful to him. I also explored with him what his emotional responses to hurting this man were likely to be. He stated that at first he would feel "fantastic." I agreed this might be so, but suggested that, based on his history, he was likely to feel extremely remorseful and guilty shortly thereafter. After thinking about it, he agreed that this was true, and later reported that my pointing this out was an important deterrent to acting on his angry feelings.

Sometimes patients voice the idea, "I can't live without Jimmy." To address this, the therapist can ask, "How old were you when you met Jimmy? How did you manage before you met him? Should you have killed yourself then?" In addition, the therapist can work with the patient to explore specific things the patient feels she cannot do without her ex-husband: Can you go to the grocery store without him? Can you go to work without him? Can you see your other friends without him? This type of discussion frequently elicits ways in which Jimmy actually interfered with the patient's activities or enjoyment.

Sometimes suicidal behavior is motivated by the wish to hurt others: "He'll be sorry." "She'll see how unfairly she treated me." "She'll suffer now!" To address these types of ideas, the therapist can ask, "Let's imagine you do kill yourself. How will life change for that other person? How miserable will that person be? How long will it last? How will you be feeling while all this is going on?"

Intervening with reasons to live

Sometimes patients who report they have no reasons to live are experiencing such distortions in their thinking that they omit vitally important reasons, such as care of their children. The patient may have forgotten about this problem, or she may be disqualifying the positive, saying, "Oh, yeah, my children would be upset if I died, but I'm so much trouble to them that they'd be better off in the end." To handle this, the therapist can help the patient flesh out the ways in which she feels her children might be better off, to look for cognitive distortions in these thoughts and the ways she has not considered that her children might actually be worse off.

The therapist can work to expose reasons for living that the patient may have forgotten about. Religious convictions, either because of the beliefs themselves (suicide is a sin) or because they reflect membership in a strong group, can provide an important reason to live. The therapist can remind the patient of important activities and interests. Even when these are not apparently of life and death significance, they can play an important role when patients consider suicide. One patient recently stated, "I can't kill myself — I'm a birder, and I want to see 500 birds." If this patient began feeling suicidal, a discussion of his bird tally might be helpful.

CHAPTER 11

Cognitive therapy for the cognitive therapist

Therapists frequently feel uncomfortable in their work. A certain level of discomfort is normal and useful; in fact, as Basch (1980) points out, if the therapist does not experience any anxiety, he is probably not seeing challenging enough patients or setting high enough standards for his work. However, if the therapist is feeling extremely uncomfortable with certain patients or in certain situations, the case formulation model tells us that his behavior and thinking in those situations are probably dysfunctional. Thus, the therapist who feels guilty due to the automatic thought, "I'm not really helping this patient," may have difficulty making and following through with a homework assignment or may delay raising issues the patient doesn't want to discuss — a drinking problem, for example. The therapist's pattern of irrational thinking and behavioral difficulties may reflect his own underlying irrational beliefs. This therapist, for example, may have the idea, "Unless I'm extremely successful I am incompetent."

The approach to managing *patients'* problems described in this book involves (1) understanding the mood, cognitive, and behavioral problems that make up the overt difficulties and the irrational beliefs underlying the overt difficulties and (2) making cognitive and behavioral changes to address the problems at both levels. This chapter uses those same methods to understand and address several common problems *therapists* experience: suicidal patients, angry patients and therapists, mistakes, treatment failure, and ruminations.

SUICIDAL PATIENTS

Fear that a patient will attempt suicide is extremely distressing to the therapist. Work with a chronically suicidal patient can take a large emotional toll. In addition, it can interfere with effective performance in numerous ways. The frightened therapist is likely to avoid asking crucial questions that will expose a patient's suicide potential (and exacerbate the therapist's fear). As a result, he may fail to take the necessary steps to protect the patient from dangerous situations. The therapeutic relationship will deteriorate if the patient feels the need to conceal suicidal thinking and behavior. If the patient perceives the therapist's fear, the patient's fear may escalate as well, and he may feel hopeless about being helped.

Three types of cognitive distortions that can underlie excessive fear about suicide are examined here: irrational perceptions of control, believing one's competence is at stake, and fearing the patient's anger. The first two seem to have a basis in underlying fears of incompetence, whereas the last seems based in the therapist's fear of disapproval. The therapist can decrease his anxiety about suicide by working to resolve these cognitive distortions. Of course, the therapist can also decrease anxiety about suicide by improving his skills at managing this problem (see Chapter 10).

Irrational perceptions of control

Anxiety about a suicidal patient is often accompanied by thoughts like, "I'm not doing enough, I should be doing more for this patient." These thoughts may be accurate and adaptive. It is possible the therapist *should* be doing more. For example, if the therapist is feeling anxious about his work with a difficult patient, a consultation with a colleague is indicated. If the patient has a potent means of killing himself readily available, active intervention to remove it is needed. Schutz (1982) provides a checklist useful for determining whether all appropriate and necessary action has been taken.

Often, however, the therapist's perception that he should be doing more is based on an irrational thought along the lines, "It's my responsibility to make certain my patient doesn't commit suicide." This thought is irrational and distorted for at least two reasons: First, the therapist does not control the patient's behavior at all times. The therapist is not expected to have this degree of control. However, without it, the therapist cannot guarantee that his patient will not commit suicide. Imagine that you expect yourself to control the amount of water that flows over Niagara Falls and that failure to do so may result in loss of life. How do you feel? Quite anxious, I expect. To alleviate this anxiety, it is necessary to give up the expectation that you can control, or ought to control, the situation. In the case of the suicidal patient, this means accepting the fact that therapists do not control patients' behavior.

Second, the therapist is not responsible for his patient's behavior. The patient is responsible for her behavior. The therapist is responsible for his behavior; that is, he is responsible for doing his job to the best of his ability so that a suicide attempt does not occur. To emphasize that his responsibility is for his own behavior, the therapist can review the steps he has taken to prevent suicidal behavior to determine whether additional interventions are needed.

Another sign of taking excessive responsibilty for the patient's behavior is the statement, after a suicide, "It's my fault the patient is dead. If I had handled my vacation differently, the patient might be alive now." To address this type of thinking, we must acknowledge that the second part of this statement may indeed be true—if the therapist had handled his vacation differently, the patient might be alive. However, even if we grant this, does this mean it is the therapist's fault that the patient is dead? Notice the grandiosity inherent in this thinking. This statement ignores the fact that it was in fact the patient, not the therapist, who committed the actions leading to death. Remember, too, that the vacation issue is not the single factor responsible for the patient's death; the idea, intent, plan, behaviors, etc., also contribute.

The therapist who takes too much responsibility for his patient's behavior is likely to experience quite a lot of anxiety and to have difficulty handling suicidal behavior appropriately. The opposite problem, taking too little responsibility, can also cause difficulties. The therapist who believes, "I can't handle this situation," or "I can't do anything to change it," may experience too *little* anxiety given the actual danger of the situation. His passivity may convey to the patient, "My therapist doesn't really care whether I kill myself or not." This therapist may adopt a distant, inactive stance, failing to intervene in a life-threatening situation.

Believing one's competence is at stake

The therapist who is excessively anxious about the risk of suicide may be having the thought, "If the patient makes a suicide attempt, that will prove I am incompetent." However, this idea is irrational. If the patient makes a suicide attempt, this does not prove the therapist is incompetent. Why not? Ask yourself these questions: If one of your therapist friends had a patient who committed suicide, would you infer that your friend is an incompetent therapist? If the same difficult patient did not commit suicide, would this show that your friend is a competent therapist? Furthermore, if we really believe that a therapist whose patient commits suicide is incompetent, then state licensing boards ought to revoke the license of every therapist whose patient commits suicide. However, no state licensing boards operate in this way.

Even if we grant that one of the contributing factors (there are always more than one) in a completed suicide was a mistake by the therapist, does this mistake indicate that the therapist is incompetent? No, it does not. In fact, four patients in a recent NIMH-funded outcome study of cognitive therapy and pharmacotherapy for depression attempted suicide. Two succeeded; both ingested a fatal dose of their prescribed antidepressant medication (Hollon, DeRubeis, Evans, Wiemer, Garvey, Grove, & Tuason, 1988).

Closely related to concerns about competence are fears like, "If my patient kills herself, my name will be on the front pages of the newspaper. All my peers will lose respect for me. I'll lose my license. The patient's family will sue me, and I'll have to go to court." Again, the therapist concerned about these issues can review her handling of the case to be confident it follows current standards of practice. A consultation with a colleague or a lawyer may be helpful. If, after these steps, the fears persist, the therapist can use a Thought Record to examine and respond to the distortions in her thinking. It may be helpful to remember that the most common reason for malpractice suits against psychologists is a dispute about fees (Roswell, 1988).

Fearing the patient's anger

Patients are often reluctant to discuss suicide. They know that if they do, the therapist is likely to ask them to give up their suicide plan and to relinquish the means to carry it out they have so carefully hoarded. They may resent the therapist's attempt to take away what they perceive as the ultimate solution to their problems. Patients may lie or evade questions in order to avoid discussing suicide, necessitating careful confrontation by the therapist.

The therapist who cannot tolerate anger, disapproval, or rejection from her patient will have a great deal of difficulty managing these situations. She may have the automatic thoughts, "If I raise the topic of suicide, the patient will feel I don't trust him and may become angry with me," or "If I press the patient on this issue, he may become upset and leave therapy." As a result, the therapist may not be assertive enough in insisting that patients discuss the issue, asking patients to make changes to remove themselves from dangerous situations, or following through with hospitalization or other interventions the patient does not want. The therapist may allow herself to be placed in an untenable position. For example, she may be willing to work on an outpatient basis with a patient who owns a loaded gun and asserts firmly that if things get bad enough he plans to kill himself. Not surprisingly, this situation will generate an enormous amount of anxiety in the therapist. The therapist's willingness to tolerate this dangerous arrangement may be supported by the irrational thought, "I should be able to cope with this situation without undue anxiety."

Related problems may include the therapist's distorted notion of the patient's degree of control over his behavior ("The patient cannot surrender the gun") or a distorted notion of the patient's degree of fragility ("He won't be able to tolerate my asking him to do this"). These types of distortions may be due to the therapist's accepting the patient's own irrational beliefs about himself.

Alternative views require the therapist's understanding that she can tolerate the patient's anger or rejection, and the perception that it would be disappointing but not the end of the world or a sign that the therapist is incompetent if the patient left therapy. In addition, the therapist might consider adopting the view that her wish to work in a situation that allows her to function without excessive anxiety is valid and reasonable. If she does not assertively arrange for this, the patient will not receive good care.

Applying the case formulation method

When the therapist feels unduly anxious about suicide, the Thought Record can be used to examine and work on the automatic thoughts that generate the fear and to understand behavioral problems that may be occurring as well. The downward arrow technique (Chapter 7, p. 124) can be useful in identifying irrational underlying beliefs that might be responsible for these difficulties, and the strategies outlined earlier in the book can be used to work on behavioral and cognitive change.

Preparation for suicide

Coping with a suicide attempt poses a great challenge for the therapist. Because any therapist who spends a professional career working with depressed patients is likely to experience more than one suicide attempt, and probably a completed suicide, active work to prepare for these events *before* they happen is indicated. To do this, the therapist can work on derivatives of irrational beliefs that cause anxiety about suicide as they occur in other situations. For example, when a patient flunks out of college or abandons a marriage, the therapist may experience automatic thoughts like, "It's my fault. I should have anticipated those problems and worked on them. I'm really a lousy therapist. My patient is angry at me," and so on. When this happens, the therapist can sit down with a Thought Record and work to respond to those irrational ideas. In this way, the therapist can detect and change his irrational perceptions of control and responsibility. Such work may be helpful in alleviating anxiety about suicide even before a suicidal crisis occurs.

ANGRY PATIENTS AND THERAPISTS

This section addresses two problems: angry patients and angry therapists. Each can spark negative mood, dysfunctional behavior, and irrational thinking on the part of the therapist. These problems can form a positive feedback loop. For example, the therapist's irrational thinking can cause him to make concessions to the patient that later lead to resentment and anger; this resentment then precipitates inappropriate behavior, and so on.

Angry patients

Hostile, attacking, critical, demanding patients can arouse intense anxiety in the therapist due to the irrational automatic thoughts, "If the patient is angry at me, I must have done something wrong," or "If the patient is angry at me, he will leave therapy, and this will be awful." The first therapist is driven by a fear of being incompetent, and the second by a fear of rejection or disapproval. Of course, both types of thinking may occur.

These thoughts motivate the therapist to do everything possible to prevent the patient from becoming angry. The therapist may be overly helpful, avoid confronting the patient on difficult or uncomfortable issues, and "forget" to assign or follow up on homework. The therapist who fears rejection may behave more like a friend and less like a professional person. The therapist who fears being incompetent may be tentative, indecisive, and passive in his interventions in order to avoid making a mistake. He may experience the urge to fire the patient in order to protect his self-esteem and emotional equilibrium.

To address these difficulties, a written Thought Record (e.g., see Figure 11.1) can be helpful in pinpointing the irrational thinking and maladaptive behavior aroused in these situations and in generating alternatives. After working through the Thought Record the therapist will be in a much more powerful position to handle the situation assertively and therapeutically.

Angry therapists

Therapists feel angry at patients in many types of situations. For example:

- hostile, attacking patients like those described in the last section may elicit anger in the therapist, who has the thought, "I shouldn't have to put up with this!"
- a patient who complains in a whiny voice about how depressed and awful he feels, and who holds the therapist responsible for his failure to improve but consistently fails to follow the therapist's recommendations;
- a patient who covertly or overtly threatens suicide whenever the therapist says or does something he doesn't like;
- a patient who puts pressure on the therapist to falsify an insurance report or an application for disability;
- a patient who repeatedly criticizes the therapist's competence;
- a patient who lies about his drug or alcohol use or about suicidal behavior;
- a patient who is regularly late to sessions, or who frequently cancels or reschedules sessions.

Angry feelings toward patients can be quite distressing to the therapist and make it extremely difficult to function with a clear and level head. The therapist may find himself acting out his angry feelings by criticizing or attacking the patient or even by getting rid of the patient. Passive-aggressive behaviors, such as changing the patient's regular appointment time or coming late to the session may also interfere.

Several common irrational beliefs that lead to angry feelings toward patients, as well as some suggestions for managing them, are described here.

"THE PATIENT SHOULD NOT ACT THAT WAY." Often the therapist's angry feelings toward the patient stem from "shoulds" the therapist has for the patient: The patient "shouldn't lie about his drug use," "shouldn't attack me," "should do homework and take an active role in getting better," "shouldn't ask me to file a fraudulent disability report," "shouldn't threaten me with suicide." The most powerful way to dispel these shoulds is through a clear understanding of the origins of the patient's behavior— that is, an understanding of why the patient *should* be acting the way he is. This understanding usually comes from the case formulation.

For example, why does the patient put pressure on the therapist to file a fraudulent disability report? One possibility can be described meta-phorically. The patient may be experiencing a state of profound panic, perhaps feeling that he is drowning. He sees the therapist standing on dry land near a life preserver. In this situation, the patient expects the thera-pist to throw him the life preserver, even if the therapist must steal it from someone else. In fact, anyone in this situation would probably have the same expectation. Thus, the patient "should" expect the therapist to file a fraudulent disability report.

The therapist's "shoulds" may be fueled by the idea, "The patient shouldn't do this, because if he does, the therapy will be a failure, and if the therapy fails, this means I'm a bad therapist." There are several distor-tions in this statement. A key one is the therapist's *need* for the patient to behave in a certain way, or to get better. If the therapist needs the patient to get better in order to feel competent or for some other reason, she is vulnerable to feeling angry at the patient whenever his behavior seems to set up obstacles to a successful treatment. This attitude makes the thera-pist emotionally dependent on the patient. In addition, of course, it may block the patient's progress, as the patient may perceive that the therapist is pushing the patient to meet the *therapist's* needs and may passively resist this pushing.

It is easy to feel angry at a depressed, suicidal patient who covertly or overtly threatens suicide on a regular basis. To cope with the idea that the patient "shouldn't do this," the therapist can work to understand why he *does* do it. I recently began working with a severely depressed young man who frequently raised the issue of suicide apparently "out of the blue," often at the end of sessions. My formulation for this young man was that his central problem was a fear of being alone, isolated, and unsupported. The reports of suicidal ideation reflected this fear, as the patient used them to engage my attention and concern and to prolong the session.

As soon as I developed this hypothesis and felt I was beginning to understand this patient's behavior, I immediately felt less resentful about it. In fact, I began to look forward to sessions, so that I could test my hypothesis. I also felt less panicky, because whenever this particular pa-

Figure 11.1 Thought record for coping with an angry patient.

Date	Situation	Behavior(s)	Emotion(s)	Thoughts	Responses
11/30	I'm avoiding pointing out James' drinking problem	→	anxiety	1. If I focus on the drinking, James and his parents will get angry at me.	1. Yes, they probably will, but this is not a good reason to avoid the problem.
				2. They'll yell at me.	2. They may yell; if they do, I can ask them to stop.
				3. They'll criticize me.	3. They may criticize; this doesn't mean I've done anything wrong. I can listen to the criticism—maybe I'll learn something.
				4. I'll get flustered, and I won't know what to do.	4. I might get a little flustered. I can plan beforehand how I'll handle the situation.
				5. They'll drop out of treatment.	

6. This will mean I'm an incompetent therapist.

5. I'll try to raise the drinking in a way they can handle without dropping out of treatment; I may or may not be successful. James' dropping out would not be a disaster, especially if he's not willing to work on the drinking. He may need to encounter several therapists who tell him this before he's willing to accept it.

6. James' difficulty accepting his drinking problem has nothing to do with my competence. Denial is common in alcoholics and their families.

tient reported suicidal thoughts, I read them not as the statement, "I'm about to kill myself" (although of course this possibility remains and must be considered), but as, "I'm feeling needy and alone, and I need to make sure you're there for me."

This hypothesis also helped me intervene more effectively. It became clear that prolonging the session in response to suicidal ideation was not a good idea, as it reinforced the patient's belief that suicidal reports are an effective way to get attention and caring from others. Instead, I began to raise the issue of suicide at the beginning of the session and to help the patient make the translation from "I feel suicidal" to "I feel lonely and unable to cope."

"I'M WORKING HARD, AND THE PATIENT DOESN'T APPRECIATE IT." This thought contains an unspoken "should": "The patient should be appreciative," or "If I make extra efforts for the patient, he should be extremely grateful to me." To manage the angry feelings that result, the therapist can work to counter the "should" in this statement.

Another coping strategy involves behavior change. The thought, "I'm working hard and the patient doesn't appreciate it," comes from the therapist who is working too hard for the patient. She has overcommitted herself. She may have committed to see the patient at a time that was not convenient for her, perhaps due to some irrational belief about the patient's inability to make another arrangement, or to the irrational idea, "If I don't do this, I'm not doing enough, and the patient won't get well." Or she may have reduced the fee to a level she is unhappy with, or she may be spending many hours of consultation to talk about the patient's problems.

Young (1988) pointed out that many—if not most—therapists are vulnerable to overextending themselves to patients. In fact, the need to be helpful to others probably played a role in the therapist's career choice. However, the therapist who is dominated by the idea, "My own needs don't count; my job is to meet others' needs" will find herself feeling overburdened and resentful—and paradoxically, will be less helpful to her patients.

The best solution to this particular difficulty is not to have it in the first place. The therapist can avoid this type of resentment if she knows herself well enough to predict what types of situations are likely to cause her to feel resentful and if she is assertive enough to prevent them from occurring. As Linehan (1987) points out, the best therapist is not one who has no limitations; all therapists have limitations, and none can be all-giving. An effective therapist knows what her limitations are and abides by them.

Of course, prevention is not always possible, and the therapist may find herself in a situation that causes her to feel overburdened and resentful. In this case, she may need to make some behavioral changes to extricate herself from the situation. A Thought Record to address any irrational and maladaptive thoughts that make it difficult to do this may be helpful. In addition, assertive behavior will be necessary. The therapist can say, "I'm realizing that the commitment I made to see you on Thursdays at 8 is not working for me, and we'll need to make another arrangement." The therapist may even wish to initiate a frank discussion of the fact that this situation is causing her to feel overburdened and resentful. She can point out that she likes the patient and doesn't wish to feel irritated with her; to prevent this, a change in scheduling is needed. The therapist's experience, of course, probably matches the experience of significant others in the patient's life, and the therapist may be able to take advantage of this opportunity to point that out.

"I SHOULDN'T FEEL ANGRY AT A PATIENT." Paradoxically, this belief can lead to anger, because it can motivate the therapist to avoid recognizing early angry feelings and managing them before they get out of hand. This thought also causes the therapist to feel angry with himself, and it undermines his confidence.

If the therapist is aware of his angry feelings, especially early on before they become strong, he can manage them effectively and use this information to help the patient. This can be done in an explicit way: "I notice that when you say that, I feel a little irritated. I'm wondering if your husband also feels that way when you say that to him."

PERSONALIZATION. The therapist struggling with a difficult patient may have the thought, "The patient is doing these things on purpose to torture me." This perception is probably distorted. To emphasize this point, the therapist can search for an alternative explanation of the patient's behavior, using the case formulation as a guide.

Labeling can also fuel the therapist's anger. Therapists working over a long period of time with a difficult patient may find that they have developed a nickname for the patient or a way of talking to themselves about the patient that sums up—and strengthens—their angry feelings. "This week, to punish me, the patient did XYZ." Again, the therapist is in need of an alternate label for and explanation of the patient's behavior.

MISTAKES

All therapists make mistakes. Excessive anxiety about mistakes signals the presence of cognitive distortions. It can also lead to a tentative, indecisive, and passive intervention style, and probably reflects an irrational belief that error-free performance is required in order to be worthwhile, competent, or acceptable to others. It can also prevent the therapist from recognizing and working to correct mistakes when they do occur.

To work on this problem, the therapist can examine his thinking, his behavior, and his underlying irrational beliefs whenever he is preoccupied with the thought, "I made a mistake." This thought may simply be incorrect. Frequently interventions I thought were mistakes turned out to be quite helpful (and others I thought were brilliant flopped completely!). On one occasion a patient I had been treating with only moderate success for many weeks announced that she had accomplished a task that she had been procrastinating on for years; moreover, she viewed this breakthrough as a direct result of our previous session. This perception (and the breakthrough) came as a complete surprise to me, because I had been kicking myself for taking too passive a role during the session!

Another irrationality is the idea, "This mistake will hurt my patient or damage the therapy." Even mistakes that are undeniably mistakes can frequently be used in a therapeutic way. One day I became so involved in a writing project that I forgot about my 4 o'clock patient. About 15 minutes after the hour, she knocked on my door and found me knee-deep in piles of papers and books. My reaction was embarrassment and anxiety, fearing the patient would feel worthless because I had forgotten about her. I asked the patient her reaction; she responded, in a very genuine way, "Oh, I feel good about it, because it shows that you're not perfect — you're human too, and you make mistakes too!" My mistake brought us closer together and made my interventions more powerful, because it showed her that my view of the world might actually be relevant to her own imperfect way of operating.

I learned this lesson again when I realized 15 minutes before the hour that I had inadvertently scheduled two severely depressed patients for the same therapy hour. One, Mrs. A., was a new patient I knew was suicidal and had traveled about two hours for the therapy session, and whose tone on the telephone when she made her appointment was hostile and intimidating. The other, Mrs. B., was another severely depressed woman whom I was seeing for the second time. She, too, was a demanding and difficult patient. When I realized my mistake, I felt extremely anxious, fearing these two patients would view me as incompetent and uncaring, and that either or both might respond by becoming hysterical, enraged, and threatening suicide. I handled the situation by asking Mrs. B. to return later in the day, explaining that I had a suicidal emergency that needed immediate attention. She agreed gracefully, and when I later asked her reaction to the situation, she responded, "It made me feel good that you asked me to help—I felt that if I ever had an emergency, you would do what was necessary to be available for me."

The view that a particular mistake will seriously damage the therapy seems to involve inflated estimates of the therapist's power and the patient's fragility. Actually, the therapist's real fear may be that he is not very competent, and therefore cannot afford to make even the usual number of mistakes. To uncover and work on this irrational belief, the therapist can use the downward arrow technique described earlier (p. 205 above).

The therapist's irrational concern may lead to the urge to telephone patients between sessions to rectify "mistakes." With rare exceptions, I find this is not a good idea, for several reasons:

1. Things I think are mistakes frequently turn out not to be.

2. Attempts to apologize or fix up the mistake are likely to be off the mark unless I know what the patient's reaction has been, and this is best done during the therapy hour when there is time to discuss the situation.

3. My need to fix up the mistake or apologize probably comes from my own anxiety, and there is no need for me to impose on my patient in order to solve my problem.

4. Tolerating anxiety and waiting to see what happened is good role modeling for the patient.

5. Telephoning to fix up a mistake reinforces ideas like, "I shouldn't make mistakes in sessions," "If I make a mistake, something terrible might happen unless I fix it up right away," "I can't tolerate the anxiety of possibly having made a mistake," and so on. I find that once I begin to yield to this sort of thinking, my confidence begins eroding and my performance deteriorates. Tolerating the anxiety, viewing my behavior as adequate and acceptable rather than defective and incompetent, reinforces my sense of competence.

6. Telephoning the patient to determine if he got very upset when I said, "Well, maybe John wasn't good for you," involves an irrational, grandiose perception of my power and influence over the patient's life and an exaggerated perception of the patient's fragility.

7. The patient may accept my view of his vulnerability and fragility, and this would be countertherapeutic.

8. The patient may expect me to be available in the future for telephone consultations about trivial matters.

Other thoughts helpful for coping with mistakes include: I do not expect error-free performance, and neither do my patients; I often learn much more from mistakes than from successes; if I'm making mistakes it means I'm seeing challenging patients and working in a way that stretches and improves my skills.

TREATMENT FAILURE

Treatment failure rarely appears in the literature (for one exception, see Foa and Emmelkamp, 1983). However, every therapist has had the experience of working with patients who do not respond to treatment or who get worse. This situation can be extremely uncomfortable for both therapist and patient. Many patients undoubtedly manage (or at least eliminate) this difficulty by dropping out of treatment. For therapists, the solution is not so simple, although they may be tempted to behave inappropriately as well. The therapist may avoid evaluating the progress of the therapy, thereby prolonging indefinitely an unsuccessful treatment, or abruptly refer the patient to another therapist without discussing the reasons for this with the patient.

Accurate assessment of failure

Strategies for coping with treatment failure are offered here. First, however, comes a discussion of whether or not the treatment has in fact failed. Both therapist and patient perceptions of failure may be distorted. Either may be too quick or too slow to perceive failure.

Some patients, particularly depressed ones, are biased toward perceiving all their efforts, including therapy, as useless and unsuccessful; these patients may be too quick to declare the therapy a failure. Others, particularly those who are excessively dependent on the therapist, may be unwilling to acknowledge lack of progress in therapy. Unwary therapists may "buy into" these distorted perceptions.

Therapists may bring distorted perceptions of their own to the therapeutic interaction. They may perceive failure as a sign that they are incompetent, or a patient's leaving treatment as a personal rejection. They may feel so anxious about failure that they fail to perceive it when it occurs, or they may overreact and view any setback or plateau as a sign that treatment has failed. To facilitate an accurate perception of the success or failure of treatment, any or all of the following strategies might be helpful:

- careful, objective specification of goals of therapy;
- periodic consultations with colleagues to review cases;
- regular reviews of progress (ideally, a collaborative review by both patient and therapist);
- elimination of cognitive distortions by both patient and therapist.

Several cognitive distortions can prevent the therapist from recognizing and coping effectively with an unsuccessful treatment.

Common cognitive distortions

"IF THE THERAPY FAILS, THIS MEANS I'M AN INCOMPETENT THERAPIST." The fact that little is written about treatment failure reinforces the notion that treatment failures "shouldn't" occur, and if they do, "I (the therapist) must be doing something wrong." It is of course possible that the therapist *has* made errors. When treatment is not going well, the therapist has a responsibility to reevaluate the formulation and treatment plan. Consultations with colleagues can be helpful in protecting the therapist from errors or blind spots.

However, recurrent ideas along the lines, "If the patient is not doing well, this proves I have done something wrong" and "This proves I'm an incompetent therapist" are likely to be distorted. First, on the face of it, the fact that the patient is not doing well doesn't prove that the treatment is inadequate or that the therapist is incompetent; there are many possible reasons for a treatment failure. Second, the therapist's labeling herself as incompetent is likely to cause her to feel anxious and guilty. Although a certain amount of anxiety can enhance performance and may lead the therapist to work harder in a productive way (e.g., doing some reading or consulting with colleagues), when these feelings are excessive, they impair the therapist's ability to function productively.

Third, if the therapist jumps to the conclusion that a treatment failure means that she is incompetent, she imposes a premature closure on the issue that prevents her from obtaining a balanced, realistic perception of the failure and its causes. Instead of labeling herself incompetent, she might take a more productive approach to the problem by asking questions like, "Why is this treatment not going well? Am I making any mistakes? What are they? How can I correct them? Are there any other reasons the treatment is not going well?" Finally, the belief, "If I fail with this patient it means I'm incompetent," may prevent the therapist from seeing and acknowledging failure when it occurs. As a result, the therapist may continue an unsuccessful treatment far beyond the point where termination will be for both patient and therapist anything other than a demoralizing, painful, and bitter event.

"I CAN'T AFFORD TO END TREATMENT WITH THIS PATIENT." The therapist may feel that he cannot afford, either financially or emotionally, to acknowledge that a treatment failure has occurred and to terminate the treatment. In this situation, the therapist is overdependent on the patient. This overdependence may be reflected in seductive irrational thoughts such as, "If we just keep trying, we may get somewhere," and "I'm doing as well as any other therapist could do." Several cognitive therapists (including Simons, et al., 1984 and Teasdale, 1985) have reported that successful treatments usually produce some benefits early.

The therapist's overdependence on his patient can be financial or emotional, as in the case when the therapist needs the patient to get well so that he (the therapist) can feel competent. In the extreme case, the therapist's need to use the patient to fulfill the therapist's needs may lead to sexual or other types of exploitation.

"MY ENDING THE TREATMENT BECAUSE IT IS UNSUCCESSFUL WILL REINFORCE THE PATIENT'S BELIEF THAT HE IS A FAILURE." To address the distortions in this thinking, it is important first to acknowledge the reality (if it is a reality) that the treatment has not been a success. Next, given this reality, the therapist can ask herself, is it to the patient's advantage to avoid facing this reality? The answer to this seems clearly to be no. If the therapy fails, this does not prove that the patient is destined to fail at everything he tries. In fact, the therapist who avoids acknowledging the fact that the treatment has failed may have "bought into" the patient's idea that this failure cannot be accepted because it means the patient is a failure and will never succeed at anything. To help the patient learn that failure at one thing does not mean failure at all things, the therapist can model and be willing to accept failure when it does occur.

"THE PATIENT WON'T BE ABLE TO COPE WITH THIS FAILURE." Again, the therapist who persists with an unsuccessful treatment in response to this distorted thought has probably accepted the patient's distorted view of his fragility and helplessness, and reinforces this helplessness by supporting the patient's denial and refusal to cope with the realities of life.

A related distortion is the idea, "I can't broach the possibility of terminating the treatment because the patient will precipitate a crisis, and may even make a suicide attempt." The therapist who prolongs a treatment for this reason can be sure she is making a mistake.

"IF I TERMINATE THE TREATMENT, THE PATIENT WILL FEEL REJECTED OR ABANDONED." This thought may very well be true. However, it is not a good reason to continue an ineffective treatment. The therapist's job is to help the patient work to correct the distortions in his thinking, not to manipulate reality so that the patient doesn't have to confront his distortions.

"FAILURE IS UNACCEPTABLE." The therapist who persists with an unsuccessful treatment is modeling this idea. Much more helpful for most patients would be an active modeling of the idea, "Failure can happen. However, it can be accepted without a loss of self-esteem, and can lead to progress in a forward direction." The therapist who thinks about treatment failure in this way can model acceptance of and productive coping with failure (generating lists of possible reasons for the failure, and lists of alternative possible solutions, etc.). This exercise is likely to be more therapeutic than continuing an unsuccessful treatment because neither therapist nor patient can face reality.

"IF I GIVE UP ON THE THERAPY, THIS WILL MEAN TO THE PATIENT THAT I DON'T REALLY CARE ABOUT HIM." Again, the therapist's expectation that the patient will feel rejected and uncared-for may be true (although mind-reading is involved here, and it may not turn out that way). Even if it is true, this perception is distorted, and the therapist's job is to teach this. This anticipated reaction on the part of the patient may mean that careful preparation is required in order to handle a termination in a therapeutic way. However, it does not mean that a termination must be avoided.

Notice also the therapist's description of herself as "giving up." This phrase implies that the therapist blames herself for not working hard enough: "I should be willing to persist with this patient for a long time; if I don't this means I'm lazy." To answer this thought, the therapist might ask herself for evidence that she is a lazy therapist and tends to give up on her patients prematurely. Perhaps the therapist who prolongs an unsuccessful treatment might be described as "lazy" in the sense that he's avoiding the hard work involved in confronting the issue.

"IF I TERMINATE THE TREATMENT, THIS WILL MEAN TO THE PATIENT THAT I THINK HE'S A HOPELESS CASE." This idea contains the implicit assumption, "If I can't treat this patient successfully, no one can." This assumption can also be present explicitly, in the form, "Although I'm not helping this patient, I don't think anyone else could do any better, so I might as well continue." This view involves an excessively grandiose view of the therapist's skills.

In general, to cope with anxiety about treatment failure, the therapist works for a nondistorted, clear perception of the degree of success or failure of the therapy, and reminds himself that no therapist is successful with all patients. Reasons for failure may lie in the patient, the therapist, the patient-therapist match, or the nature of the treatment. If the therapist can view a treatment failure in a matter-of-fact way, it can be accepted and discussed without undue anxiety, guilt, or loss of self-esteem.

RUMINATIONS

The therapist struggling with any of the problems described above — a suicidal patient, angry feelings, or a treatment that is not going well — can find himself more preoccupied with the problem than he would like. Intrusive, repetitive ruminations can consume large amounts of the therapist's energy and time. The therapist caught in this cycle is probably feeling inadequate and incompetent. A Thought Record can be helpful in uncovering the sources of the therapist's anxiety.

In addition, the therapist is probably having some version of the covert thought, "Ruminating will help." To address this thought, the therapist can list the advantages and disadvantages (Burns, 1980) of ruminating about this particular patient. Under the "advantages" column, the therapist can ask herself, "Has the ruminating led to any productive treatment ideas?" In my own experience, the answer to this question is usually "No." Under the "disadvantages" column, the therapist may find a surprising number of items, as I did when I did this exercise for myself:

1. Ruminating impairs my ability to help this patient. When I notice how many hours I've spent ruminating and working on this case, I get the thought, "I really must be doing something wrong here; otherwise, I wouldn't need to keep working so hard." This idea saps my confidence and makes me tentative in the sessions.
2. I feel resentful at the patient for "making" me work so hard and for "making" me so uncomfortable.
3. Ruminating feels awful and spoils my time at home with my family.
4. Ruminating reinforces this particular patient's pathology. Ruminating reinforces my own idea that I'm not doing enough for the patient, the idea that I need to think of something more and different, to make a superhuman effort, or this patient won't get well. These are irrational, distorted, thoughts. In fact, they are the *patient's* irrational, distorted thoughts ("my therapist needs to do something significant so I

can get well"). This problem is in fact this patient's central problem, and if I buy into this idea, I am actually making it more difficult to get well.

After completing this exercise, I was ready to severely limit my ruminating. I decided to limit my treatment planning for this patient to 15 minutes before each therapy hour (I had already spent many hours consulting with colleagues on this case). When I was able to do this, I found that my anxiety decreased considerably and my functioning improved.

The general strategy of stimulus control can be used to control the garden-variety stresses and strains that therapists experience on a daily basis. To prevent the strains of clinical work from intruding at home and during evening and weekend hours, I make it a point to carry out patient business only in my office, never at home. This strategy is recommended for confidentiality reasons as well.

CONCLUSION

The theme of this chapter is the notion that if the therapist is experiencing a lot of discomfort in his work, his functioning and thinking are probably dysfunctional as well. The negative mood and dysfunctional behavior and cognitions probably reflect underlying vulnerabilities that are responsible both for the difficulty at hand and for other difficulties the therapist experiences, both inside and outside of therapy sessions. The strategies outlined in this book can be used to address these difficulties. Thus, the therapist can take advantage of discomfort in his work to learn something about his own cognitive vulnerabilities and to do some work to prevent them from interfering with his work with patients.

References

Alexander, J. F., Barton, C., Schiavo, R. S., & Parsons, B. V. (1976). Systems-behavioral intervention with families of delinquents: Therapist characteristics, family behavior, and outcome. *Journal of Consulting and Clinical Psychology, 44,* 656–664.

Arieti, S., & Bemporad, J. (1980). The psychological organization of depression. *American Journal of Psychiatry, 136,* 1365 1369.

Barlow, D. H., & Waddell, M. T. (1985). Agoraphobia. In D. H. Barlow (Ed.) *Clinical handbook of psychological disorders: A step-by-step treatment manual* (pp. 1–68). New York: Guilford

Basch, M. F. (1980). *Doing psychotherapy.* New York: Basic Books.

Beck, A. T. (1972). *Depression: Causes and treatment.* Philadelphia: University of Pennsylvania Press.

Beck, A. T. (1976). *Cognitive therapy and the emotional disorders.* New York: International Universities Press.

Beck, A. T. (1983). Cognitive therapy of depression: New perspectives. In P. J. Clayton & J. E. Barrett (Eds.) *Treatment of depression: Old controversies and new approaches.* New York: Raven Press.

Beck, A. T., Brown, G., Steer, R. A., Eidelson, J. I., & Riskind, J. H. (1987). Differentiating anxiety and depression: A test of the cognitive content-specificity hypothesis. *Journal of Abnormal Psychology, 96,* 179–183.

Beck, A. T., Emery, G., & Greenberg, R. L. (1985). *Anxiety disorders and phobias: A cognitive perspective.* New York: Basic Books.

Beck, A. T., Kovacs, M., & Weissman, A. (1979). Assessment of suicidal ideation: The Scale for Suicide Ideation. *Journal of Consulting and Clinical Psychology, 47*, 343–352.

Beck, A. T., Resnick, H. L. P., & Lettieri, D. J. (Eds.) (1974). *The prediction of suicide*. Bowie, MD.: Charles Press.

Beck, A. T., Rush, A. J., Shaw, B. F., & Emery, G. (1979). *Cognitive therapy of depression*. New York: Guilford.

Beck, A. T., Schuyler, D., & Herman, I. (1974). Development of suicidal intent scales. In A. T. Beck, H. L. P. Resnick, & D. J. Lettieri (Eds.) *The prediction of suicide* (pp. 45–56). Bowie, MD: Charles Press.

Bernstein, D. A., & Borkovec, T. D. (1973). *Progressive relaxation training: A manual for the helping professions*. Champaign, IL: Research Press.

Blaney, P. H. (1977). Contemporary theories of depression: Critique and comparison. *Journal of Abnormal Psychology, 86*, 203–223.

Blatt, S. (1974). Levels of object representation in anaclitic and introjective depression. *The Psychoanalytic Study of the Child, 29,* 107–157.

Bloom, B. L. (1981). Focused single-session therapy: Initial development and evaluation. In S. Budman (Ed.), *Forms of brief therapy*. New York: Guilford.

Boice, R. (1982). Increasing the writing productivity of "blocked" academicians. *Behaviour Research and Therapy, 20*, 197–207.

Boorse, C. (1976). What a theory of mental health should be. *Journal for the Theory of Social Behavior, 6*, 61–84.

Bornstein, P. H., Hamilton, S. B., & Bornstein, M. T. (1986). Self-monitoring procedures. In A. R. Ciminero, K. S. Calhoun, & H. E. Adams, (Eds.) *Handbook of behavioral assessment* (2nd ed.) (pp. 176–222). New York: Wiley.

Bower, G. H. (1981). Mood and memory. *American Psychologist, 36*, 129–148.

Burns, D. D. (1980). *Feeling good: The new mood therapy*. New York: William Morrow.

Burns, D. D. (1985). *Intimate connections*. New York: New American Library.

Burns, D. D., Adams, R. L., & Anastopoulos, A. D. (1985). The role of self-help assignments in the treatment of depression. In E. E. Beckham & W. R. Leber, Eds., *Handbook for the diagnosis, treatment and research of depression*. Homewood, IL: Dorsey Press.

Burns, D. D. & Persons, J. B. (1982). Hope and hopelessness: A cognitive approach. In L. E. Abt & I. R. Stuart (Eds.) *The newer therapies: A workbook*. New York: Van Nostrand Reinhold.

Cannon, D. S., & Baker, T. B. (1981). Emetic and electric shock alcohol aversion therapy: Assessment of conditioning. *Journal of Consulting and Clinical Psychology, 49*, 20–33.

Carson, T. P. (1986). Assessment of depression. In A. R. Ciminero, K. S. Calhoun, & H. E. Adams (Eds.) *Handbook of behavioral assessment* (2nd edition) (pp. 404–445). New York: Wiley.

Cautela, J. R. (1967). Covert sensitization. *Psychological Reports, 20*, 459–468.

Cautela, J. R. (1970). Covert reinforcement. *Behavior Therapy, 1*, 33–50.

Ciminero, A. R., Calhoun, K. S., & Adams, H. E. (Eds.) (1986). *Handbook of behavioral assessment* (2nd edition). New York: Wiley.

Corcoran, K., & Fischer, J. (1987). *Measures for clinical practice: A sourcebook*. New York: Free Press.

Coyne, J. C. (1976). Depression and the response of others. *Journal of Abnormal Psychology*, *85*, 186–193.

Crisp, A. H. (1966). 'Transference,' 'symptom emergence,' and 'social repercussion' in behaviour therapy: A study of fifty-four treated patients. *British Journal of Medical Psychology*, *39*, 179–196.

DeVoge, J. T., & Beck, S. (1978). The therapist-client relationship in behavior therapy. In M. Hersen, R. M. Eisler, & P. M. Miller (Eds.), *Progress in Behavior Modification*, vol. 6. (pp. 203–248). New York: Academic Press.

Eaves, G., & Rush, A. J. (1984). Cognitive patterns in symptomatic and remitted unipolar major depression. *Journal of Abnormal Psychology*, *93*, 31–40.

Emery, G. (1982). *Own your own life: How the new cognitive therapy can make you feel wonderful*. New York: New American Library.

Farberow, N. I. (1974). *Suicide*. Morristown, NJ: General Learning Press.

Foa, E. B., & Emmelkamp, P. M. G. (Eds.) (1983). *Failures in behavior therapy*. New York: John Wiley.

Foa, E. B., & Kozak, M. J. (1985). Treatment of anxiety disorders: Implications for psychopathology. In A. H. Tuma & J. D. Maser (Eds.), *Anxiety and the anxiety disorders* (pp.421–452). Hillsdale, NJ: Lawrence Erlbaum.

Foa, E. B., & Kozak, M. J. (1986). Emotional processing of fear: Exposure to corrective informaton. *Psychological Bulletin*, *99*, 20–35.

Foa, E. B., Steketee, G., Turner, R. M., & Fischer, S. C. (1980). Effects of imaginal exposure to feared disasters in obsessive-compulsive checkers. *Behaviour Research and Therapy*, *18*, 449–455.

Ford, J. D. (1978). Therapeutic relationship in behavior therapy. *Journal of Consulting and Clinical Psychology*, *46*, 1302–1314.

Fordyce, W. E., & Steger, J. C. (1979). Chronic pain. In O. F. Pomerleau, & J. P. Brady (Eds.) *Behavioral Medicine: Theory and practice* (pp. 125–153). Baltimore: Williams and Wilkins.

Frank, J. D. (1961). *Persuasion and healing: A comparative study of psychotherapy*. Baltimore: Johns Hopkins University Press.

Garcia, J., & Koelling, R. A. (1966). The relation of cue to consequence in avoidance learning. *Psychonomic Science*, *4*, 123–124.

Goldfried, M. (1985). In-vivo intervention or transference? In W. Dryden (Ed.), *Therapists' dilemmas* (pp. 63–74). London: Harper & Row.

Goldfried, M. R., & Davison, G. C. (1976). *Clinical behaivor therapy*. New York: Holt, Rinehart & Winston.

Goldfried, M., & Pomeranz, D. M. (1968). Role of assessment in behavior modification. *Psychological Reports*, *23*, 75–87.

Goldstein, A. P. (1975). Relationship enhancement methods. In F. H. Kanfer & A. P. Goldstein (Eds.), *Helping people change*. New York: Pergamon.

Guidano, V. F., & Liotti, G. (1983). *Cognitive processes and emotional disorders*. New York: Guilford.

Hall, R. G., Sachs, D. P. L., & Hall, S. M. (1979). Medical risk and therapeutic effectiveness of rapid smoking. *Behavior Therapy*, *10*, 249–259.

Hall, R. G., Sachs, D. P. L., Hall, S. M., & Benowitz, N. L. (1984). Two-year efficacy and safety of rapid smoking therapy in patients with cardiac and pulmonary disease. *Journal of Consulting and Clinical Psychology*, *52*, 574–581.

Hamilton, E. W., & Abramson, L. Y. (1983). Cognitive patterns and major depressive disorder: A longitudinal study in a hospital setting. *Journal of Abnormal Psychology, 92*, 173–184.

Hammen, C., & Glass, D. (1975). Depression, activity, and evaluation of reinforcement. *Journal of Abnormal Psychology, 84*, 718–721.

Hammen, C., Marks, T., Mayol, A., & deMayo, R. (1985). Depressive self-schemas, life stress, and vulnerability to depression. *Journal of Abnormal Psychology, 94*, 308–319.

Heide, F. J., & Borkovec, T. D. (1984). Relaxation-induced anxiety: Mechanisms and theoretical implications. *Behaviour Research and Therapy, 22*, 1–12.

Hersen, M., & Bellack, A. S. (Eds.) (1988). *Dictionary of behavioral assessment techniques*. New York: Pergamon.

Hollon, S. D., DeRubeis, R. J., Evans, M. D., Wiemer, M. J., Garvey, M. J., Grove, W. M., & Tuason, N. V. (1988). Cognitive therapy, pharmacotherapy, and combined cognitive-pharmacotherapy in the treatment of depression: I. Differential outcome in the CPT project. Unpublished manuscript, University of Minnesota.

Horowitz, M., Marmar, C., Krupnick, J., Wilner, N., Kaltreider, N., & Wallerstein, R. (1984). *Personality styles and brief psychotherapy*. New York: Basic.

Jacobson, E. (1938). *Progressive relaxation*. Chicago: University of Chicago Press.

Jannoun, L., Munby, M., Catalan, J., & Gelder, M. (1980). A home-based treatment program for agoraphobia: Replication and controlled evaluation. *Behavior Therapy, 11*, 294–305.

Kazdin, A. E., & Mascitelli, S. (1982). Covert and overt rehearsal and homework practice in developing assertiveness. *Journal of Consulting and Clinical Psychology, 50*, 250–258.

Klein, D. F., Gittelman, R., Quitkin, F. & Rifkin, A. (1980). *Diagnosis and drug treatment of psychiatric disorders: Adults and children*, Baltimore: Williams & Wilkins.

Kornblith, S. J., Rehm, L. P., O'Hara, M. W., & Lamparski, D. M. (1983). The contribution of self-reinforcement training and behavioral assignments to the efficacy of self-control therapy for depression. *Cognitive Therapy and Research, 7*, 499–527.

Krantz, S. (1985). When depressive cognitions reflect negative realities. *Cognitive Therapy and Research, 9*, 595–610.

Krantz, S., & Hammen, C. (1979). Assessment of cognitive bias in depression. *Journal of Abnormal Psychology, 88*, 611–619.

Kreitman, N. (1977). *Parasuicide*. London: John Wiley.

Lang, P. J. (1977). Imagery in therapy: An information processing analysis of fear. *Behavior Therapy, 8*, 862–886.

Lang, P. J. (1979). A bio-informational theory of emotional imagery. *Psychophysiology, 16*, 495–512.

Lewinsohn, P. M. (1974). Clinical and theoretical aspects of depression. In K. S. Calhoun, H. E. Adams, and K. M. Mitchell (Eds.), *Innovative treatment methods in psychopathology*. New York: John Wiley.

Lewinsohn, P. M., & Graf, M. (1973). Pleasant activities and depression. *Journal of Consulting and Clinical Psychology, 41*, 261–268.

Lewinsohn, P. M., Hoberman, T., & Hautzinger, M. (1985). An integrative theory of depression. In S. Reiss & R. Bootzin (Eds.), *Theoretical issues in behavior therapy*. New York: Academic Press.

Lewinsohn, P. M., & Libet, J. (1972). Pleasant events, activity schedules, and depression. *Journal of Abnormal Psychology, 79*, 291–295.

Lewinsohn, P. M., Muñoz, R. F., Youngren, M. A., & Zeiss, A. M. (1978). *Control your depression*. Englewood Cliffs, NJ: Prentice-Hall.

Linehan, M. M. (1981). A social-behavioral analysis of suicide and parasuicide: Implications for clinical assessment and treatment. In H. Glazer & J. Clarkin (Eds.), *Depression: Behavioral and directive intervention strategies* (pp. 229–294). New York: Brunner/Mazel.

Linehan, M. M. (1987). Dialectical behavioral therapy: A cognitive behavioral approach to parasuicide. *Journal of Personality Disorders, 1*, 328–333.

Linehan, M. M., Camper, P., Chiles, J. A., Strosahl, K., & Shearin, E. (1987). Interpersonal problem solving and parasuicide. *Cognitive Therapy and Research, 11*, 1–12.

Luborsky, L., McLellan, T., Woody, G. E., O'Brien, C. P., & Auerbach, A. (1985). Therapist success and its determinants. *Archives of General Psychiatry, 42*, 602–610.

Mandler, G., Mandler, J. M., & Uviller, E. T. (1958). Autonomic feedback: The perception of autonomic activity. *Journal of Abnormal and Social Psychology, 56*, 367–373.

Marks, I. M. (1981). *Cure and care of neuroses: Theory and practice of behavioral psychotherapy*. New York: John Wiley.

Maultsby, M. C. (1971). Systematic written homework. *Psychotherapy: Theory, research, and practice, 8*, 195–198.

Miller, R. C., & Berman, J. S. (1983). The efficacy of cognitives behavior therapies: A quantitative review of the research evidence. *Psychological Bulletin 94*, 39–53.

Minkoff, K., Bergman, E., Beck, A. T., & Beck, R. (1973). Hopelessness, depression, and attempted suicide. *American Journal of Psychiatry, 130*, 455–459.

Miranda, J., & Persons, J. B. (1988). Dysfunctional attitudes are mood-state dependent. *Journal of Abnormal Psychology, 97*, 76–79.

Miranda, J., Persons, J. B., & Byers, C. N. (1988b). Endorsement of dysfunctional beliefs depends on current mood state. Manuscript submitted for publication.

Morris, R. J. & Suckerman, K. R. (1974a). The importance of the therapeutic relationship in systematic desensitization. *Journal of Consulting and Clinical Psychology, 42*, 148.

Morris, R. J., & Suckerman, K. R. (1974b). Therapist warmth as a factor in automated systematic desensitization. *Journal of Consulting and Clinical Psychology, 42*, 244–250.

Osmond, H., Mullaly, R., & Bisbee, C. (1984). The pain of depression compared with physical pain. *Practitioner, 228*, 849–853.

Padesky, C. (1988). Schema-focused CT: Comments and questions. *International Cognitive Therapy Newsletter, 4*, 1.

Persons, J. B. (1986a). Generalization of the effects of exposure treatments for phobias: A single case study. *Psychotherapy, 23*, 160–166.

Persons, J. B. (1986b). The advantages of studying psychological phenomena rather than psychiatric diagnoses. *American Psychologist, 41*, 1252–1260.

Persons, J. B., & Burns, D. D. (1985). Mechanisms of action of cognitive therapy: The relative contributions of technical and interpersonal interventions. *Cognitive Therapy and Research, 9*, 539–551.

Persons, J. B., Burns, D. D., & Perloff, J. M. (1989). Predictors of dropout and outcome in cognitive therapy for depression in a private practice setting. *Cognitive Therapy and Research, 12*, 557–575.

Persons, J. B., & Miranda, J. (1988). Depressive symptoms reflect underlying cognitive vulnerabilities. Manuscript submitted for publication.

Persons, J. B., & Rao, P. A. (1985). Longitudinal study of cognitions, life events, and depression in psychiatric inpatients. *Journal of Abnormal Psychology, 94*, 51–63.

Pope, K. S. (1985). The suicidal client: Guidelines for assessment and treatment. *California State Psychologist, 20*, 1–7.

Premack, D. (1962). Reversibility of the reinforcement relation. *Science, 136*, 235–237.

Rabavilas, A. D., Boulougouris, J. C., & Perissaki, C. (1979). Therapist qualities related to outcome with exposure *in vivo* in neurotic patients. *Journal of Behavior Therapy and Experimental Psychiatry, 10*, 293–299.

Rachman, S. (1981). The primacy of affect: Some theoretical implications. *Behaviour Research and Therapy, 19*, 279–290.

Rachman, S. (1981). The primacy of affect: Some theoretical implications. *Behaviour Research and Therapy, 19*, 279–290.

Rachman, S. J., & Wilson, G. T. (1980). *The effects of psychological therapy*. New York: Pergamon.

Rehm, L. P, Kaslow, N. H., & Rabin, A. S. (1987). Cognitive and behavioral targets in a self-control therapy program for depression. *Journal of Consulting and Clinical Psychology, 55*, 60–67.

Rogers, C. R. (1951). *Client-centered therapy*. Boston: Houghton Mifflin.

Rogers, C. R. (1957). The necessary and sufficient conditions of therapeutic personality change. *Journal of Consulting and Clinical Psychology, 21*, 95–103.

Rosen, D. H. (1976). The serious suicide attempt: Five-year follow-up study of 886 patients. *Journal of the American Medical Association, 235*, 2105–2109.

Roswell, V. A. (1988). Professional liability: Issues for behavior therapists in the 1980s and 1990s. *The Behavior Therapist, 11*, 163–171.

Ryan, V. L., & Gizynski, M. N. (1971). Behavior therapy in retrospect: Patients' feelings about their behavior therapies. *Journal of Consulting and Clinical Psychology, 37*, 1–9.

Safran, J., D., & Greenberg, L. S. (1986). Hot cognition and psychotherapy process: An information processing/ecological perspective. In P. C. Kendall (Ed.), *Advances in cognitive-behavioral research and therapy* (Vol. 5). New York: Academic Press.

Safran, J. D., Vallis, T. M., Segal, Z. V., & Shaw, B. F. (1986). Assessment of core cognitive processes in cognitive therapy. *Cognitive Therapy and Research, 10*, 509–526.

Schutz, B. M. (1982). *Legal liability in psychotherapy*. San Francisco: Jossey-Bass.

Schwartz, B. (1984). Psychology of learning and behavior, 2nd edition, New York: Norton.

Seligman, M. E. P. (1970). On the generality of the laws of learning. *Psychological Review, 77*, 406–418.

Silverman, J. S., Silverman, J. A., & Eardley, D. A. (1984). Do maladaptive attitudes cause depression? *Archives of General Psychiatry, 41*, 28–30.

Simons, A. D., Epstein, L. H., McGowan, C. R., Kupfer, D. J., & Robertson, R. J. (1985). Exercise as a treatment for depression: An update. *Clinical Psychology Review, 5*, 553–568.

Simons, A. D., Garfield, S. L., & Murphy, G. E. (1984). The process of change in cognitive therapy and pharmacotherapy for depression. *Archives of General Psychiatry, 41*, 45–51.

Simons, A. D., Murphy, G. E., Levine, J. L., & Wetzel, R. D. (1986). Cognitive therapy and pharmacotherapy for depression. *Archives of General Psychiatry, 43*, 43–49.

Steketee, G., & Foa, E. B. (1985). Obsessive-compulsive disorder. In D. H. Barlow (Ed.), *Clinical handbook of psychological disorders: A step-by-step treatment manual* (pp. 69–144). New York: Guilford.

Strupp, H. H. (1973). On the basic ingredients of psychotherapy. *Journal of Consulting and Clinical Psychology, 41*, 1–8.

Suinn, R. M., & Richardson, F. (1971). Anxiety management training: A nonspecific behavior therapy program for anxiety control. *Behavior Therapy, 2*, 498–510.

Sweet, A. A. (1984). The therapeutic relationship in behavior therapy. *Clinical Psychology Review, 4*, 253–272.

Taylor, C. B., & Agras, S. (1981). Assessment of phobia. In D. H. Barlow (Ed.), *Behavioral assessment of adult disorders* (pp. 181–208). New York: Guilford.

Teasdale, J. D. (1985). Psychological treatments for depression: how do they work? *Behaviour Research and Therapy, 23*, 157–165.

Telch, M. J. (1981). The present status of outcome studies: A reply to Frank. *Journal of Consulting and Clinical Psychology, 49*, 472–475.

Thorndike, E. L. (1935). *The psychology of wants, interests, and attitudes.* New York: Appleton-Century-Crofts.

Truax, C. G., & Carkhuff, R. R. (1967). *Toward effective counseling and psychotherapy: Training and practice.* Chicago, Aldine.

Turkat, I. D. (Ed.) (1985). *Behavioral case formulation.* New York: Plenum.

Turkat, I. D., & Brantley, P. J. (1981). On the therapeutic relationship in behavior therapy. *The Behavior Therapist, 4*, 16–17.

Turkat, I. D., & Carlson, C. R. (1984). Data-based versus symptomatic formulation of treatment. The case of a dependent personality. *Journal of Behavior Therapy and Experimental Psychiatry, 15*, 153–160.

Turkat, I. D., & Maisto, S. A. (1985). Personality disorders: Application of the experimental method to the formulation and modification of personality disorders. In D. H. Barlow (Ed.), *Clinical handbook of psychological disorders: A step-by-step treatment manual* (pp. 502–570). New York: Guilford.

Weissman, A. (1979). The Dysfunctional Attitude Scale: A validation study. *Dissertation Abstracts International, 40*, 1389–1390B. (University Microfilm No. 79-19, 533).

Weissman, A., & Beck, A. (1978, November). Development and validation of the dysfunctional attitude scale. Paper presented at the meeting of the Association for Advancement of Behavior Therapy, Chicago.

Wilson, G. R. (1978). Alcoholism and aversion therapy: Issues, ethics and evidence. In G. A. Marlatt & P. E. Nathan (Eds.), *Behavioral approaches to alcoholism*. New Brunswick, NJ: Rutgers Center of Alcohol Studies.

Wilson, G. R. (1984). Fear reduction methods and the treatment of anxiety disorders. In *Annual review of behavior therapy: Theory and practice* (pp. 95–131). New York: Guilford.

Wilson, G. R., & Evans, I. M. (1977). The therapistlient relationship in behavior therapy. In A. S. Gurman and A. M. Razin (Eds.), *Effective psychotherapy: A handbook of research* (pp. 544–565). New York: Pergamon.

Wolpe, J. (1973). The practice of behavior therapy (2nd ed.). Elmsford, NY: Pergamon Press.

Wolpe, J., & Lang, P. J. (1969). Fear survey schedule. San Diego: Educational and Industrial Testing Service.

Young, J. (1987). Schema-focused cognitive therapy for personality disorders. Unpublished manuscript, Cognitive Therapy Center of New York, 111 W. 88 Street, New York, N. Y. 10024.

Young, J. (1988). Cognitive therapy for personality disorders. Workshop presented with George Lockwood, Palo Alto, California, October 1, 1988.

Youngren, M. A., & Lewinsohn, P. M. (1980). The functional relation between depression and problematic interpersonal behavior. *Journal of Abnormal Psychology, 89*, 333–341.

Zajonc, R. (1980). Feeling and thinking: Preferences need no inferences. *American Psychologist, 35*, 151–175.

Zeiss, A. M., Lewinsohn, P. M., & Muñoz, R. F. (1979). Nonspecific improvement effects in depression using interpersonal skills training, pleasant activity schedules, or cognitive training. *Journal of Consulting and Clinical Psychology, 47*, 427–439.

Zuroff, D. C., & Mongrain, M. (1987). Dependency and self-criticism: Vulnerability factors for depressive affective states. *Journal of Abnormal Psychology, 96*, 14–22.

Index

223